Research Series on the Chinese Dream and China's Development Path

Drawing on a large body of empirical studies done over the last two decades, the *Research Series on the Chinese Dream and China's Development Path* seeks to provide its readers with in-depth analyses of the past and present, and forecasts for the future course of China's development. Thanks to the adoption of Socialism with Chinese characteristics, and the implementation of comprehensive reform and opening, China has made tremendous achievements in areas such as political reform, economic development, and social construction, and is making great strides towards the realization of the Chinese dream of national rejuvenation. In addition to presenting a detailed account of many of these achievements, the authors also discuss what lessons other countries can learn from China's experience. This series will be an invaluable companion to every researcher who is trying to gain a deeper understanding of the development model, path and experience unique to China.

More information about this series at http://www.springer.com/series/13571

Zhiguo Kong

The Making of a Maritime Power

China's Challenges and Policy Responses

SSAP

Springer

Zhiguo Kong
Beijing Energy Development Research
Center
North China Electric Power University
Beijing
China

Translated by Mr. Jin Bao
Polished by Ms. Sun Xiao, Ms. Luo Hongyan

ISSN 2363-6866 ISSN 2363-6874 (electronic)
Research Series on the Chinese Dream and China's Development Path
ISBN 978-981-10-1785-8 ISBN 978-981-10-1786-5 (eBook)
DOI 10.1007/978-981-10-1786-5

Jointly published with Social Sciences Academic Press

Library of Congress Control Number: 2016950898

Printed on acid-free paper

This Springer imprint is published by Springer Nature
The registered company is Springer Nature Singapore Pte Ltd.
The registered company address is: 152 Beach Road, #22-06/08 Gateway East, Singapore 189721, Singapore

Series Preface

Since China's reform and opening began in 1978, the country has come a long way on the path of Socialism with Chinese Characteristics, under the leadership of the Communist Party of China. Over thirty years of reform, efforts and sustained spectacular economic growth have turned China into the world's second largest economy, and brought many profound changes in the Chinese society. These historically significant developments have been garnering increasing attention from scholars, governments, and the general public alike around the world since the 1990s, when the newest wave of China studies began to gather steam. Some of the hottest topics have included the so-called "China miracle", "Chinese phenomenon", "Chinese experience", "Chinese path", and the "Chinese model". Homegrown researchers have soon followed suit. Already hugely productive, this vibrant field is putting out a large number of books each year, with Social Sciences Academic Press alone having published hundreds of titles on a wide range of subjects.

Because most of these books have been written and published in Chinese, readership has been limited outside China—even among many who study China—for whom English is still the lingua franca. This language barrier has been an impediment to efforts by academia, business communities, and policy-makers in other countries to form a thorough understanding of contemporary China, of what is distinct about China's past and present may mean not only for her future but also for the future of the world. The need to remove such an impediment is both real and urgent, and the *Research Series on the Chinese Dream and China's Development Path* is my answer to the call.

This series features some of the most notable achievements from the last 20 years by scholars in China in a variety of research topics related to reform and opening. They include both theoretical explorations and empirical studies, and cover economy, society, politics, law, culture, and ecology, the six areas in which reform and opening policies have had the deepest impact and farthest-reaching consequences for the country. Authors for the series have also tried to articulate their visions of the "Chinese Dream" and how the country can realize it in these fields and beyond.

All of the editors and authors for the *Research Series on the Chinese Dream and China's Development Path* are both longtime students of reform and opening and recognized authorities in their respective academic fields. Their credentials and expertise lend credibility to these books, each of which having been subject to a rigorous peer-review process for inclusion in the series. As part of the Reform and Development Program under the State Administration of Press, Publication, Radio, Film and Television of the People's Republic of China, the series is published by Springer, a Germany-based academic publisher of international repute, and distributed overseas. I am confident that it will help fill a lacuna in studies of China in the era of reform and opening.

Xie Shouguang

Acknowledgments

After a relatively short gestation period, the *Research Series on the Chinese Dream and China's Development Path* has started to bear fruits. We have to thank, first and foremost, the books' authors and editors for making this possible. And it was the hard work by many people at Social Sciences Academic Press and Springer, the two collaborating publishers, that made it a reality. We are deeply grateful to all of them.

Mr. Xie Shouguang, President of Social Sciences Academic Press (SSAP), is the mastermind behind the project. In addition to defining the key missions to be accomplished by it and setting down the basic parameters for the project's execution, as the work has unfolded, Mr. Xie has provided critical input pertaining to its every aspect and at every step of the way. Thanks to the deft coordination by Ms. Li Yanling, all the constantly moving parts of the project, especially those on the SSAP side, are securely held together, and as well synchronized as is feasible for a project of this scale. Ms. Gao Jing, unfailingly diligent and meticulous, makes sure every aspect of each Chinese manuscript meets the highest standards for both publishers, something of critical importance to all subsequent steps in the publishing process. That high quality if also at times stylistically as well as technically challenging scholarly writing in Chinese has turned into decent, readable English that readers could see on these pages then largely thanks are due to Ms. Liang Fan, who oversees translator recruitment and translation quality control.

Ten other members of the SSAP staff have been intimately involved, primarily in the capacity of in-house editor, in the preparation of the Chinese manuscripts. It is a time-consuming work that requires attention to details, and each of them has done this, and is continuing to do this with superb skills. They are, in alphabetical order: Mr. Cai Jihui, Ms. Liu Xiaojun, Mr. Ren Wenwu, Ms. Shi Xiaolin, Ms. Song Yuehua, Mr. Tong Genxing, Ms. Wu Dan, Ms. Yao Dongmei, Ms. Yun Wei and Ms. Zhou Qiong. In addition, Xie Shouguang, and Li Yanling have also taken part in this work.

Ms. Yun Wei is the SSAP in-house editor for the current volume.

Our appreciation is also owed to Ms. Li Yan, Mr. Chai Ning, Ms. Wang Lei, and Ms. Xu Yi from Springer's Beijing Representative Office. Their strong support for the SSAP team in various aspects of the project helped to make the latter's work that much easier than it would have otherwise been.

We thank Mr. Jin Bao for translating this book and Ms. Sun Xiao, Ms. Luo Hongyan for their work as the polishers. The translation and draft polish process benefited greatly from the consistent and professional coordination service by China Translation Corporation. We thank everyone involved for their hard work.

Last, but certainly not least, it must be mentioned that funding for this project comes from the Ministry of Finance of the People's Republic of China. Our profound gratitude, if we can be forgiven for a bit of apophasis, goes without saying.

Contents

1 China's Maritime Rise as a Historical Trend 1
1.1 The Needham Puzzle 1
1.2 Unintentional Rise and Decline of a "Maritime Power" 3
1.3 Passive Awakening and Low-Profile Growth 10
1.4 The Irresistible Trend of Passive Rise 16
1.5 The World Calls for a Maritime China 26

2 The Great Maritime Power Dream: Challenges and Problems 31
2.1 The Taiwan Question 31
2.2 Possible Deadlock in Sovereignty Disputes 34
2.3 Nationalism Adds to Uncertainty 41
2.4 Formidable Rivals Nearby 43
2.5 Military Expenditure and the "China Threat" Theory 48
2.6 Hidden Risks in Overseas Security 52
2.7 Underdeveloped Seas 55
2.8 The Harm of Seeking Regional Balance 59
2.9 The Lack of Strategic Awareness 64

3 Evolution of International Sea Power: Trend and Influence 69
3.1 Piratical-Style Competition and Mahan's Contribution 69
3.2 Sovereignty and Sea Rights Do not Come for Free 74
3.3 The Rise of Peaceful Competition on the Sea 77
3.4 Comparable Elements of Sea Power 79
3.5 "Spoon-Shaped Chain" of Sea Power 84
3.6 In Search of Equilibrium 87
3.7 Cost–Benefit Analysis of China's Sea Power 90

4 Peaceful Growth: Dilemma and Prerequisites 97
4.1 Growing Pains 97
4.2 Promoting an Evolution in International Rules Through Self-development 98
4.3 Head-on Conflict, Full-on Engagement 100

4.4 Issues and Tensions 106
4.5 Necessary Conditions for Future Development 112

5 Learning from *Tuntian* of Western Han 117
5.1 Why Learn from the Western Han? 117
5.2 About the *Tuntian* Policy During the Western Han 120
5.3 Military and Tax Substitution 126
5.4 The Formation of Assimilation, Deterrence and Borders 133
5.5 Border Regions and the Creation of Property Rights 134

6 Peaceful Rise: Strategic Prospect and Recommendations 145
6.1 The Strategy Must Come First 145
6.2 Prerequisites for the Implementation of *Tunhai* 147
6.3 Establishing the *Tunhai* Policy 152
6.4 Implementation and Examples 164
6.5 However, *Tunhai* Is not the Be-All and End-All 167
6.6 Possible Scenarios for Dispute Resolution 171

About the Author

Zhiguo Kong received a Ph.D. in Economics (Shandong University) and Master of Laws (Beijing University). He is a research fellow at the North China Electric Power University, Beijing Energy Development Research Center, a senior research fellow at Tsinghua-Grandview Oceanographic Research Center, and a part-time research fellow at the Zhejiang University Center for Ocean Law and Governance. As one of the proponents of the *tunhai* theory, his recommendations have been reported at length or commented on by *Southern Weekend*, *South Reviews*, *21st Century Business Herald*, *China Law*, and *Ta Kung Pao*.

Introduction

The topic of this book is not a novel one. Whether China can achieve a maritime rise, what are the challenges against such rise, and how can China achieve it as soon as possible—these are three questions that scholars on Chinese matters—political, economic, military, maritime, and historical—and international China hands have long tried to answer.

However, the answer given in this book may differ in many ways from the conclusions of previous research and discussions.

First of all, regarding China's maritime rise, this book eschews the ambiguity in characterizing most China studies and foreign researchers' indulgence in blinkered guesswork about China's military strength. Instead, it points out with eloquence and clarity that China's maritime rise is irresistible, as it is necessitated by both the internal demand for continued development and the greater responsibility China has to shoulder due to the political and economic restructuring of the international community.

Second, in terms of the challenges against China's maritime rise, this book partially agrees that China's wrestling and confrontation with a few neighboring countries over sovereignty disputes and with the great powers seeking strategic control in waters near the China seas are challenges that one cannot turn a blind eye to. However, China cannot evade a more important challenge, i.e., how to emerge as a universally acknowledged maritime power in the ever intensifying competition for the provision of global sea-related public goods.

Finally, as a recommendation for accelerating China's maritime rise, this book posits that *tunhai* (i.e., the establishment of military-economic settlements on the sea—translator's note), derived from the Western Han practice of *tuntian* (the establishment of military-agricultural settlements—translator's note), can be a feasible way for China to gradually obtain complete maritime sovereignty and make the best use of its seas under the current conditions of sea power competition. China needs to reshape the relationship between state and sea on the basis of *tunhai* in the full awareness that, in the context of globalization, it would be impossible for it to confine itself to the land. Development toward the sea is not a general strategy of a departmental or thematic nature, but a change in the country's orientation.

This book is also structured around these three answers.

Chapter 1, "China's Maritime Rise as a Historical Trend," analyzes China's relationship with the sea in different historical periods and notes that, in the twenty first century, the sea has become China's inevitable choice for survival and voluntary option for development. This is unlike the link between China and the sea before the Opium Wars, which was dispensable and intermittent, and also unlike China's passive posture on maritime issues from the end of the Opium Wars through the entire twentieth century, from being bullied to awakening and growth.

This general trend, however, does not mean that China's maritime rise would be plain sailing. Chapters 2 to 4 aim to find out what challenges China has to overcome and what efforts it has to make before it becomes a real great maritime power.

Chapter 2, "The Great Maritime Power Dream: Challenges and Problems," presents a panoramic view of the real pressure facing China on the sea from its own perspective. Such pressure is of a multifaceted and multidimensional nature, coming from neighboring countries, traditional great maritime powers, and China itself; it is related to military strength and the ability to make use of the sea, to maritime awareness, tradition and voice, and to policy orientation and strategic vision.

It is true, though, that China's sea power cannot grow on its own or in a wild way, in view of the quickening tempo of globalization and the shrinking of the globe into a village by the Internet and modern means of transport. Chapter 3, "Evolution of International Sea Power: Trend and Influence," attempts to provide the international and historical coordinates of China's sea power in terms of the evolution of and international competition for sea power. Now that "peaceful competition" is becoming the mainstream and emphasis is placed on the provision of global sea-related public goods, though the jungle law still has some influence on international maritime order; it is impossible for China to follow the course taken by Britain, the US, and other countries, which achieved their maritime rise through the exercise of military power. Apart from possessing a security capability commensurable with its expanding maritime interests, China needs to set an example for the world in the deep and sustainable development and utilization of marine resources.

Chapter 4, "Peaceful Growth: Dilemma and Prerequisites," outlines the course of China's growth into a great maritime power. The growth of China's sea power and the tendency toward peaceful competition in production in international sea power competition determine that, behind the frustration, repression, and challenge accompanying China's advance toward the sea, China has a mixture of goals to pursue represented by the tension between competition and cooperation, including the urgent need for maritime rise and the strong wish for peace, strategic aggressiveness through tactical conservatism, and the creation of a new maritime order under the existing framework. Therefore, given the shortfall in both related public goods provided by the government and the ability to develop and utilize the sea, China must come up with a strategy that can guarantee its maritime security and enable itself to cope with interferences and provocations while making no trouble itself and, at the same time, to make the best use of the sea, enhance the whole nation's interest in it, and forge closer ties between the country and the sea.

Chapter 5, "Learning from *Tuntian* of Western Han," represents a wise approach that can shed light on the design of this strategy—tuntian. Western Han was confronted with much the same adverse situation on its land border as today's China is facing on the sea: both need complete sovereignty and rights to win space for lasting economic development despite the insufficiency of security support. The Western Han government achieved the goal through the *tuntian* system, in which soldiers were ordered to cultivate land and civilians were encouraged to live in the border region and asked to engage in both production and self-defense. The people involved in *tuntian* effectively relieved problems like the shortage of soldiers and logistic support for the military. Moreover, they highlighted the importance of the *tuntian* fields to the state through frontier development, the spread of agricultural technology, and integration. Those people depended on the *tuntian* fields for their livelihood, and those fields played an indispensable part in the state's cost-and-benefit system. As a result, Western Han eventually gained complete land power in its competition with the Xiongnu.

Chapter 6, "Peaceful Rise: Strategic Prospect and Recommendations," which builds on the logic of *tuntian* of Western Han, makes a systematic proposal for China to become a great maritime power based on the strategy of *tunhai*. First, China should develop systems and laws conducive to its advance toward the sea, e.g., by revising applicable articles in the Constitution and introducing Law of the Sea as a fundamental law, and creating a system of rules featuring mutual support between laws and regulations of the central government and those of local authorities. Second, China should establish a sea governance structure with the emphasis on practical effects as a strong institutional support. Finally, China should adopt specific *tunhai* measures such as expanding the Maritime Silk Road, encouraging the scientific development of islands, giving full·play to the role of ex-service personnel, and abolishing "restraining" policies on the growth of coastal economy.

It must be emphasized that, during the writing of this book, I was torn between two forces—an infinite longing for peace and a feeling of helplessness at the jungle law that still sways the mentality of governments.

On the one hand, I sincerely hope that this book could contribute to the creation of a new maritime order dominated by peaceful competition around the world, and I also expect my country to become one of the advocates and founders of this new order, which, barring any unforeseen circumstances, will be the case in the future. On the other hand, however, reason keeps reminding me that the concept of nation-state remains prevalent nowadays and that a participant in the competition should meet the higher demand of "being able to compete by not competing" (an allusion to what Lao Tzu said: "It is exactly because she does not contend, that nobody can contend with her"—translator's note). To achieve a peaceful rise, China may have to possess a high deterrence capacity.

Therefore, towards the end of this book, I note with some reluctance that although the importance of *tunhai* should not be underestimated, China's maritime rise must involve the development of military power on the sea, the encouragement of relevant technological innovation, and the demonstration of a view on the sea that can stand up to test and scrutiny. I wish that some day, when China has become a real great maritime power, there will be no more contention for power in a world that is a happy home for all mankind, with the seas being nothing more than an Eden for the pursuit of a better life.

Chapter 1
China's Maritime Rise as a Historical Trend

Is China a maritime state? Will it become a great maritime power? For this increasingly influential country that is about to overtake the US as the world's largest economy, is the vast expanse of water a springboard or a short board? Opportunities or risks? Should there come a day when China replaces the US as the greatest maritime power? How would its rise differ from the power shift from Portugal, to Spain, to Holland, to Britain, and finally to the US in the previous centuries?

To answer these questions, one must find out, first of all, why is it that China's past attempts to "look at the world with wide-open eyes" only invited war and unrest, and what changes, if any, are there in the sea's life-and-death significance for China today?

1.1 The Needham Puzzle

According to the research conducted by the British scholar Angus Maddison, a universally acknowledged authority on China studies in the West, China was the world's strongest economy in 1820. Her GDP was larger than the sum of those of the US, Japan, and Europe, and more than twice that of India, which had almost the same population (Fig. 1.1). However, only two decades later, in 1840, China suffered foreign aggression. From then on until 1949, China had little autonomy in terms of sovereignty, governance, and even her economy and people's livelihood. Why is it that the curve of her fortune went south for as long as 109 years?

Quite a few Western scholars have expressed their puzzle at such an abrupt downturn in China's course of development.

A similar question was posed by the British scholar Joseph Needham, who specialized in Chinese history, and Max Weber, the German scholar with great accomplishments in sociology, history, and economics, namely, why is it that the Industrial Revolution did not originate in China, which had been so far ahead of

Z. Kong, *The Making of a Maritime Power*, Research Series on the Chinese Dream and China's Development Path, DOI 10.1007/978-981-10-1786-5_1

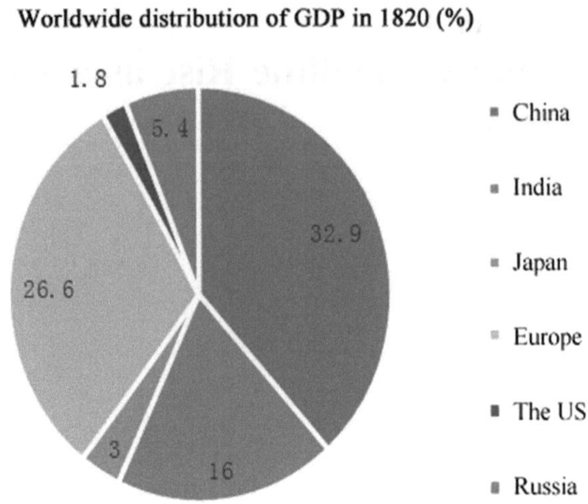

Fig. 1.1 *Source* Maddison, Angus. *Chinese Economic Performance in the Long Run, 960–2030 AD*. Tr. Wu Xiaoying and Ma Debin. Shanghai People's Publishing House, 2011, 39

other countries in science, technology, and economy, and where capitalism had already sprouted, and that it did not catch up with the West even long after the Industrial Revolution had begun there? Paul Kennedy, an expert on international politics, was also surprised at China's choice to "turn its back on the world" despite "the opportunities that beckoned overseas."

Their puzzle was shared by Adam Smith, the father of economics. Smith, however, tried to trace the puzzle to the root causes. He attributed it to the rigid culture, believing that there is a causal link between China's long stagnation and the acquisition of the "full complement of riches" permitted by its laws and institutions. First of all, trade was affected; the opening of only one or two ports would apparently mean much less for the flourishing of foreign trade than the full opening of all the coastal and river ports. Furthermore, the dynamics of the flow of wealth from the have-nots to the haves further stifled economic vitality. "Under alternative laws and institutions," China might have produced greater wealth that its soil, climate, and situation might admit of.

However, Adam Smith only provided part of the answer. In retrospect it seems, on the surface at least, that China's downturn had something to do with the sea and sea power. By the time nation-states were in the ascendant, warships, and cannons were throwing their weight about, and vessels from Britain, France, Portugal, Spain and Holland had roamed the Atlantic and the Pacific for more than 300 years. In an age when colonies around the world had changed hands over and over again among those great powers, China was still slumbering in the illusion of a "celestial empire," which was coupled with a host of internal troubles, including corruption, conflict between bureaucrats and common people, ethnic tension, and civil unrest. Ignorant about the maritime world and indifferent to the rise of sea power, how could it continue to turn up her nose at the rest of the world?

A wealthy but weak nation would inevitably end up in jeopardy. In the international jungle, the wealthier China became, the more easily it would fall prey to great powers that had long cast their covetous eyes on her. And it would be theirs for the taking—the wealth it had accumulated with such pains could be plundered and split in a blink of an eye. That was exactly what happened. The Opium Wars were followed by incessant territorial cession and payment of reparations. The Boxer Protocol alone took away nearly one billion taels of silver–an epitome of China's gloomy modern history (Table 1.1).

A series of defeats at war taught the Chinese a hard lesson. Chinese history since 1840 is in some way one of repeated efforts to revive the country's sea power and to catch up with the more advanced world. What China is doing now in terms of sea power and the sea is a new and important part of that history.

To truly understand history and find out what China expects from the sea and what the sea means to her today is essential for a sound judgment about the country's maritime future. "Today," as we call it, is a logical continuation and product of numerous "yesterdays." For any serious study of China's tragic early modern history, the interaction between the country and the sea is not to be neglected.

In other words, only by looking back upon the past can we properly evaluate China's performance at sea, draw lesson from the country's humiliating and costly defeats at sea battles, and see why it will certainly become a great maritime power.

The interaction between the sea and China can be roughly divided into three periods, depending on the role the sea has played in each of them.

1.2 Unintentional Rise and Decline of a "Maritime Power"

The first period refers to the time before the Opium Wars. Apart from its intermittent role as a trade channel, the sea, which had long been regarded as a less important supplement to the land, served primarily as natural borders in east and south China where it joined the land. A passive pattern characterized human interaction with the sea in this period with this vast unknown realm often overlooked and undervalued. Whether or not the sea should be explored or otherwise used was solely at the government's free discretion. With neither a long-term maritime plan nor conscious efforts, China became what might be called a "maritime power." And then, ironically enough, it was its ill-prepared navy that suffered the first defeat before the Western powers, thus beginning a century of humiliation and sufferings.

There are people who miss China's past glories on the sea. They would argue, for instance, the Maritime Silk Road, which started from Xuwen (now Xuwen County in Guangdong) and Hepu (now Beihai City in Guangxi) and later from Guangzhou and Quanzhou, took shape as early as the Western Han Dynasty; the Tang and Song dynasties boast the 14,000-km Guangzhou Sea Route to Foreign Lands that led to over 100 countries and regions in the Persian Gulf, East Africa and

Table 1.1 Provisions for territorial cession and payment of reparations in some of the unequal treaties signed by China in early modern times

Title	Signed in	Signed by	Provisions for territorial cession and payment of reparations
Treaty of Nanking	1842	China and Britain	Payment of 21 million silver dollars; cession of Hong Kong Island to Britain; tariffs to be agreed upon by the two countries
Treaty of Aigun	1858	China and Russia	Cession to Russia of over 600,000 km^2 of land north of Heilongjiang and south of the Outer Khingan; about 400,000 km^2 of land east of the Wusuli River would be controlled by both China and Russia
Treaty of Tientsin	1858	China, the US, Britain and France	Foreign merchant ships and warships could sail freely to the ports along the Yangtze River; payment of two million taels of silver to Britain and France, respectively for military expenditures; payment of two million taels of silver for the losses sustained by British merchants
Convention of Peking	1860	China, Britain and France	Cession of Tsim Sha Tsui of Kowloon to Britain; payment of 8 million taels of silver to Britain and France, respectively for military expenditures
Convention of Peking	1860	China and Russia	Cession to Russia of about 400,000 km^2 of land east of the Wusuli River, including Sakhalin
Treaty of Tarbagatai	1864	China and Russia	Cession to Russia of over 440,000 km^2 of land east and south of Lake Balkhash

(continued)

Table 1.1 (continued)

Title	Signed in	Signed by	Provisions for territorial cession and payment of reparations
Agreement Between the High Commissioner Plenipotentiary of Japan and the Chinese Ministers of Foreign Affairs	1874	China and Japan	The Qing government would pay 500,000 taels of silver to Japan as condition for the withdrawal of Japanese troops from Taiwan
Treaty of Ili	1881	China and Russia	China would recover Ili and cede the area west of the Khorgos River to Russia and pay 9 million rubles of reparations
Boundary Protocol of Khobdo	1883	China and Russia	Cession to Russia of extensive land east and south of Lake Zaysan
Treaty of Shimonoseki	1895	China and Japan	Cession to Japan of Liaotung Peninsula, Taiwan and the Penghu Islands; payment of 200 million taels of silver
Boxer Protocol	1901	China, Britain, Russia, Germany, France, the US, Japan, Italy, Austria, Belgium, Holland and Spain	Payment of 450 million taels of silver over a period of 39 years, plus an interest of 530 million taels of silver; designation of Dongjiaominxiang as the Legation Quarter, in which foreign troops could be stationed but no Chinese might live
Twenty-one Demands	1915	China and Japan	Transfer to Japan of all the rights Germany enjoyed in Shandong; privileges for Japan in South Manchuria and East Mongolia in terms of industry and commerce, land, railways and mines, consultation, and loan
Treaty of Hulun	1915	China and Russia	Hulunbuir would be a "special zone," which the Chinese military could not enter without Russia's permission

Source Li Kan et al. *A Modern History of China.* Zhonghua Book Company, 1994

Europe across South China Sea and the Indian Ocean; Zheng He, the Ming Dynasty explorer who led the world's most advanced ships on seven voyages to the "Western Seas," anticipated and outshone Columbus and Vasco da Gama, both some 80–90 years his junior.

These research findings are echoed by a number of scholars around the world. American writer Louise Levathes, among others, has shown great admiration for those glories of China in her book *When China Ruled the Seas*,[1] which was based on her discussions with experts on Chinese history and oceanology including Joseph Needham and Huang Xingzong, and her travels to countries in Asia and Africa. She is not only surprised at the gigantic "tower ships" and "bridge ships" of the Han Dynasty and the regular shipping service between China and Indonesia, but is also certain that, during the period between 1405 and 1433, the era of Zheng He and his "treasure ships," it was perfectly possible for China to rule the world one century before Europe's great maritime expansion.

However, one could not refute the fact that, like other countries of the time, China's knowledge and utilization of the sea was confined to aquatic products and shipping. On a macroeconomic level, the value of the sea to China was quite limited.

Even for the Southern Song Dynasty that was less affluent than its predecessor the Northern Song and thus relied more heavily on foreign trade, trade activities via the sea brought merely 10 % (a figure which soon slipped to 3 %) of its revenue in the early years due to the policy of monopoly plus heavy tax. More often than not, the economic value of the sea was little more than nothing. Since China tended to exchange its handicrafts such as silk, porcelain and lacquerware for exotic luxury goods, such as agate and amber, maritime trade only served to reduce rather than increase its wealth.[2]

From the Western Han to the Ming and Qing Dynasties, China spent well more than what it got from maritime trade.[3] Even Zheng He's reputed voyages to the Western Seas were little more than a grandiose and costly diplomatic show.[4] As a result, foreign trade, especially maritime trade, meant very little to Chinese rulers.

An unspoken tenet of governance is that peace within a country leads it to prosperity while unrest to decline. This is why the Ming Dynasty declined despite its dominance on the sea and the steady influx of silver from foreign trade,[5] and

[1]Levathes, Louise (2004). *When China Ruled the Seas*. (Qiu, Zhonglin, trans.) Guilin: Guangxi Normal University Press.

[2]Yu, Ying-shih (2005). *Trade and Expansion in Han China: A Study in the Structure of Sino-Barbarian Economic Relations*. (Wu, Wenling etc., trans.) Shanghai: Shanghai Ancient Books Publishing House, p. 158.

[3]Chao Zhongchen (2005). *Overseas Trade and the Ban on Maritime Trade during the Ming Dynasty*. Beijing: People's Publishing House, p. 117.

[4]Levathes, Louise (2004). *When China Ruled the Seas*. (Qiu, Zhonglin, trans.) Guilin: Guangxi Normal University Press, pp. 72–177.

[5]Chao Zhongchen (2005). *Overseas Trade and the Ban on Maritime Trade during the Ming Dynasty*. Beijing: People's Publishing House, pp. 264–278.

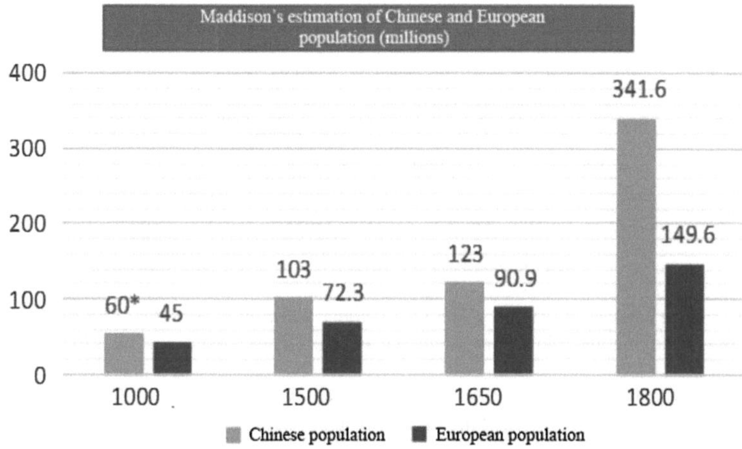

Fig. 1.2 *Source* Maddison, Angus. *Chinese Economic Performance in the Long Run, 960–2030 AD*. Tr. Wu Xiaoying and Ma Debin. Shanghai People's Publishing House, 2011, 33–34. *An approximate number based on Maddison's estimation that China had a population of 55 million in 960 AD plus consideration given to population increase

why China's maritime adventures ceased abruptly after Zheng He's seven voyages, whereas the West engaged in wild expansion for "Christianity and gold."[6]

For the Ming Dynasty, opening up to the outsideû world was really not worth it when China was ahead of the rest of the world in science and technology[7] and superior in farming,[8] with a larger and more unified market than anywhere else in the world.[9] In comparison with Europe, one of China's salient features is the sheer size of its market. For most of its history, China maintained a unified market on the continent despite the change of dynasties. Europe, however, was often divided, all the more so between 1000 and 1800, a period marked by the splitting, collapse, and reconstruction of states. During that period, the ratio between China's population and that of Europe stayed around 1.3:1 until the time around 1800, when it spiked to nearly 2.3:1 (Fig. 1.2). Besides, there was an even wider gap in the quality of the market. China had long been ahead of Europe in such farming techniques as cultivation and irrigation. "The farming practices (in China) in the 12th century did not emerge (in Europe) until the 20th century." Moreover, with much less arable land

[6]Stavrianos, L.S. (1999): *The World Since 1500: A Global History*. (Wu, Xiangying, and Liang, Chimin, trans.) Shanghai: Shanghai Academy of Social Sciences Press, p. 13.

[7]Stavrianos, L.S. (1999): *The World Since 1500: A Global History*. (Wu, Xiangying, and Liang, Chimin, trans.) Shanghai: Shanghai Academy of Social Sciences Press, pp. 331–334, 14, 17, 23.

[8]Maddison, Angus (2011). *Chinese Economic Performance in the Long Run, 960-2030 AD*. (Wu, Xiaoying, and Ma, Debin, trans.) Shanghai: Shanghai People's Publishing House, pp. 28–29.

[9]Kennedy, Paul (2006). *The Rise and Fall of the Great Powers: Economic Change and Military Conflict from 500 to 2000*. (Chen, Jingbiao, et al., trans.) Beijing: China International Culture Press, p. 6.

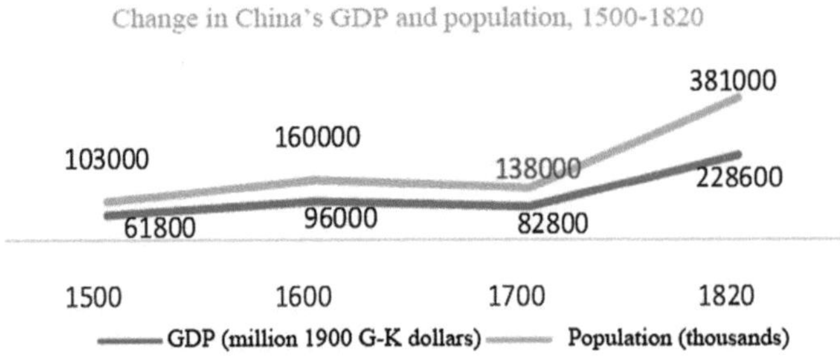

Fig. 1.3 *Source* Maddison, Angus. *Chinese Economic Performance in the Long Run, 960–2030 AD*. Tr. Wu Xiaoying and Ma Debin. Shanghai People's Press, 2011, 33, 39, 176, 186

per capita, China had a per capita GDP, at a conservative estimate, comparable to that of Europe in (Fig. 1.3).[10]

Zheng He's voyages and the so-called "trade of tribute"[11] were, if truth be told, costly vanity undertakings. While the inflow of silver was most welcome to the merchants involved in foreign trade,[12] the benefit for the government was no match for the costs of defense against Japanese pirates and control over maritime commerce. The imbalance between loss and gain was aggravated by the effect of price inflation on the economy.

Under such circumstances, the ban on maritime trade (*haijin*) became the principal policy on foreign trade for the Ming and the subsequent Qing Dynasty. Most people have attributed China's isolation from the rest of the world after the Ming Dynasty and its continental tradition to political considerations such as the famous uncle-nephew strife within the imperial family[13] or ethnics rivalries,[14] or well-justified tactics of avoiding simultaneous threats from the land and the sea.[15]

[10]Maddison, Angus (2011). *Chinese Economic Performance in the Long Run, 960–2030 AD*. (Wu, Xiaoying, and Ma, Debin, trans.) Shanghai: Shanghai People's Publishing House, pp. 18–29.

[11]Chao, Zhongchen (2005). *Overseas Trade and the Ban on Maritime Trade during the Ming Dynasty*. Beijing: People's Publishing House, pp. 64–77.

[12]The inflow of silver created a number of wealthy people in Fujian and Guangdong. These people would carry "cheap and shoddy goods" to "Luzon and other foreign states" and "return with shiploads of silver", "gaining profits that were always more than 100 times the costs of their goods". As cited in Chao, Zhongchen (2005). *Overseas Trade and the Ban on Maritime Trade during the Ming Dynasty*. Beijing: People's Publishing House, p. 276.

[13]Zhu Di (Emperor Chengzu of Ming) and his nephew Zhu Yunwen (Emperor Huidi of Ming).

[14]Zheng Chenggong was a leading figure of the movement to topple the Qing Dynasty and restore the Ming Dynasty.

[15]Most scholars believe that security threats from the west and the north were the major factor that shaped China's land tradition. Invasions by northern nomadic peoples like the Xiongnu, the Turks, the Khitans and the Jurchens were the nightmare of the ruler of every dynasty. Keeping distance from the sea was therefore a natural decision.

These may indeed have played a part, but based on the analysis above we may easily conclude that economy was the intrinsic long-term factor behind the age-old policy.

Not only the government, but the ordinary people also chose to be away from the sea. The preference was well proven by the demographic change between 1381 and 1391 during the Ming Dynasty: the population declined in the south (coastal provinces like Nanzhi, or present-day Jiangsu, Zhejiang, Fujian, and Guangdong), as opposed to a growth in the north (interior provinces like Shanxi, Shaanxi and Sichuan).[16] An important reason for the change is that many moved inland as they believed interior provinces were more promising for livelihood.[17]

As a natural consequence, the sea was more valued for its border-defining role in an extended period prior to 1840. Due to wars, riots, and government policies, maritime trade was intermittent and so were the profits from the sea. However, ever since the First Emperor of Qin unified China, no matter how China's territory might change, the East China Sea and the Yellow Sea have remained the country's eastern border while the South China Sea[18] the southern border. For any of the rulers, the conservative strategy for sea power was "inaction." There seemed to be a "gate" between sea and land, which, once closed, would ward off any foreign threat from the sea.

However, the Opium Wars marked the end of the policy of "inaction." In 1840, British warships forced their way through the "gate." Though still ignorant about the other parts of the world and the jungle law in the modern struggle for sea power, China felt the pain of being attacked front and rear. It knew for the first time that enemies on the sea could advance all the way to the seat of government in the same way as enemies on land.

Sea and land have since ceased to be either-or options for China. They are interdependent as problems with either may undermine national sovereignty and security, and the other would hardly stay unharmed. While the importance of sea as

---

[16]Wang, Yuquan (ed.) (2007). *A General History of Chinese Economy: The Ming Dynasty (vol. 1).* Beijing: China Social Sciences Press, pp. 40–41.

[17]In the opinion of the author of *A General History of Chinese Economy: The Ming Dynasty*, all the migrants in the Jiangnan region moved between the provinces in that region and none of them moved out to any of the northern provinces. However, it seems that this could not explain the population increase in inland provinces and the decrease in coastal ones, considering the social stability, economic recovery and the rise of living standards at the beginning of the Ming Dynasty despite the stern measures to curb the under-reporting of population and land. Wang, Yuquan (ed.) (2007). *A General History of Chinese Economy: The Ming Dynasty.* China Social Sciences Press, pp. 40–41.

[18]The ambitious Emperor Wudi of Han and Kublai Khan waged wars to conquer Japan and Korea but never succeeded. For Emperor Wudi of Han's attack on Korea, see *Book of Han: The Southwestern Barbarians, the Two Yues, and Korea* (Chap. 65). For the Yuan Dynasty's expeditions to Japan in 1274 and 1281, see Masaaki, Sugiyama (2013). *Kublai Khan's Challenge.* (Zhou, Junyu Trans.) Beijing: Social Sciences Academic Press, pp. 191–192. During the Ming Dynasty, China and Japan were alternately on the offensive in their rivalry, and Japanese pirates frequently intruded upon China during the 100-odd years after the founding of the dynasty; in 1495, the Ming government helped Korea to defeat the Japanese invaders. The Chinese territory was never affected.

natural borders declined, the traditional system of ideas on national security began to crumble. In comparison to land security, maritime security, which had rarely been addressed in the country's defense framework, was more meaningful and more complicated.

1.3 Passive Awakening and Low-Profile Growth

The more than 150 years from the end of the Opium Wars to 2000 marked the second period of the relationship between China and the sea. While the previous period was characterized by the country's unintentional rise and decline in maritime strength, this period saw the sea playing a more active role because many attacks on China started or occurred on the sea. China was in a state of "passive awakening" most of the time. While enduring humiliations and bully from the maritime powers, China adopted a conservative posture of *baoyuan shouyi.*[19] It worked hard to gain a better understanding of the sea and sea power, and to improve its strength and performance. During the first half of this period, in its struggle for independence, China was in a vulnerable position in international relations; during the second half, it emphasized peaceful coexistence[20] and kept a low profile due to the need to maintain a climate of peaceful development.

An important fact about the independence struggle between 1840 and 1949 is that while China could put up effective defense against ground forces on the strength of its vast interior, complicated terrain, and large population, it was almost powerless to attacks from the sea—at least by 1949. This explains why China was never fully colonized though it had been humiliated and invaded by one or more Western industrialized powers and had many places fall into foreign control; and why it eventually triumphed over Japan after 8 years of resistance. It is precisely for the same reason, however, that after the American warships entered the Taiwan Strait, the People's Liberation Army (PLA) failed to recover Taiwan despite its hitherto irresistible momentum of victory.

The occupation and cession of land and related damages during more than a century due to its weakness in sea power were merely the beginning and a most unforgettable part of China's sea-related pains. Despite the tough position of Mao Zedong and Deng Xiaoping, the two top leaders after 1949 who believed in the

[19] *Baoyuan shouyi* ("maintaining the primordial unity") is one of the earlier methods of practicing Taoism. The main idea is to maintain the human essence, energy and spirit in such a way that they would neither be consumed nor escape, so that they would fill the body all the time and become one with the physical form.

[20] On December 31, 1953, Zhou Enlai put forward the Five Principles of Peaceful Coexistence: mutual respect for sovereignty and territorial integrity, mutual nonaggression, noninterference in each other's internal affairs, equality and mutual benefit, and peaceful coexistence. In 1990, these principles were advocated by Deng Xiaoping and became China's tenet for the building of a new international political and economic order.

Table 1.2 Change in the regional structure of China's foreign trade in 1950–1952 (million USD)

Countries/regions receiving exported goods	1950		1951		1952	
	Amount	Percentage (%)	Amount	Percentage (%)	Amount	Percentage (%)
USSR and other communist countries	395	33.5	1282	65.4	1577	81.3
Capitalist countries	735	66.5	678	34.6	363	18.7

Source Wu Chengming and Dong Zhikai (ed.). *A History of the Economy of the PRC*. Social Sciences Academic Press, 2010, 539

"power of the gun," China continued to be in an embarrassing situation in sea-related affairs, as it could not afford to offend the great powers while having difficulty getting along with small countries. China was never fully capable of taking over the maritime assets left by its ancestry: the control over nearly forty islands, including the Diaoyu Islands in the East China Sea and Nanzi Island in the South China Sea, was seized or encroached upon by neighboring countries. The economic blockade by the West handicapped China's peaceful utilization of the sea. Though foreign trade increased by USD810 million from 1950 to 1952, trade with "capitalist countries" declined from USD735 million to USD363 million (see Table 1.2). Moreover, for a rather long period of time, China's foreign trade was mainly conducted by land or via Hong Kong (Fig. 1.4).

The situation did not improve until the historic visits of Richard Nixon and Kakuei Tanaka, which started the process of the normalization of China-US and China-Japan diplomatic relations in 1972. China's imports and exports, after chronic single-digit growth, jumped 30.2 % in 1972 over the previous year. The momentum of growth continued in the years that followed, with imports and exports up 74.29 % in 1973 and 32.7 % in 1974 (see Figs. 1.5 and 1.6). In 1979 when China and the United States reestablished diplomatic relations, imports and exports rose 40.41 % year-on-year and in 1980, a similarly impressive increase of 42.1 % was reported.

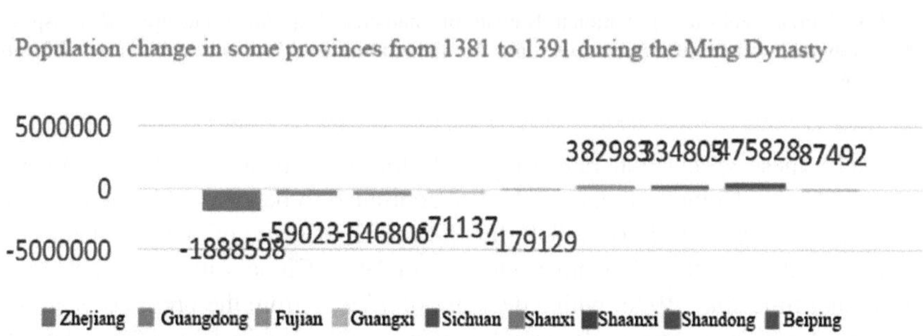

Fig. 1.4 Population change in some Chinese provinces during Ming Dynasty (1381–1391). *Source* Wang Yuquan (ed.). *A General History of Chinese Economy: The Ming Dynasty*. China Social Sciences Press, 2007, 40–41. These data only serve as a frame of reference

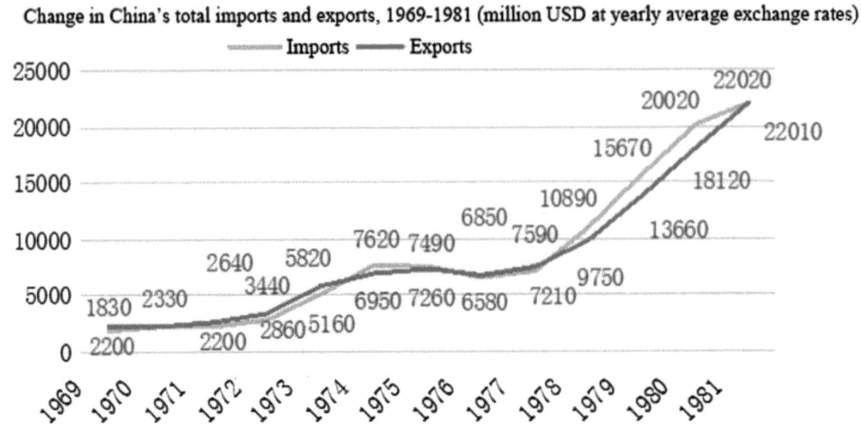

Fig. 1.5 Change in China's total imports and exports, 1969–1981 (million USD). *Source* Website of National Bureau of Statistics, http://data.stats.gov.cn/workspace/index?m=hgnd

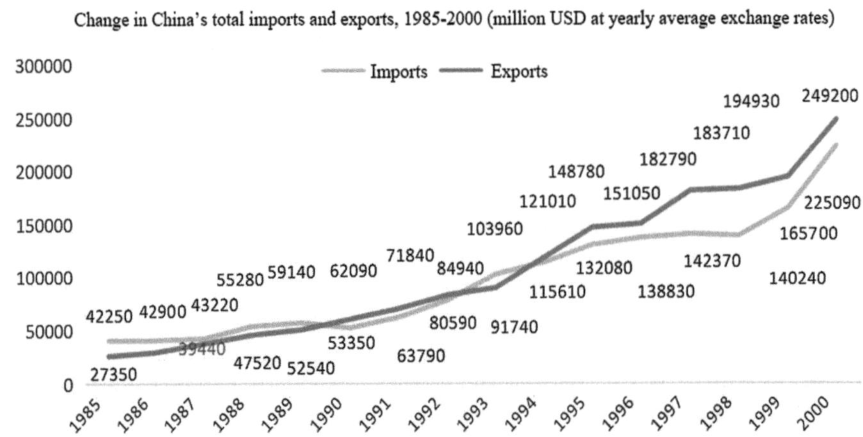

Fig. 1.6 *Source* Website of National Bureau of Statistics, http://data.stats.gov.cn/workspace/index?m=hgnd; website of National Oceanic Administration, http://www.soa.gov.cn/zwgk/hygb/zghyjjtjgb/

Despite these spectacular rates of growth, the sea was, as it had been, no free range for China. China's foreign trade data continued to be affected by its relations with great powers, especially the US. In 1990, partly because of Western countries' sanctions following the Tiananmen incident in 1989, China's imports went down for the first time since 1976, with a decrease of 9.79 % from the previous year (see Fig. 1.6). China's marine trade activities were often inhibited by great maritime powers like the US, and the Yinhe incident is a case in point. On July 23, 1993, the US alleged that the Yinhe was a dangerous ship carrying thiodiglycol and thionyl chloride, precursors for chemical weapons, from Dalian to Bandar Abbas in Iran. On August 3, the US demanded that the Chinese government should order the ship to return home, or allow American inspectors to board the ship, or leave the anchored ship at their disposal. Despite the protests of the Chinese government and the ship crew, the Yinhe, after being made to stop for 25 days by American warships in international waters, accepted an exceptionally severe inspection conducted jointly by Saudi Arabia, the host country of its port of call at Dammam, China, and the United States. Having found nothing in the suspected containers from August 28 to 30, the Americans asked for a thorough search, and it was not until all the other containers were examined from September 2 to 4 that they agreed to leave.

The inspection and related investigations proved the innocence of the Yinhe. It was an ordinary cargo ship departing from Tianjin New Harbor instead of the alleged Dalian port. More importantly, there was not a single Iranian harbor in the places it passed (Shanghai, Hong Kong, Singapore, and Jakarta) or was destined for (Dubai, Damman and Kuwait). In clear contrast with America's arrogance and peremptoriness was China's passivity and helplessness on the sea.

This was not an isolated case. Apart from the capacity of ensuring trade activities, China's capacity of protecting overseas Chinese was also inadequate. On May 14, 1998, violence against Chinese took place in Indonesia. Within 50 h, riots broke out in 27 areas of Jakarta. Over 5000 Chinese-owned shops and houses were burned, nearly 1200 died, and 468 women and girls were raped, the youngest among whom was only nine. Like the mob violence against Chinese in May 1969 in Malaysia, this incident sent a ruthless warning to China: a great power with nuclear weapons is still incapable of effective protection of its citizens abroad if it had no control over the sea.

Each coin has two sides. Such painful and embarrassing experiences reflected to some degree the deepening of China's relationship with and its understanding of the sea.

From the arrogant belief that all under the heaven belonged to the emperor to the panic at losing sovereignty and land, from desperate resistance to the common enemy to the defense of and emphasis on sovereignty and territorial integrity, from worries about maritime security to the advocacy of maritime rights and interests, China has come to value and rely on the sea more, and it has become more confident in the face of greater challenges from the sea.

It is perhaps the painful maritime experiences that helped shape the Chinese view of the sea. Due to the passivity of its awakening and the lack of understanding and study of sea-related international rules of interaction, China has yet to develop a system of mature ideas about how to use the sea. Some ideas are single-tracked, such as the development of the navy, the building of ships, and rights to sail across international waters; some practices are merely experimental, such as the adjustment of a series of relationship between land and sea, armament and commerce, domestic trade and overseas trade, domestic demand and external demand, introducing foreign capital and making overseas investment, maritime economy and support for related industries, state guidance, and the civil society's enthusiasm to participate.

However, it was a major turning point and step forward when China ceased to turn its back on the sea and came to examine its insufficient understanding of the sea and the lack of a maritime strategy. Moreover, China is seeking to make the sea a great strength rather than a soft spot in its national security and development strategy. China has abandoned the policy of maritime defense and development characterized by passive offshore defense and shifted its vision from coastal waters to more distant waters and the open sea. Apart from the security of territorial land and waters, China's national security has extended to encompass nontraditional elements, such as security of overseas Chinese citizens, trade, investment, and energy resources. The goal is now not just to ensure the independence and integrity of national sovereignty, but to continuously support national rejuvenation.

However, these changes do not mean that China has entirely cast off its conservative and defensive posture. Following the case of Wen Ho Lee[21] in March 1999 and the bombardment of the Chinese embassy in Yugoslavia by the US military in May 1999,[22] China chose to exercise restraint in order to avoid too much impact on its relations with America. It was not until September 2000 that President Jiang Zemin prudently and publicly remarked on both incidents on "60 min" hosted

[21]The case of Wen Ho Lee: In 1996, while investigating the so-called possibility of China stealing secrets about the design of nuclear weapons from Los Alamos National Laboratory, the FBI identified Chinese American scientist Wen Ho Lee as the suspect. In March 1999, Secretary of Energy Richardson gave orders to fire Lee on the ground of violation of security regulations. In April, the spokesperson for the Chinese Foreign Ministry refuted the "nuclear spy" case as sheer nonsense. In May, Congressman Christopher Cox and others issued the notorious Cox Report, which accuses China of collecting confidential data about nuclear warheads and high-performance computer technology through academic exchange, tourism and contact with laboratory employees conducted by so-called shell companies in the United States. Though the report contains no convincing evidence for the allegations and assumptions, Wen Ho Lee was once again victimized by the anti-China politicians' slanders and attacks on China. On September 10, Los Alamos National Laboratory announced disciplinary actions against three of the persons in charge of the lab (including blocking salaries and issuing letters of reprimand) who had wrongly accused Wen Ho Lee of espionage. In November, Lee re-asserted his innocence. The US government decided not to seek to indict him for espionage because no evidence showed he had deliberately passed nuclear secrets. On December 11, the Department of Justice arrested Lee on 59 charges. On December 20, Attorney General Janet Reno stated that there was no sufficient evidence to show Lee's involvement in espionage. On December 21, Lee struck back and sued the US government for serious violation of his privacy that led to his being considered a spy. On March 19, 2000, Lee's children set up a legal defense foundation to raise judicial funds for their father. On August 22, the Department of Justice openly admitted that the data downloaded by Lee were not confidential. At the same time, however, it rejected Lee's request to reduce the number of charges against him. On August 24, Federal Judge Parker agreed to release Wen Ho Lee on bail.

[22]On May 8, 1999, the United States bombed the Chinese embassy in Yugoslavia, causing injuries and deaths and vast damage of property. The US government stated that it was accidental.

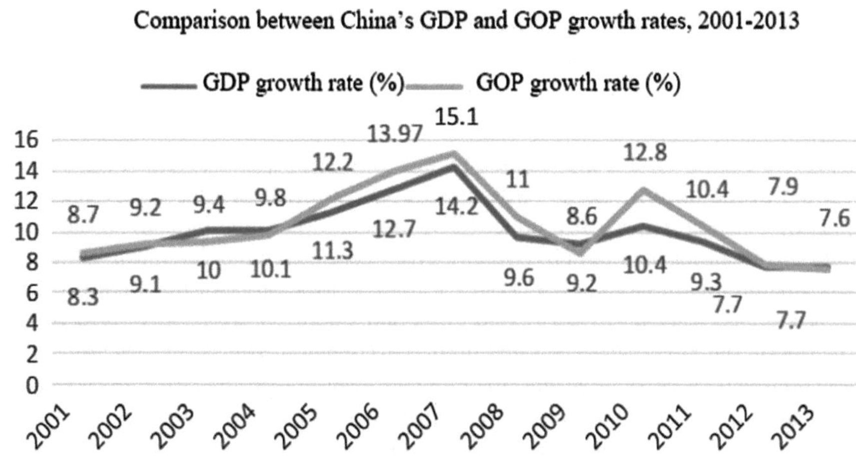

Fig. 1.7 *Source* Website of National Bureau of Statistics, http://data.stats.gov.cn/workspace/index?m=hgnd

by Mike Wallace. "Was he (Wen Ho Lee) really a spy?" he asked Wallace. Regarding the bombardment of the Chinese embassy, he said that, considering the technological capability of America, the "accidental bombing" explanation was "hardly convincing".[23] The belated statement from the top leader contained no criticism nor accusation; it was not even a counterattack (Fig. 1.7).

Soon, however, there was a turn for the better. In 2001, with the collision between a Chinese military aircraft with an American one[24] and China's entry into the WTO,[25] another qualitative change took place in China's relationship with the sea. Thanks to the sea, many of China's essential socioeconomic data increased by leaps and bounds, and rise became an irresistible trend that would sweep the world.

[23]Kuhn, Robert Lawrence (2005). *The Man Who Changed China: the Life and Legacy of Jiang Zemin*. (Tan, Zheng, Yu, Haijiang et al. trans.) Shanghai: Shanghai Century Publishing Group and Shanghai Translation Publishing House, pp. 310–311, 346–348.

[24]On April 1, 2001, an EP-3 reconnaissance aircraft of the United States was operating above waters near Hainan when China sent two J-8II fighters for surveillance and interception. The wingman's aircraft collided with the American aircraft above the Chinese exclusive economic zone 70 nautical miles (110 km) southeast of Hainan. The Chinese fighter crashed and the pilot, called Wang Wei, bailed out. His whereabouts after that became unknown and he was eventually confirmed by China to be dead. China accused the American aircraft of intentionally hitting the J-8II fighter and making a crash landing on Chinese territory without notice and permission. The United States said that the EP-3 was hit by the J-8II fighter which had gone out of control and was led to the airfield by the other J-8II.

[25]On December 11, 2001, the PRC officially joined the WTO after 15 years of negotiation.

1.4 The Irresistible Trend of Passive Rise

The internal driving force for China's "passive rise" is its growing reliance on the sea.

Since 2001, the following major changes have taken place in China:

Maritime economy has grown rapidly, with industrial structure effectively upgraded. The gross ocean product (GOP) (mainly maritime industries) has generally grown faster than the GDP in any given period (see the diagram). While the GOP (mainly maritime industries) only accounted for 6.66 % of the GDP in 2001, the percentage went up to 9.19 % in 2004 and stabilized above 9 % most of the time during the next couple of years until 2010, when it rose again to 9.56 %. For three consecutive years after that, the rate was even higher and close to 10 % (see the diagram). More importantly, the structure of maritime industries has been optimized. In 2003, the proportions of the three industries were: primary industry, 28 %; secondary industry, 29 %; tertiary industry, 43 %; in 2013, the proportions became: primary industry, 5.4 %; secondary industry, 45.8 %; tertiary industry: 48.8 %. This has narrowed the gap between China and the world in the structure of maritime industries.[26] In fact, China's is already a well-developed structure, with such pillars as maritime transportation, coastal tourism, marine fishery, offshore oil and gas, marine vessel manufacturing, marine chemical industry and sea salt engineering, covering marine mining, marine biopharmaceutics, marine electric power, and seawater utilization.

A large population has flown to coastal regions, the powerhouse of economic development. In terms of registered permanent residents only, in 2000, the 11 province-level administrative coastal regions[27] had 35.94 % (approx. 455 million) of China's population with 10.19 % of its mainland territory and created 52.33 % (approx. RMB5.13 trillion) of the national GDP; in 2010, they had 37.67 % (approx. 505 million) of China's population and created 56.45 % (approx. RMB22.56 trillion) of the national GDP (see Table 1.3). During this period, these regions' superiority as a magnet for population and economy has further increased.

If other factors are considered (e.g., the support the coastal regions have provided for the inland areas, the massive influx of people into the regions who form

[26]The global structure of maritime industries in 2003: primary industry, 8 %, secondary industry, 59 %, tertiary industry: 33 %. See China Institute for Marine Affairs Research Group of State Oceanic Administration (2007). *China's Ocean Development Report*. Beijing: China Ocean Press, pp. 126. The United States' structure of maritime industries in 2005: primary industry, 2 %, secondary industry, 29.2 %, tertiary industry, 68.8 %. See Zhao, Zhen (2007). China's Structure of Maritime Industries and Its Optimization. *Maritime Development and Management*, no. 7, pp. 43–46.

[27]These are Liaoning Province, Hebei Province, Tianjin City, Shandong Province, Jiangsu Province, Shanghai City, Zhejiang Province, Fujian Province, Guangdong Province, the Zhuang Autonomous Region of Guangxi, and Hainan Province. The statistical scope of National Bureau of Statistics also includes Beijing among the coastal regions. If so, the economic performance of the coastal regions would be even more impressive.

Table 1.3 Comparison in population and GDP between province-level regions in the Chinese mainland in 2000 and 2010

Region (coastal/inland)	Area (10,000 km^2)	GDP (100 million RMB)		Population (10,000)		Percentage (%)	
		2000	2010	2000	2010	2000	2010
Total	954.76	98,000.45	399,579.94	126,583	133,973	100	100
Beijing	1.68	3161.66	14,113.58	1382	1961	1.09	1.46
Tianjin (coastal)	1.19	1701.88	9224.46	1001	1294	0.79	0.97
Hebei (coastal)	19	5043.96	20,394.26	6744	7185	5.33	5.36
Shanxi	16	1845.72	9200.86	3297	3571	2.60	2.67
Inner Mongolia	118	1539.12	11,672.00	2376	2471	1.88	1.84
Liaoning (coastal)	15	4669.06	18,457.27	4238	4375	3.35	3.27
Jilin	18	1951.51	8667.58	2728	2746	2.16	2.05
Heilongjiang	45	3151.40	10,368.60	3689	3831	2.91	2.86
Shanghai (coastal)	0.59	4771.17	17,165.98	1674	2302	1.32	1.72
Jiangsu (coastal)	10	8553.69	41,425.48	7438	7866	5.88	5.87
Zhejiang (coastal)	10	6141.03	27,722.31	4677	5443	3.69	4.06
Anhui	13	2902.09	12,359.33	5986	5950	4.73	4.44
Fujian (coastal)	12	3764.54	14,737.12	3471	3689	2.74	2.75
Jiangxi	16	2003.07	9451.26	4140	4457	3.27	3.33
Shandong (coastal)	15	8337.47	39,169.92	9079	9579	7.17	7.15
Henan	16	5052.99	23,092.36	9256	9402	7.31	7.02
Hubei	19	3545.39	15,967.61	6028	5724	4.76	4.27
Hunan	21	3551.49	16,037.96	6440	6568	5.09	4.90
Guangdong (coastal)	18	10,741.25	46,013.06	8642	10,430	6.83	7.79
Guangxi (coastal)	23	2080.04	9569.85	4489	4603	3.55	3.44
Hainan (coastal)	3.5	526.82	2064.50	787	867	0.62	0.65
Chongqing	8.2	1791.00	7925.58	3090	2885	2.44	2.15
Sichuan	48	3928.20	17,185.48	8329	8042	6.58	6.00
Guizhou	17	1029.92	4602.16	3525	3475	2.78	2.59
Yunnan	38	2011.19	7224.18	4288	4597	3.39	3.43
Tibet	123	117.80	507.46	262	300	0.21	0.22
Shaanxi	20	1804.00	10,123.48	3605	3733	2.85	2.79
Gansu	45	1052.88	4120.75	2562	2558	2.02	1.91
Qinghai	72	263.68	1350.43	518	563	0.41	0.42
Ningxia	6.6	295.02	1689.65	562	630	0.44	0.47
Xinjiang	166	1363.56	5437.47	1925	2181	1.52	1.63
People in active military service	–	–	–	250	230	0.20	0.17
People whose permanent places of residence are uncertain	–	–	–	–	465	–	0.35
Coastal regions	97.28	51,286.65	225,549.95	45,496	50,448	35.94	37.67

Source Website of National Bureau of Statistics, http://data.stats.gov.cn/workspace/index?m=hgnd. The 2010 data are used because the fourth census had just been completed that year the majority of the 200 million floating population, and the economic balance policies the central government has developed in favor of western and inland regions), the coastal region's contribution to development would be even greater and the actual population and economic contribution data would be even more impressive. The role of the coastal regions as the economic powerhouse reflects the choice of the people who "vote with their feet," and the competitive edges of the regions despite the fact that the competition has been somewhat reduced by the balance policy. The land, which used to be the center of development, is losing the lead to the sea.

The economy has become more externally dependent, giving prominence to the "maritime economy and energy lifeline." A well-known trend is the widening gap between China's total energy output and total energy consumption. In 2001, consumption only exceeded output by 65 million tons of standard coal, but the gap had increased to 362 million tons by 2013 (Fig. 1.8).

The gap has to be filled by imports. As a result, China became the world's largest energy consumer and net importer of coal in 2009, the largest coal importer in 2011, and the largest oil importer in 2012. By 2013, China's external dependence for energy, oil, natural gas and coal had reached 9.65, 58.1, 31.6, and 8.13 %, respectively.

Meanwhile, imports and exports have risen to a new level every 3 or 4 years, and dependence on foreign trade has remained high. China's total import and export value exceeded USD1 trillion in 2004, and USD2 trillion and USD3 trillion in 2007 and 2011, respectively. In 2013, it soared by another trillion US dollars to USD4.16 trillion (Fig. 1.9), making China the world's largest trader in goods. Accordingly, dependence on foreign trade has fluctuated at high levels. Such dependence rarely

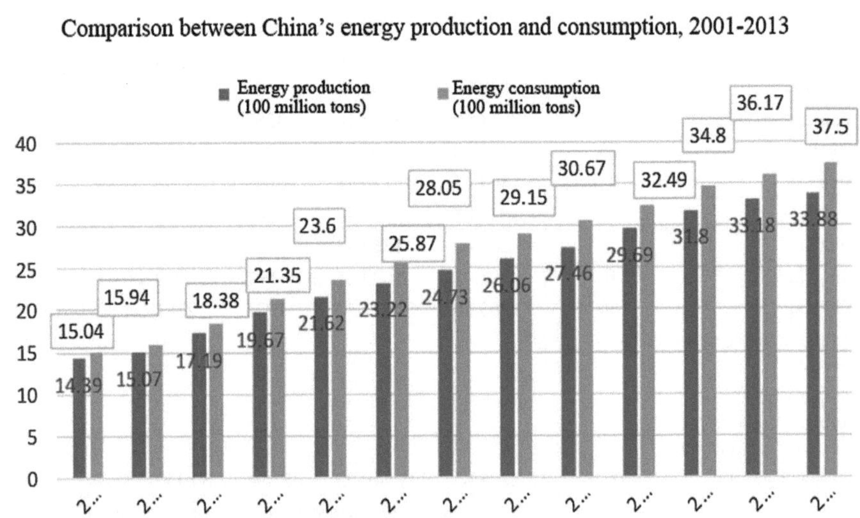

Fig. 1.8 *Source* Website of National Bureau of Statistics, http://data.stats.gov.cn/workspace/index?m=hgnd

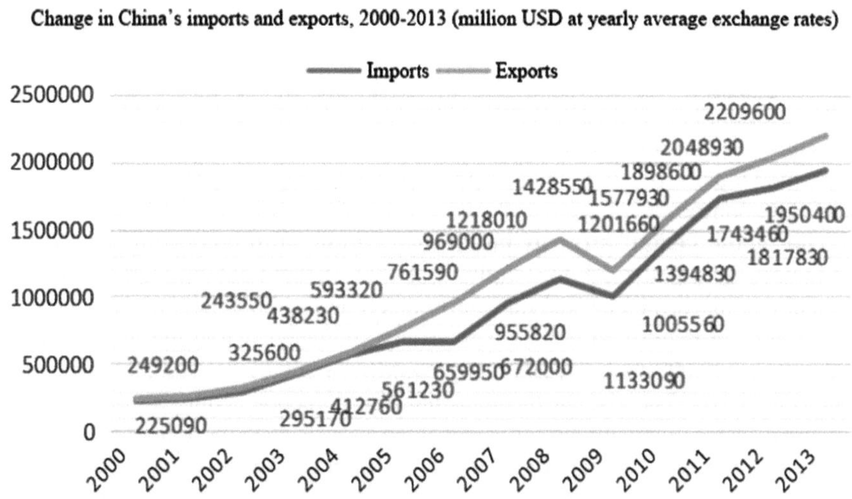

Fig. 1.9 *Source* Website of National Bureau of Statistics, http://data.stats.gov.cn/workspace/index?m=hgnd

went beyond 40 % before 2000, but a radical change took place in the twenty-first century. After it exceeded 50 % in 2002, it shot up to 67 % in 2006. There was a period of decline after the financial crisis in 2008: dependence dropped to 50.1 % in 2011 and below 50 % in 2012 and 2013 (47 and 46 % respectively). Nevertheless, the fundamentals have remained unchanged. In view of the global depression which has seriously affected foreign trade, the fact that China's dependence on foreign trade has remained steady at a high level of 50 % (way higher than the American and Japanese level of around 30 %) undoubtedly reflects the vitality of its export-oriented economy.

Since around 90 % of international trade in goods is conducted through maritime transportation, the importance of the sea to economic and energy security is self-evident. The brilliant achievements in recent years in the provision of ships, the opening of shipping routes and the construction of harbors and docks related to international shipping can be seen as China's response to the situation and an essential part of that situation.

According to statistics, by the end of 2013, eight of the ten busiest ports in the world were in China, including the two that ranked first and second (Table 1.4); China had 2457 oceangoing ships with a total net capacity of 63.666 million tons, which transported 712 million tons of cargo with a turnover of 4,870,537 million ton-km (Table 1.5). These differed markedly from the figures in 2001 and 2002.[28] In 2001, China had only four of the ten busiest ports in the world and none of them was among the top three (Table 1.4). In 2002, though China owned 2337

[28]For reasons related to the collection of data, the data on China's international ocean transport in 2001 cannot correspond to those in 2013. As a result, the data of 2002 are used in this book.

oceangoing ships, their total net capacity was only 23.1617 million tons; the total weight of cargo transported by ocean shipping and the cargo turnover were only 300 million tons and 2,173,270 million ton-km respectively (Table 1.5).

Now China has opened more than 30 routes connecting over 2000 harbors in 170 countries and regions in the five continents. As a member of the International Maritime Organization, China has signed bilateral shipping agreements with more than 100 countries.[29]

The "going global" strategy builds momentum, with increasing people and businesses going abroad for study, work or investment opportunities. The number of Chinese people studying abroad exceeded 100,000 in 2002, and the time it took for the number to double was greatly shortened: while the increase from 100,000 to 200,000 took 7 years, the growth from 200,000 to 400,000 took only four (Fig. 1.10). The rise in the total number of people going abroad and the number of those going abroad for personal purposes is even more impressive. Over the period of merely 12 years from 2001 to 2013, those numbers had increased 7.09 times and 12.24 times, respectively (Fig. 1.11). There was also a remarkable increase in the number of Chinese citizens staying abroad at the end of the year for contracted foreign projects: it increased more than 4.43 times from 2001 to 2013, and peaked in 2010 at 6.28 times the number in 2001 (Fig. 1.12). The number of Chinese citizens staying abroad as workers for foreign employers at the end of the year has stabilized between 400,000 and 500,000, yet it was not until after 2001 that it exceeded 400,000 (Fig. 1.12).

The "going global" strategy for enterprises was proposed at the Third Session of the Ninth National People's Congress in March 2000. Shortly after that, in October the same year, it was reemphasized at the Fifth Plenary Session of the 15th National Congress of the CPC. It was listed as one of the four new major strategies along with the development of China's western region, urbanization, and personnel development in the CPC Central Committee's Recommendations on the Formulation of the Tenth Five-Year Plan for the Development of National Economy and Society. Boosted by the strategy, during the 10th Five-Year Plan period, the enterprises approved for outward investment rose 33.01 % annually, up 12.35 % points from the previous five-year period.[30] During the 11th Five-Year Plan period, the number and performance of Chinese enterprises going global attained a new height.[31] First of all, central state-owned enterprises (SOEs) put up a brilliant performance. About 100 central SOEs set up subsidiaries or managing

[29]Ye, Xiangdong and Chen, Sizeng (ed.) (2013). *Modern Maritime Economy: Theory and Practice*. Beijing: Publishing House of Electronics Industry, p. 11.

[30]The Economic Information Department of China Council for the Promotion of International Trade. Analysis of the Formation of China's 'Going Global' Strategy and the System of Promotional Policies", January, 2007, http://www.ccpit.org/Contents/Channel_1276/2007/0327/30814/content_30814.htm.

[31]Information Office of the Ministry of Commerce. Leapfrog Development in China's "Going Global" Strategy during the 11th Five-Year Plan Period, October 2010. http://www.mofcom.gov.cn/aarticle/ae/ai/201010/20101007200262.html.

Table 1.4 The ten busiest ports in the world (2013 and 2001)

Top ten Ports in 2013				Top ten Ports in 2001			
Rank	Name	Country	Cargo throughput (100 million tons)	Rank	Name	Country	Cargo throughput (100 million tons)
1	Port of Ningbo-Zhoushan	China	8.10	1	Port of Rotterdam	Holland	3.15
2	Port of Shanghai	China	7.76	2	Port of Singapore	Singapore	3.14
3	Port of Singapore	Singapore	5.58	3	Port of South Louisiana	The United States	2.53
4	Port of Tianjin	China	5.01	4	Port of Shanghai	China	2.21
5	Port of Guangzhou	China	4.55	5	Port of Hong Kong	China	1.78
6	Port of Suzhou	China	4.54	6	Port of Chiba	Japan	1.59
7	Port of Qingdao	China	4.50	7	Port of Nagoya	Japan	1.54
8	Port of Tangshan	China	4.46	8	Port of Antwerp	Belgium	1.30
9	Port of Rotterdam	Holland	4.41	9	Port of Ningbo-Zhoushan	China	1.29
10	Port of Dalian	China	3.33	10	Port of Guangzhou	China	1.28

Source http://www.chineseport.cn/

Table 1.5 China's international ocean transport data in 2013 and 2002

2013		2002	
Berths for production at coastal harbors	5675	Berths for production at coastal harbors	3822
Berth at/above the 10,000-ton level at coastal harbors	1607	Berth at/above the 10,000-ton level at coastal harbors	700
Throughput of goods for foreign trade at coastal harbors (100 million tons)	30.57	Throughput of goods for foreign trade at coastal harbors (100 million tons)	6.0
Oceangoing ships	2457	Oceangoing ships	2337
Container slots on oceangoing ships (10,000 TEU)	117.66	Container slots on oceangoing ships (10,000 TEU)	45.09
Capacity of oceangoing ships (10,000 tons)	6366.6	Capacity of oceangoing ships (10,000 tons)	2316.17
Cargo in coastal transport (100 million tons)	16.47	Cargo in coastal transport (100 million tons)	3.6
Turnover of cargo in coastal transport (100 million ton-km)	19216.14	Turnover of cargo in coastal transport (100 million ton-km)	4269.2
Cargo in ocean transport (100 million tons)	7.12	Cargo in ocean transport (100 million tons)	3.0
Turnover of cargo in ocean transport (100 million ton-km)	48705.37	Turnover of cargo in ocean transport (100 million ton-km)	21732.7

Source Website of Ministry of Transport, http://www.moc.gov.cn/zhuzhan/tongjigongbao/

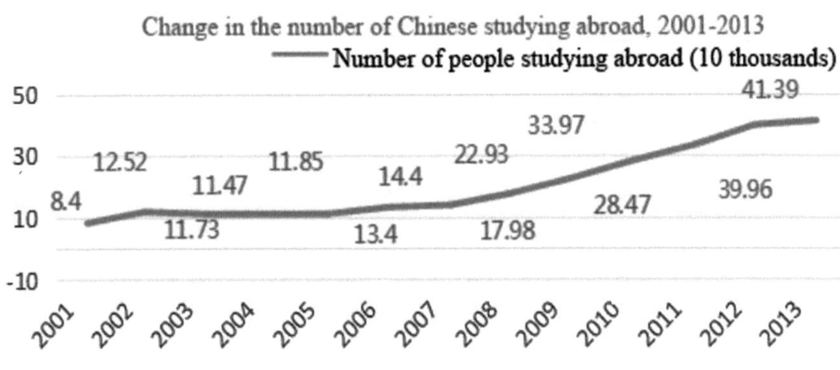

Fig. 1.10 *Source* Website of National Bureau of Statistics, http://data.stats.gov.cn/workspace/index?m=hgnd

agencies abroad, and the proportion of overseas profits and assets kept increasing in the asset and revenue structure of such SOEs as China Minmetals Corporation, China Nonferrous Mining Group, China National Petroleum Corporation, and China Ocean Shipping (Group) Company. Second, the quality of projects has steadily improved. Projects worth above USD100 million numbered 240 in 2009; in contrast, in 2005 toward the end of the 10th Five-Year Plan, there were only 49 of

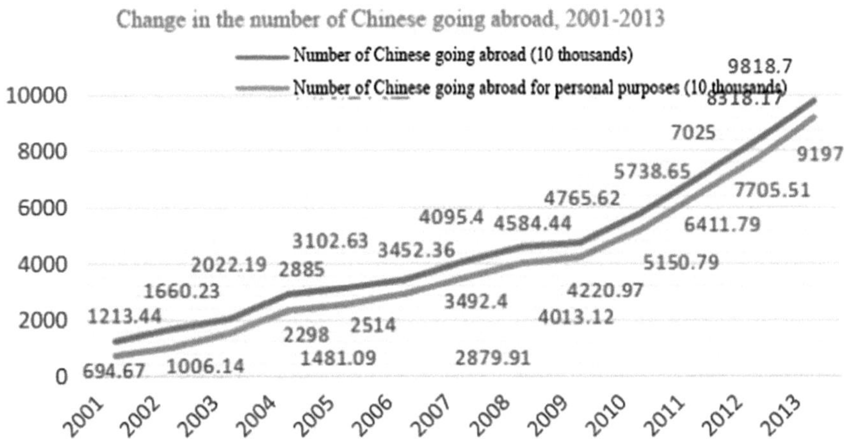

Fig. 1.11 *Source* Website of National Bureau of Statistics, http://data.stats.gov.cn/workspace/index?m=hgnd

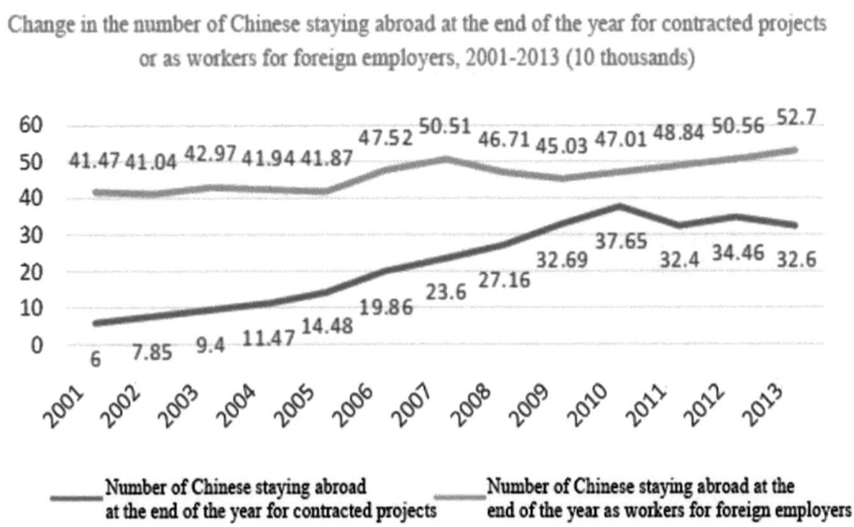

Fig. 1.12 *Source* Website of National Bureau of Statistics, http://data.stats.gov.cn/workspace/index?m=hgnd

such projects. The range of areas covered by projects has also expanded from simple processing and packaging to infrastructural construction and the manufacturing of high-end products.

The "going global" of businesses has fueled the outstanding performance of foreign direct investment (FDI) and foreign contracted projects (Figs. 1.13 and 1.14). In terms of foreign direct investment, both the flow and the stock had started

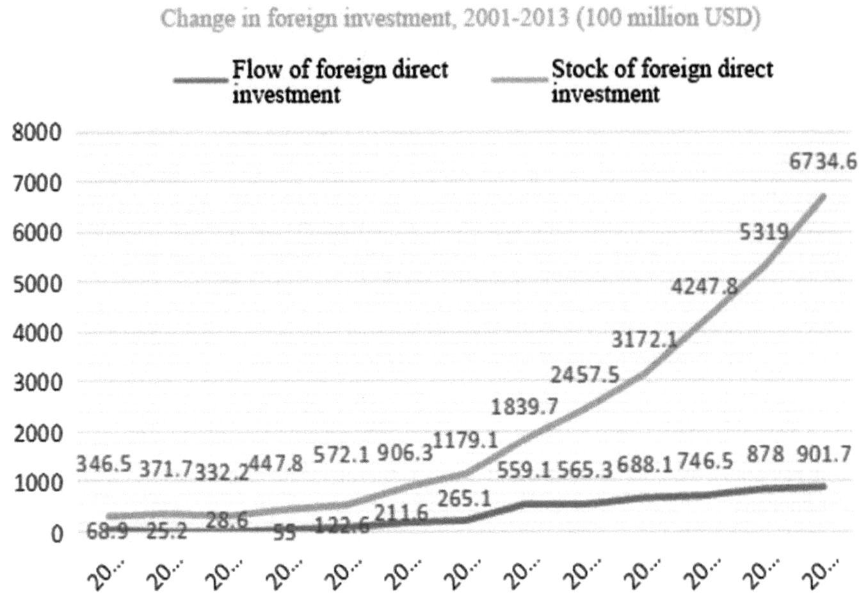

Fig. 1.13 *Source* Website of National Bureau of Statistics, http://data.stats.gov.cn/workspace/index?m=hgnd

Fig. 1.14 *Source of data* Website of National Bureau of Statistics, http://data.stats.gov.cn/workspace/index?m=hgnd

from a low level and risen to an impressive height in 10-odd years. The annual flow of FDI exceeded USD10 billion in 2005, USD20 billion in 2006, and USD50 billion in 2008; in 2013, it went beyond USD90 billion and approached the strategic level of USD100 billion, making China one of the world's three greatest investors along with the United States and Japan for 2 years running. The performance in the stock of FDI has also been brilliant. Having exceeded USD100 billion in 2007, it went beyond USD500 billion in 2012. By the end of 2012, 16,000 Chinese investors had established nearly 22,000 FDI businesses abroad in 179 countries and regions around the world.

Foreign contracted projects have developed as fast as FDI. In terms of the total worth of such projects and the worth of the completed ones among them, the figures of 2013 were 13.16 times and 15.41 times those of 2001, respectively, at a growth rate comparable to that of FDI flow (The FDI flow of 2013 was 13.09 times that of 2001).

With the rapid growth of maritime economy and the optimization of the maritime industry structure, the coastal regions have become the focus of economic development. This has resulted in increased external reliance and accelerated flow of enterprises, personnel and funds across the globe. This not only reflects China's greater capability of using the sea as an impetus of development in terms of transport and energy, but also means that the sea has acquired an indispensable role for China's national security on multiple levels including industry, energy, social administration and public services. China has developed an inextricable relationship with the sea. It not only needs to obtain impetus of development from or through the sea, but it must also be able to maintain this state of affairs.

China must have the courage and ability to protect its investments, factory premises, and infrastructure from external threats or infringement. This was the underlying reason for the aforementioned incident of 2001 in which the Chinese military aircraft intercepted the more advanced American one. China must also be able to guarantee the safety of its citizens, enterprises, and capital abroad. The withdrawal of Chinese citizens from Egypt and Libya, the participation in the search for Malaysia Airlines flight 370, and many other events since 2011 indicate that, in response to the demand from overseas Chinese citizens and enterprises for public service in security provided by the Chinese government, the government is trying to build its capacity in this respect.

Therefore, apart from becoming a strong nation in maritime economy and technology, China has to be a major military power on the sea. The combination of strength in these three aspects would undoubtedly outline a veritable great maritime power. This is probably the road map for China's "rise on the sea."

A closer observation would reveal that the rise would happen in stages and on various levels. However, it is distinctly "passive" regardless of any particular stage, level or sense. Superficially, the economic and technological rise seems more proactive thanks to the existence of less controversy and resistance. In fact, it is merely a continuation of the "passive awakening," for without it China would have to stand by and see other countries vie with each other on the vast waves and tolerate their control over and appropriation of its marine resources. The "passivity" of the military rise, which would meet with more significant resistance, is evident. Without that, China would have difficulty preserving its achievements in the economic and technological rise, let alone sustainable development in a more rapid and effective way.

Thus the internal causes not only prompt China to "rise passively" on the sea, but also demand a successful rise. This would be a natural result of China's development in the context of deepening international intercourse. It is also an inevitable step toward China's rejuvenation, and an overall agenda China would not allow any force to disrupt.

1.5 The World Calls for a Maritime China

This, of course, is only one aspect of China's "passive rise" on the sea, which mainly reflects the driving force behind China's self-reliance in this respect. On the other hand, various signs indicate that China's "maritime rise" has also been the result of interactions and changes in the international political and economic situation. International forces are staging a drama of international politics in which China is compelled to build its maritime strength.

China's growing economic reliance on other countries is only part of the picture; the other side of the coin is the increasing reliance of the rest of the world on China. The weakening of China's comparative advantage in labor price has undermined its status in the world system of industrial division of labor and cooperation; while China is seeking for a new orientation, "made in China" may give way to "made in India," "made in Vietnam," and "made in Indonesia," so that cheap Chinese goods can no longer play the vital role of a bridge between China and other countries—if so, the Chinese market is no doubt one of the best links between China and the world. The aforementioned increasing Chinese FDI may soon become yet another. In 2011, China became a major trade partner with 124 countries and regions. The interest in the Chinese market taken by the United States, Europe, Russia, and the Middle East, the expectation for Chinese investment among China's neighbors in Southeast Asia and Central Asia as well as its partners in Africa and South America, and the motivational role played by China in the global economic recovery after the financial crisis of 2008—these, among others, are impressive indicators in their own right. China and the world are being brought closer together, despite the decrease of cheap Chinese goods. The vast majority of the countries and regions around the world are in need of more mutually beneficial economic cooperation with China.

It is apparent that China must have the capacity for tapping this potential for cooperation to the full. For example, it can develop as many trade routes as possible and increase trade channels and support. Under special circumstances, it can accomplish a series of tasks single-handedly according to agreements and in the interest of cooperation, such as the circulation of goods and services, the prospecting and development of resources, the construction of infrastructure, and the completion of industrial projects. China must also be able to make cooperation happen, ensuring the quality, and timely availability of both imported and exported goods and services, and guaranteeing that collaborative projects are completed on time and up to the standard in both quality and quantity, or in a manner that meets the expectations.

To this end, it has become an inevitable trend to step up the development of overseas resources, construction, and the operation of factories and businesses, to open more international ocean routes, to form a secure and interconnected ocean transport network and to reach a wider market as well as optimize and restructure the market as needed. All these require considerable maritime strength that is built upon busy ocean fleets, a dense network of trade destinations, technology for prospecting and developing resources under complex and unfamiliar topographical conditions, marketing skills and international cooperation for maritime security and the protection of legitimate commercial interests as well as preparedness for overseas security emergencies.

Apart from the impetus from the international community's economic expectations, the wish among other countries for China to bear more international responsibility implies a demand for greater contribution to maritime affairs (e.g., cooperation in assistance and salvage at sea, the provision of public goods for security in international waters, and the protection of environment and resources) and propels China's bid to become a strong maritime nation.

Nowadays, thanks to the rapid progress of science and technology, mankind is enjoying the benefits of globalization and industrialization and will be enjoying more of them. However, every coin has two sides; mankind is also facing unprecedented challenges. Terrorism, the proliferation of weapons of mass destruction, space garbage, environmental pollution and damage, and endangered species are universally recognized as common challenges for mankind. Addressing these challenges calls for strong cooperation between countries.[32] As a country with many ethnic groups and a major country in terms of nuclear and space capability and energy consumption, China is as a matter of course an indispensable party to jointly solving these issues related to global public governance.

Terrorist attacks know no boundary between land and sea, weapons of mass destruction are basically free from spatial restrictions, and blue waters are as seriously polluted as inland areas. These are coupled with piracy, a trouble with a long history. The sea is a principal locale, sometimes the origin, for these issues of global public governance. This also increasingly calls for China's contribution in money, measures and action.

This becomes particularly noticeable when the US-led Western community comes up short in addressing issues of global public governance. For instance, the dispatch of ships by the Chinese navy for continuous participation in the joint international operations against piracy off the coast of Somalia since 2009 has been a result of strong request by the international community. Powerful as the United

[32]Zhang, Yuyan and Li, Zenggang (2008). *International Economic Politics*. Shanghai: Shanghai People's Publishing House, pp. 189–195.

States and its allies might be, they were overwhelmed by the unpredictability of the Somalian pirates and the advantage of being world police was outweighed by the troubles they made. Given the difficulty in continuing to provide at a loss the global public goods of order and security in the waters in question, getting China to share the cost and responsibility, in view of its thriving economy and growing activity along ocean routes, became a more viable option.

The presence of Chinese naval ships in the waters off Somalia is just an epitome of the situation. Today's popular topics also include the Sino-Russian joint military exercise at sea in 2012 and China's role in Exercise RIMPAC in 2014 (Table 1.6). In fact, as early as November 11, 2004, China signed the Regional Cooperation Agreement on Combating Piracy and Armed Robbery against Ships in Asia with the ten ASEAN countries, Japan, the Republic of Korea, India, Sri Lanka and Bangladesh et al. However, the agreement, which became effective on September 4, 2006, has not made much difference. Till now, the waters of South China Sea are still considered a second Gulf of Aden by the International Maritime Organization. With the United States unwilling and other Asian countries willing but unable to contribute, China may eventually become the de facto provider of order and security as public goods in those waters.

Table 1.6 Influential international joint military exercises at sea participated in by China

Participants	Time	Place	Forces sent by China
China and Russia	Sept. 18, 2009	Western area of Gulf of Aden	One destroyer and one AOR
China and Russia	April 22–27, 2012	Waters of the Yellow Sea off Qingdao	Two submarines and 16 surface vessels including destroyers, frigates, missile boats, AORs and a hospital ship
China and Russia	July 5–12, 2013	Peter the Great Bay, the Sea of Japan	Four destroyers, two frigates, and one AOR
China and Russia	May 20–26, 2014	Northern part of the East China Sea	Two submarines, eight surface vessels including destroyers, frigates, missile boats and AORs, and nine fixed-wing aircraft
22 countries including China, the US, Britain, Japan, the Republic of Korea and India	June 26–August 1, 2014	Waters off Hawaii	One destroyer, one frigate, one AOR, and one hospital ship

Source Based on open-source materials

While people have talked a lot in recent years about how China will replace the United States as the world's largest economy, they are also interested in how its role will change in areas other than economy, how important its position will be in the global security order, and how different it will be from Britain, America and other great powers in the road leading up to the rise at sea. This is probably the most fundamental context.

China's road to a real great maritime power will be fraught with difficulty and uncertainty. For instance, America's new Asia-Pacific policies of "return to Asia" and "rebalance toward Asia" as well as the neighboring countries with which China has disputes over maritime borders or those whose maritime strategy is in conflict with that of China will impede China's bid to go far and deep at sea. Moreover, whether China can contribute a new view of sea power and the sea and what it will be like are yet to be seen.

Given the basic conclusion that the world needs security and order and China relies more on international peace for its development, China will begin to contribute or contribute more to the provision of global public goods not only in the neighboring international waters, but also in a number of important waters around the world. With the war in Afghanistan, the Iraq war, the Arab Spring and the incident in Ukraine, America's global values have been roundly criticized for being selfish and domineering. Moreover, economic slowdown and cut in military spending have significantly weakened its motivation and ability to be the world police, resulting in continuous aggravation of conflict or terrorism in areas around the world. In addition, the readjustment of America's armed forces abroad has created more and larger loopholes in the global security and order system. This has been the cause for the acceleration of arms race between countries, the increase of paramilitary and military conflict, and terrorism becoming a common enemy of all governments.

Facts will prove that the result from international demand or the game at sea may be similar to China's natural course of development. Though China faces more complicated and daunting challenges on the sea, it also enjoys greater leeway and opportunity for maneuvering and showcasing itself. China has entered a period of progress at sea in many ways. Both the world and China have to be ready for a future that can hardly be changed: China will become a real great maritime power, not only economically and technologically, but also politically and militarily. The economic and technological strength from the sea will lead to magnitude in sea-related international voice and influence. As time goes by, the latter will increasingly become what is expected of the former. Any attempt to separate the two would be unrealistic and impossible.

It is clear to everyone that, without strong military power at sea, China would not only fail to become a great maritime power, but its economic and technological achievement would eventually prove to be a castle in the air. As long as nation-states and sovereign states exist, no country would allow any other country to manipulate and control its destiny. China cannot be an exception.

There are voices, organizations and countries that tend to play up the so-called potential threat of China's rise on the sea; they are doing so to prevent China from becoming strong. The "peaceful rise" they advocate is essentially to make China an economic giant but a political follower that looks to other countries for the trend and tempo of its development. This is obviously at odds with China's idea of peaceful rise. Self-reliance and national power are crucial for a large independent country like us. Without them, economic prosperity would be just an illusion. It would be reduced to rubbles by war, just like the period before and after the Opium Wars when the economy was impressive but crises were imminent. If so, what would be the significance of the national independence that has been won since 1840 by generations of Chinese with their patriotic devotion, blood and even lives?

Chapter 2
The Great Maritime Power Dream: Challenges and Problems

The future is bright, yet the road to that future is full of twists and turns.

China will eventually rise to become a great maritime nation that deserves this title in every respect. This will be an irresistible historical trend, but the process will not be plain sailing. In fact, it will be fraught with challenges from within to without.

Though China has accelerated its efforts to build its maritime capability, it is an indisputable fact that it still faces a risky situation marked by intertwining conflicts and impediments. Given the world's political and economic patterns and interactions, China is in the embarrassing situation that it cannot afford to offend the great powers while having difficulty getting along with less internationally influential ones.

2.1 The Taiwan Question

The importance of Taiwan to China is self-evident.

As the old proverb goes, blood is thicker than water. China would not be a complete nation state if the mainland and Taiwan were not reunified. If political reintegration were achieved for both sides of the Taiwan Straits, the most immediate benefit would be an economy growing in size and influence, market expansion, upgraded business cooperation, and increased welfare for the people.[1]

More importantly, it will significantly improve China's status in the geopolitical structure of Asia.

China's access to the Pacific Ocean is surrounded or restricted by a number of straits and sea routes, including the Korean Strait, Osumi Kaikyo, Bashi Channel,

[1]Kong Zhiguo. "The Next Step: Breaking Down Trade Barriers", in *Cenfortuna*, 2009 (2).

Z. Kong, *The Making of a Maritime Power*, Research Series on the Chinese Dream and China's Development Path, DOI 10.1007/978-981-10-1786-5_2

and the Strait of Malacca. There are three principal routes to the Pacific: the north route which passes the Korean Strait and the Kuril Islands, the east route made up of the seaways between the Japanese Archipelago, the Ryukyu Islands, the Diaoyu Islands, and Taiwan, and the south route via the Taiwan Straits or through the waters off Guangdong or Guangxi straight to the Pacific and then to the Indian Ocean. If Taiwan is reunified with the mainland, China will enjoy ample leeway along the eastern and southern routes, and Taiwan will become an unsinkable "aircraft carrier," a fortress and a business hub on the border between the East China Sea and the South China Sea.

However, there is a striking difference between reality and what people have wished for.

Compared with the days when all the mails, telegrams, and phone calls from the mainland had to go through Hong Kong before reaching Taiwan, great changes have occurred in the cross-strait relations since the beginning of the reform and opening up in 1978, as evident in the "mini three links,"[2] the subsequent "greater three links,"[3] and the signing of the Service and Trade Agreement[4] (Table 2.1). Despite the closer contacts, however, enhancing the mutual understanding between the mainland and Taiwan and preventing the United States, Japan and the secessionists from intervening in the peaceful reunification process remain an important issue for the Chinese government and one of the most pressing challenges for China's maritime rise.

Unless it is reunified with the mainland, Taiwan cannot help but being taken advantage of against the mainland by America, Japan, and some other countries for their own interests; on its part, the mainland has to explore, use and manage the sea at the risk of being contained any time.

As we know, the control over the three island chains led by the United States and participated in by its allies including Japan, the Philippines, and Australia is the primary constraint on China's entry into the Pacific. Taiwan is the hub in the first island chain, which is made up of the Aleutian Islands, the Chiba Islands, the Japanese Archipelago, the Ryukyu Islands, the Taiwan Island, the Philippines, and the islands of Indonesia. The lack of control over Taiwan has not only deprived China of a manageable route to the ocean, which has seriously undermined its overall strength and interests, but it has also added a threat from within. Taiwan can be used by America anytime to bargain with or even impose a blockade on China.

---

[2]This refers to the Measures for the Trial Opening of Traffic between Jinmen, Mazu and the Mainland unilaterally ratified by the Taiwan authorities without prior discussion with the mainland. It is popularly known as the "mini three links".

[3]First proposed by the mainland, this refers to direct mail service, transport and trade across the Taiwan Straits.

[4]On June 22, 2013, ARATS (Association for Relations across the Taiwan Straits) of the mainland and SEF (Straits Exchange Foundation) of Taiwan signed the Cross-straits Service and Trade Agreement.

Table 2.1 Milestones in cross-strait relations (1979–2013)

Time	Milestones events or agreements
1979	The mainland opened its market to Taiwan products and offered tax exemption/reduction and other favorable policies
1989	Mail packages were transported across the Straits via Hong Kong; Taiwan started telegram and telephone services to the mainland via a third place
April 1997	Direct shipping service between Fuzhou/Xiamen and Kaosiung became operational on a trial basis
The spring festival of 2003	To make it easier for businesspeople to return to Taiwan for the Spring Festival, the mainland permitted 16 flights from six Taiwan airlines to come to Shanghai from Taipei or Kaosiung via Hong Kong or Macao. It was the first time since the founding of the PRC for any aircraft of Taiwan airlines to be allowed to be landed at a mainland airport
The spring festival of 2005	For the first time, airlines on both sides of the Taiwan Straits joined the Spring Festival chartering program, enabling bidirectional cross-straits flights which did not have to land in Hong Kong or Macao but had to pass the Hong Kong flight information region
June 2008	ARATS and SEF signed in Beijing the minutes of the conference on cross-straits chartered flights. On July 4, weekend chartered flights officially started across the straits
November 4, 2008	ARATS and SEF signed the cross-straits air transportation agreement, the cross-straits shipping agreement, and the cross-straits mail service agreement
December 15, 2008	Direct shipping, direct flights, and direct mail service official started across the Straits
April 26, 2009	ARATS and SEF signed the cross-straits financial cooperation agreement, the supplementary agreement on cross-straits air transportation, and the agreement on cross-straits fight against crimes and judicial cooperation
June 29, 2010	ARATS and SEF signed the framework agreement on cross-straits economic cooperation and the agreement on cross-straits cooperation in the protection of intellectual property
August 9, 2012	ARATS and SEF signed the cross-straits customs cooperation agreement and the agreement on cross-straits protection and promotion of investment
June 21, 2013	ARATS and SEF signed the cross-straits service and trade agreement

Moreover, since most of the supporters of "Taiwan independence" are pro-Japan,[5] they may easily become a pawn in Japan's attempt to make trouble for China.

Therefore, to reintegrate Taiwan into China as soon as possible is not only an important step toward complete sea power, but also the most important of the sovereignty issues to be addressed by China.

---

[5]The Central Committee of RCCK (the Revolutionary Committee of the Chinese Kuomintang): The Organized Factions of "Taiwan Independence". Sept. 25, 2008, http://www.minge.gov.cn/minge/txt/2008-09/25/content_2492375.htm.

2.2 Possible Deadlock in Sovereignty Disputes

From North to South, China is surrounded by the Bohai Sea, the Yellow Sea, the East China Sea, and the South China Sea, which cover a total area of 4.73 million m^2 (Table 2.3). According to the United Nations Convention on the Law of the Sea,[6] with a mainland coastline of over 18,000 km, an island coastline of over 14,000 km, and 6961 offshore islands with an area over 500 m^2 (not including Taiwan, Hong Kong and Macao), China can claim control over more than 3 million m^2 of maritime space. The abundant maritime resources in this vast "blue territory" and its benefit in transportation and national defense are obviously essential parts of China's gains from its sea power (Table 2.2).

According to statistics, China's maritime space has a great variety of resources such as marine life, oil and gas, solid minerals, renewable energy, and coastal tourism, which indicate a tremendous potential for development. These include over 20,000 species of marine life, over 3000 species of sea fish, 27.53 billion tons of oil, and 10.6 trillion cubic meters of natural gas; over 3.1 billion tons of coastal placer reserves; 630 million KW theoretical reserves of renewable energy; over 1500 coastal tourist attractions and more than 100 coastal beaches; over 400 km of deep water coastline, 60-odd deep water harbor sites, 150-odd bays with an area greater than 10 km^2 along mainland shores, and over 200 bays above 5 km^2;

Table 2.2 China's Maritime Rights and Interests

Category	Sea		
	The Yellow Sea	The East China Sea	The South China Sea
Political rights and interests	Territorial waters	Territorial waters	Territorial waters
	Exclusive economic zone	Exclusive economic zone	Exclusive economic zone
	Continental shelf	Continental shelf	Continental shelf
Economic rights and interests	Fishery	Fishery	Fishery
	Oil and gas development	Oil and gas development	Oil and gas development
	Other uses	Other uses	Other uses
Security rights and interests	Prevention of invasion from the sea	Prevention of invasion from the sea	Prevention of invasion from the sea
	Forestalling conflict at sea	Forestalling conflict at sea	Forestalling conflict at sea
Research rights and interests	Oceanographic issues particular to the waters	Oceanographic issues particular to the waters	Oceanographic issues particular to the waters

Source Yang Jinsen. "The Current State of Oil and Gas Exploitation on the Seas by Surrounding Countries", in *Study of Maritime Development Strategies*, 1989 (3)

[6]On July 1, 1996, the Convention became effective for China.

Table 2.3 Basic information of the four seas around China

Name	Basic information	Remarks
The Bohai Sea	A quasi-closed shallow continental shelf sea, about 300 nautical miles long from North to South, 160 nautical miles wide from East to West, with an area of 77,000 km^2, an average depth of 18 m, and a maximum depth of 82 m	China's continental sea
The Yellow Sea	Located between the Chinese mainland and the Korean Peninsula, 432 nautical miles long from North to South, 351 nautical miles wide from East to West, with an area of 380,000 km^2, an average depth of 44 m, and a maximum depth of 140 m	Bordered by China, DPRK and ROK
The East China Sea	A sea to the East of the Chinese mainland and on the northwest margin of the Pacific, 700 nautical miles from northeast to southwest, less than 400 nautical miles wide, with an area of 770,000 km^2, an average depth of 370 m, and a maximum depth of 2719 m in the Okinawa trough	Bordered by China, ROK and Japan
The South China Sea	A sea to the South of the Chinese mainland and on the northwest margin of the Pacific, with complex terrain at the bottom, a shallow rim, and a deep sea basin at the center; with an area of 3.5 million km^2, an average depth of 1212 m, and a maximum depth of over 5500 m	Bordered by China, Vietnam, Philippines, Malaysia, Brunei and Indonesia

Source The research group of the Development Strategy Institute of the State Oceanic Administration. *China's Ocean Development Report*. China Ocean Press, 2007

38,000 km^2 of tidal-flat areas, and 124,000 km^2 of shallow sea with a depth of 0–15 m.[7]

However, due to geographic factors like closed sea, semi-closed sea, and island chains, there exist maritime boundary issues between China and eight neighboring countries from North to South, namely, the Democratic People's Republic of Korea, the Republic of Korea, Japan, the Philippines, Malaysia, Brunei, Vietnam, and Indonesia (Table 2.4). The total length of maritime borders yet to be demarcated is more than 7000 km. Whether China can really own 3 million km^2 of "blue territory" may depend to some degree on the decision of the International Court of Justice or the International Tribunal for the Law of the Sea. However, it has to be agreed upon, either explicitly or implicitly, by the neighboring countries involved.

Apart from the countries' consideration of nationalist demands and their own interests as nation states, the United Nations Convention on the Law of the Sea has sown the seeds for disputes between two or more countries neighboring or facing each other that do not have a vast expanse of sea between them.

[7]The research group of the Development Strategy Institute of the State Oceanic Administration. *China's Ocean Development Report*. China Ocean Press, 2007, 16.

Table 2.4 Maritime boundaries to be demarcated between China and neighboring countries

Neighboring country	Maritime boundary to be defined	Current status
DPRK	Neighboring sea to the North Yellow Sea, the exclusive economic zone, the continental shelf	Not demarcated. The China-DPRK Agreement on the Joint Development of Petroleum at Sea was signed on Dec. 24, 2005
ROK	The exclusive economic zones in the South Yellow Sea and the East China Sea, the continental shelf	Not demarcated The China-ROK Fishery Agreement was signed and took effect on June 30, 2001
Japan	The exclusive economic zone in the East China Sea, the continental shelf	Not demarcated. The China-Japan-ROK Fishery Agreement was signed and took effect on June 1, 2000. Controversy exists over the Diaoyu Islands and The Rock of Okinotori, among other issues
Vietnam	The exclusive economic zone in the South China Sea, the continental shelf	The agreement on the demarcation of the territorial waters in Beibu Gulf, the exclusive economic zone and the continental shelf and the agreement on fishery in Beibu Gulf were signed in 2000. The other waters are not demarcated. 29 of China's Nansha island reefs are occupied
The Philippines	The exclusive economic zone in the South China Sea, the continental shelf	Not demarcated Eight of China's Nansha island reefs are occupied
Malaysia	The exclusive economic zone in the South China Sea, the continental shelf	Not demarcated Five of China's Nansha Island Reefs are occupied
Indonesia	The exclusive economic zone in the South China Sea, the continental shelf	Not demarcated There do not exist any territorial or sovereignty disputes between China and Indonesia
Brunei	The exclusive economic zone in the South China Sea, the continental shelf	Not demarcated Brunei has laid sovereignty claims to Nantong Reef

Source The research group of the Development Strategy Institute of the State Oceanic Administration. *China's Ocean Development Report*. China Ocean Press, 2007

The Convention has been widely acclaimed for it was designed to bring about a new pattern of international maritime competition under the guidance of the sea power concept of "peace and development." However, as the demarcation rules are sometimes flexible or ambiguous and the countries are asked to settle their disputes over maritime sovereignty through negotiations, the tremendous interests the

Convention attaches to islands and the introduction of precise demarcation for land borders by nation states after the Peace of Westphalia into the division of marine territories have given rise to a host of problems.

First of all, the enormous interests attached to islands would lure some countries to take an aggressive stance and bargain hard for their own advantages.

Article 121 (2) of the Convention provides that islands have the same rights as land territory.[8] According to foreign scholars, for an islet with a diameter of one mile and an area of about 0.8 square mile, its territorial sea, if defined as the waters within 12 nautical miles from the baselines around it, can measure up to an area of 155 square miles, or 190 times its land area.[9] Considering the possibility to demarcate a 12-nautical mile-wide contiguous zone around the islet, an additional territorial sea 200 nautical miles wide, and up to 350 nautical miles of continental shelf, and considering the renewable and nonrenewable resources that could exist in such a vast sea area, the stakes are astonishingly high.[10]

---

[8]Article 121 of the Convention says,

1. *An island is a naturally formed area of land, surrounded by water, which is above water at high tide.*
2. *Except as provided for in paragraph 3, the territorial sea, the contiguous zone, the exclusive economic zone and the continental shelf of an island are determined in accordance with the provisions of this Convention applicable to other land territory.*
3. *Rocks which cannot sustain human habitation or economic life of their own shall have no exclusive economic zone or continental shelf.* (*A Little Encyclopedia of Law*. Law Press, 2002, 8–73).

[9]Zhang Haiwen. "Studies on China's Maritime Rights", in *Study of Maritime Development Strategies*, 1996 (8).

[10]The applicable provisions in the Convention are as follows:

1. *The sovereignty of a coastal State extends, beyond its land territory and internal waters and, in the case of an archipelagic State, its archipelagic waters, to an adjacent belt of sea, described as the territorial sea.*
2. *This sovereignty extends to the airspace over the territorial sea as well as to its bed and subsoil.* (Article 1)

Every State has the right to establish the breadth of its territorial sea up to a limit not exceeding 12 nautical miles, measured from baselines determined in accordance with this Convention. (Article 3)

1. *In a zone contiguous to its territorial sea, described as the contiguous zone, the coastal state may exercise the control necessary to:*
   (a) *prevent infringement of its customs, fiscal, immigration or sanitary laws, and regulations within its territory or territorial sea;*
   (b) *punish infringement of the above laws and regulations committed within its territory or territorial sea.*
2. *The contiguous zone may not extend beyond 24 nautical miles from the baselines from which the breadth of the territorial sea is measured.* (Article 33)
   The exclusive economic zone shall not extend beyond 200 nautical miles from the baselines from which the breadth of the territorial sea is measured. (Article 57)

As a result, it is easy to understand why some uninhabited islets have become the focus of international disputes. The contention between China and Japan for the Diaoyu Islands, the serious difference between China and countries like Vietnam and the Philippines on sovereignty over certain islets among the South China Sea Islands, and the utmost care taken at all costs for the Rock of Okinotori (which consists of two reefs)[11] by Japan and for Suyan Rock by the Republic of Korea[12]–all these have more or less to do with that article. China had clear historical sovereignty over these islands and only lost control over them through neglect due to war and internal strife. Without that article, other countries would at least be less aggressive in laying sovereignty claims to them.

The same kind and amount of maritime resources may be of higher value to countries with a larger population, a greater size, and a higher level of socioeconomic development.[13] However, the physical manifestation is the same for all countries. Therefore, since mankind has just started the in-depth development of the

---

(Footnote 10 continued)

In the exclusive economic zone, the coastal state has:

(a) *sovereign rights for the purpose of exploring and exploiting, conserving and managing the natural resources, whether living or nonliving, of the waters superjacent to the seabed and of the seabed and its subsoil, and with regard to other activities for the economic exploitation and exploration of the zone, such as the production of energy from the water, currents, and winds;*
(b) *jurisdiction as provided for in the relevant provisions of this Convention with regard to*
  (i) *the establishment and use of artificial islands, installations, and structures;*
  (ii) *marine scientific research;*
  (iii) *the protection and preservation of the marine environment;*
(c) *other rights and duties provided for in this Convention.* (Article 56)

1. *In the exclusive economic zone, the coastal State shall have the exclusive right to construct and to authorize and regulate the construction, operation and use of:*
   (a) *artificial islands;*
   (b) *installations and structures for the purposes provided for in article 56 and other economic purposes;*
   (c) *installations and structures which may interfere with the exercise of the rights of the coastal State in the zone.*
2. *The coastal State shall have exclusive jurisdiction over such artificial islands, installations and structures, including jurisdiction with regard to customs, fiscal, health, safety and immigration laws and regulations.* (Article 60)
   (*A Little Encyclopedia of Law*. Law Press, 2002, 8–20, 8–73).

[11]Huang Shao'an and Kong Zhiguo. *Tunhai*: One Approach to Realize Maritime Benefits for China. *Quan Heng*, 2006 (6).

[12]Gao Zhiguo. The Strategic Threat Posed to China by the Management of Suyan Rock and the Rock of Okinotori by South Korea and Japan and Suggested Coping Strategies. *Study of Maritime Development Strategies*, 2006(15).

[13]Security for example. This is well known yet hardly spoke of by the States due to the principle of "equality between States".

sea and the exact magnitude of its economic benefit to coastal countries is still unknown or only theoretical, it seems not altogether inexcusable for countries to claim their maximum interests.

Such logic may be all right when coastal countries neighboring or facing each other do not have overlapping maritime spaces as defined by the Convention. However, **if such spaces exist and the countries insist on enforcing the Convention's demarcating principles and rules on attached interests, the conflict will come out into the open and render it virtually impossible to define the border**.

The reasons are simple. If a country's cost of governance, strength, and capability of developing maritime resources is not considered and included into the demarcation process, any method–median line, fair line, mediation, arbitration, or litigation might lead to unexpected consequences as follows:

The first consequence is a high probability of conflict. If there is dispute over a maritime boundary and a settlement is not agreed upon, the parties may keep quarreling before demarcation and bear grudges against each other and wrestle under the table after that. As time goes by, when one country experiences a significant change in the independent variable of the cost-benefit function, including for example, a rapid growth in its national strength, or a far greater ability to develop maritime resources, it may seek to take steps beyond international law, or reject the legally defined border and lay new border claims. This may trigger fresh disputes or even war, and conflict would likely arise in disputed areas with strategic location and abundance in energy resources like oil and gas.

The second possible consequence is the disuse or predatory exploitation of the waters in question. In the enforcement of the Convention, whether a maritime or coastal country has the necessary ability to develop maritime resources and bear the costs for routine maintenance and the keeping of law and order is not considered for the demarcation of territorial seas. Even less consideration is given to the settlement of disputes over islands and waters before demarcation. If a country gains a maritime space incommensurable with its capability or strength through usurpation or seizure, it may result in the disuse or excessive exploitation of some of the maritime resources.

The third consequence is that the Convention may be resisted or disregarded. The United States announced that it would not join the Convention, which was by no means good news for it. Today, two-thirds of the disputes over maritime space around the world are crying out for settlement. Should a couple of countries that have joined the Convention announce that they would follow in the steps of America and refuse to acknowledge the Convention or even withdraw from it, or refuse to recognize the effect of arbitration or litigation conducted according to its judicial procedures, its credibility and prestige would be in grave danger.

Frequent disputes between China and its neighbors over the waters around such islands would then be a sequel to that drama.

In 1974, Japan and the Republic of Korea signed the Agreement on the Development of the Continental Shelf of the East China Sea for the prospecting of

Table 2.5 Intrusion across China's discontinuous boundary through oil exploitation by countries around the South China Sea

Country	Area of encroachment (km^2)	Remarks
Vietnam	22,000	Vietnam has frequently obstructed and interfered with China's oil and gas prospecting in Nansha. It intruded across China's discontinuous boundary through the continental shelf agreement it signed with Indonesia in 2003, and an invitation to bid for oil in 2004. It has claimed sovereignty over the Xisha and Nansha Islands
The Philippines	93,000	Philippines has illegally defined part of the waters in Nansha as the Kalayaan area. An invitation to bid for oil intruded across China's discontinuous boundary
Malaysia	205,000	The continental shelf agreement it signed with Indonesia in 1969 intruded across China's discontinuous boundary. Part of the announced limit of the continental shelf goes beyond the scope of 200 nautical miles. Most of the maritime areas involved in invitations to bid for oil and gas fall within China's discontinuous boundary
Brunei	35,000	Brunei claims an exclusive economic zone of 200 nautical miles and sovereignty over China's Nantong Reef. It has two areas involved in invitations to bid for oil within China's discontinuous boundary
Indonesia	35,000	The continental shelf agreements Indonesia signed with Malaysia in 1969 and with Vietnam in 2003 intruded across China's discontinuous boundary
Total	390,000	

Source Gao Zhiguo and Zhang Haiwen (ed.). *Research Papers on State Sea Policy*. China Ocean Press, 2007, 253

oil and gas resources without China's consent. The Agreement, which was implemented later, involves part of the continental shelf China lays claim to.

In recent years, "the Democratic People's Republic of Korea unilaterally built more than ten exploratory wells" in an undefined area of the Yellow Sea, and the Republic of Korea has conducted geological and topographical survey on the undefined continental shelf of the Yellow Sea. Japan has made trouble over the Chunxiao oil field and made every attempt to prevent China from developing oil and gas fields in the East China Sea. Through the introduction of foreign investment and technology, among other means, Brunei, the Philippines, Malaysia, Vietnam, and Indonesia have actively prospected and exploited oil and gas resources in the continental shelf of the waters near the Nansha Islands over which they have disputes with China (Table 2.5).[14]

[14]Zhang Haiwen. "Studies on China's Maritime Rights", in *Study of Maritime Development Strategies*, 1996 (8).

These countries have more than 1000 wells within China's discontinuous boundary, which exploit over 50 million tons of oil and gas each year. Nowadays they are still intensifying their efforts to develop oil and gas resources at sea.[15]

Meanwhile, Japan has had fishery disputes with China in waters near the Diaoyu Islands. Fishery disputes between China and Vietnam, the Philippines and Malaysia in the South China Sea are frequently reported by the media.

However, peace has become the keynote for international maritime competition; moreover, due to the advance in war technology and the greatly increased destructive power of weapons, war may go out of control once it is started. Under such circumstances, it can be anticipated that sovereignty disputes over islands will fall into a perpetual deadlock.

2.3 Nationalism Adds to Uncertainty

Uncertainty may lurk behind sovereignty disputes over islands and waters.

Disputes over islands between China and its neighboring countries have already caused tension in the surrounding waters. The consequent surge of nationalism in the countries involved has aggravated the situation.

Nationalism is no doubt a double-edged sword.

When China's maritime neighbors, particularly the governments of Japan, Philippines, and Vietnam, attempt to use their nationalists' tough position on the disputes with China for gaining popular support or as a legitimate excuse for arms buildup and exert pressure on the Chinese government, they are pushing such disputes toward a direction that is opposite to peaceful settlement.

First of all, this will stimulate the growth of nationalism in China. When the Japanese government detained the captain of a Chinese fishing boat in December 2010 and when it announced the "nationalization" of the Diaoyu Islands in September 2012, there were demonstrations and protests not only in Japan, but also in China. In addition, China protested by the cancelation of a large number of visits and tourism trips. When anti-China demonstrations were staged in Vietnam in June and December 2012 and June 2013 (over oil and gas exploitation in waters with overlapping claims) and in May 2014 (over the operation of drilling platform Sea Oil-981), Chinese nationalists also voiced their growing outrage over Vietnam's utter disregard for the great help China had given the country in the past years. East Asia and South Asia are probably among the regions where nationalist sentiments are at their highest. Owing to the surge of such sentiments in Japan, Philippines, and Vietnam, the argument that "there is bound to be a war" between China and Japan,

---

[15]The research group of the Development Strategy Institute of the State Oceanic Administration. *China's Ocean Development Report*. China Ocean Press, 2007, 83–4.

China and Vietnam, or China and Philippines has been gaining popularity in these countries.[16]

Besides, as nationalism gains opportunity for development, moral legitimacy, and steadily increasing influence because of such disputes, the situation may develop in a way beyond the control of the governments, especially the elected governments of Japan and the Philippines.

The reasons are simple. The development of modern telecommunications, the Internet, and media have facilitated the exchange of information in society. On the other hand, it has brought about the probability of information asymmetry between government and populace and the decline of the government's control. Under such circumstances, for any country, public opinion has to be considered when the government makes a decision. Sometimes, it may have to pander to public opinion, possibly without reservation, for the sake of legitimacy.

However, one of the salient features of a globalized and network-connected society is that common citizens have a lower capacity for bearing pressure, propensity for dramatic emotional fluctuations, and a strong tendency toward arbitrary judgment. As a result, extreme and irrational thinking spreads more easily and may even develop into mainstream public opinion. Nationalism is in line with such thinking to the extent that its assessment of national interests and the threat facing a nation sometimes leads to radical and bigoted conclusions due to narrow mindedness. Therefore it may also become mainstream public opinion.

In a couple of cases, nationalism may indeed be a good leverage for countries like Japan, Philippines, and Vietnam when they bargain with China. However, who know whether their policies will end up being hijacked by nationalism? This is well proven in history. Before either WWI or WWII, even though public opinion did not exert an impact as strong as it has today on policymakers, Japan was still at the mercy of the militarists, who were radical nationalists.

Such nationalism, with both sides refusing to back down, has made it more difficult for China and its neighboring countries to reach a peaceful settlement for sovereignty over the islands and rights and interests in the surrounding waters. When the Chinese government adopts certain measures, it not only has to assess time and again the extent to which the governments involved are influenced by nationalism in their countries as well as the possibility that the nationalist forces might react in a way beyond government control, but it also has to keep a close watch over the consequent actions taken by Chinese nationalists.

[16]In March 2012, there were open discussions in both China and the Philippines about the possibility of a war between the two countries. In March 2013 and June 2014, there were open discussions in both China and Japan about the possibility of a war between them. In June 2011 and June 2014, there were open discussions in both China and Vietnam about the possibility of a war between them.

2.4 Formidable Rivals Nearby

As an old Chinese saying goes, how can you allow anybody else to sleep beside your bed?

If the islands or waters over which China has disputes with its neighboring countries are likened to a bed, there are not only people who would not talk reason, trying hard to sleep beside the bed or keep the bed all for themselves, but also those who "fish in troubled waters" with a covetous eye on the bed and the treasures around. An important way to play the rogue, act tough, or bend the rules is to build up arms or show military presence.

In terms of military security, multipolar competition and cooperation and multilevel wrestling may be an accurate description of this complicated situation.

Multipolar coopetition (competition and cooperation). China has a relationship of competition, cooperation, or both with the countries it has island or maritime disputes with, and with those having or seeking strategic and economic interests in the surrounding waters, such as the United States, Russia, India, Australia, Britain, France, and Norway. Moreover, the relationship between these countries also varies in the degree of amity or enmity. For instance, the US and Japan, Philippines, and Australia are allies; Russia is one of the major arms providers to Vietnam and India; India is friendly with Vietnam, which is on good terms with Philippines; there are signs of improvement in the relations between Vietnam and the United States, but the shadow of Vietnam War is unlikely to dissipate in the near future.

Multilevel wrestling. This refers to the conflict and competition between China and the aforementioned countries regarding sovereignty over the islands and waters in question. Its military implications are all-dimensional, including the change of strategy, the deployment of armament, and military spending, which are supplemented by propaganda campaigns and the imposition of fait accompli.

On the strategic level, the most eye-catching role is of course played by the United States.

In July 2009, the then Secretary of State Hilary Clinton announced that the United States would "return to Asia" during her visit to Thailand. In November 2010, President Obama called himself the first "Pacific president" of America in a speech given to a Japanese audience; later, at the 18th informal meeting of the APEC leaders, he said, "In the 21st century, the security and prosperity of the American people is linked inextricably to the security and prosperity of Asia. That's why this was not my first trip here, and why it will not be my last. America is leading again in Asia." In June 2012, the then Secretary of Defense Leon E. Panetta proposed the strategy of "rebalancing toward Asia-Pacific". With the Middle East giving way to Asia-Pacific, to turn the twenty-first century into "America's Pacific Century"[17] has become a focus of the United States' global strategy.

[17]Hillary Rodham Clinton. "America's Pacific Century", in *Foreign Policy*, October 11, 2011.

The strategies of many other countries are blatantly aggressive and well targeted.[18]

Since it passed a series of laws and decrees aimed at rendering the Peace Constitution useless, including the Cabinet's Resolution on Lifting the Ban on Collective Self-defense, Japan has shown apparent strategic aspirations to become a major military power and a strong sea power.[19] Its defensive posture has changed from "the protection of sea routes" to "responding to the situation in surrounding areas" and developing ocean-going operational capability. The new defense plan, the Mid-term Defense Program (2014–2018), and the National Security Strategy adopted on December 17, 2013 call for the development of ballistic missiles targeting China's maritime activities and the Democratic People's Republic of Korea, strengthening remote island defense, and building capability of amphibious operation and response to ballistic missiles.

As members of the ASEAN, Vietnam, and Philippines have sought common ground in competition for maritime interests among the eastern countries through coordination of the organization's internal policies. On the other hand, they have held joint exercises or signed defense cooperation agreements with the United States, Britain, France, and Australia in order to check what they perceive as the "threat" from China as a "great power." These make their intention self-evident to confront China through the strategy of inward alliance and outward collaboration.

As the stronger of the two, Vietnam views the sea as the foundation of its nationhood and seeks strategic depth from the sea. It has changed its military strategy from "defense in the north and attack toward the south" to "attack on land and advance at sea", with focus on "defending maritime territory and resources." It considers response to emergencies at sea and local war as its operational priority, sees the United States as a potential adversary on a global scale, and regards the "neighboring great powers posing threat to Vietnam" as the main target of regional operation. It has formulated the Navy's Ten-year Development Plan and the Three-step Navy Development Plan. It is scheduled to acquire capabilities of ocean escort and maritime operation by 2015 and form forces for high seas and integrated joint operation[20] by 2050.

India's naval strategy has shifted from "offshore defense" and "regional deterrence and control" to "ocean attack." The strategic goal is to create a "world-class" navy, which is to be realized in three steps: (1) establishing the largest aircraft carrier fleet in Asia; (2) building a force capable of nuclear strikes from land, air, and sea; (3) founding a naval task force, implementing the "eastern maritime strategy," breaking the tradition of "defending the homeland," expanding its forward military presence, and building a "blue-water navy" that can "control the

---

[18]Kong Zhiguo. *Sea Power, Competitive Property Rights and the Tunhai Strategy*. Social Sciences Academic Press, 2011, 66–73.

[19]Ju Hailong. *The Strategy of China's Sea Power*. Current Affairs Press, 2010, 156–201.

[20]Cheng Hanping. "Vietnam's Maritime Security Strategies and China's Countermeasures" in *Forum of World Economics & Politics*, 2011 (3).

Indian Ocean and go eastward to the Pacific, westward out of the Atlantic, and southward to Africa."[21]

The Republic of Korea has changed its maritime strategic goal from "coastal defense" to "ocean defense." It has announced that it will strengthen the control over East Asian waters and "play a major role in the Pacific age of the 21st century." It will defend its mainland against threat from the sea and destroy the enemy's effective strength before they enter its territorial sea.

In all these strategies, China is explicitly or implicitly considered the main target or one of the main targets.

On the level of armament upgrading and deployment, which can be regarded as tactical deterrence in some sense, the United States, Japan, Vietnam, and India show a clear tendency of seeing China as an imaginary enemy.

In June 2013, as the successor to Panetta, Chuck Hagel reiterated the plan announced by Panetta one year before for the deployment of 60 % of the naval ships to the Asia-Pacific region by 2020. He also stated that the United States would commit more air and land forces and high-tech weapons, and deploy 60 % of the air force to the same region. Related work had started before this: the goal proposed in Quadrennial Defense Review 2006 to raise the proportion of nuclear-powered attack submarines permanently deployed in West Pacific to 60 % had been accomplished in 2009.[22] Moreover, six of the ten aircraft carriers in active service are deployed in the Pacific, and America has planned to increase the number to seven in 2016. More importantly, apart from their number, the American ships in the Pacific are excellent in performance. Several Virginia ships, the most advanced nuclear-powered attack submarines, have entered active service. The aircraft carrier to join the current ones in the Pacific in 2016 will be the Ford, the first ship of the most advanced class of nuclear-powered aircraft carriers.

Besides its heavy military presence in the Pacific, America's deployment of troops is being steadily optimized. For instance, it had reduced the strength, but not the effectiveness, of the troops at Okinawa. It has maintained a deterrence capability by adding new aircrafts,[23] building a new airfield, and transferring the majority of the withdrawn personnel to Guam.[24] It has intensified efforts for the balance between branches and armament upgrading at the Yokosuka, Yokota, and Iwakuni bases in Japan and the Chinhae base in the Republic of Korea. It has also formed a logistic supply and maintenance center for the US navy in West Pacific with the HQ of the Seventh Fleet and Yokosuka, the home port of the George Washington Carrier Strike Group as the nucleus, which extends to other ports including Sasebo, Busan, Pohang, Chinhae, and Naha. It has started to station troops in Australia and

---

[21]Zhao Chuanheng. "India's Eastern Fleet Upgraded, Targeting South China Sea", in *Elite Reference,* Sept. 1, 2011.

[22]Zhang Wenmu. "The Significance of America's 'Return to Asia'", in *China Entrepreneur 2011*.

[23]Anonymous. "US Military Jets Streaming to Settle in Okinawa, Making it an Asia-Pacific 'Eagle's Nest'", http://news.xinhuanet.com/mil/2012-10/18/c_123836639.htm.

[24]Anonymous. "9,000 US Troops in Okinawa to Shift to Guam, Etc., to Strengthen Deterrence." http://news.xinhuanet.com/mil/2012-04/26/c_123039906.htm.

to build Port Darwin into a backup base for the US navy. Despite the withdrawal from the Subic base in Philippines on November 24, 1992, the US military may return there in the near future,[25] or share the Palawan base in the southwest of the country with Philippine military.[26] Meanwhile, the United States has shown its importance in Asia through a series of military and diplomatic activities. These include frequent, large-scale military exercises,[27] the forging of closer ties with traditional allies such as Japan, the Republic of Korea, Australia,[28] Philippines and Thailand, intervention in the South China Sea issues to estrange China from the ASEAN, full-out effort to win India's support, and enhancement of relationship with Pakistan, etc.

In March 2009, Japan's first helicopter carrier Hyuga went into active service. This was followed by the commissioning of its second helicopter carrier Ise in March 2011. August 2013 saw the launching of Japan's third helicopter carrier Izumo, which was expected to be commissioned in 2015. According to public information, at least three ships of the same category are being built. This alone has made the Japan Maritime Self-Defense Force "the world's second largest navy,"[29] with the average tonnage of its ships, operational capability, the age of ships, and total tonnage among the top rank of the world.

However, Japan is not content with the superiority of its navy in Asia. In February 2014, the Japan Ground Self-Defense Force created an amphibious operation unit specifically designed for the capture of islands. It will be equipped with 52 amphibious vehicles and attain a strength of 2000–3000 by 2018.[30] In June 2014, Japan deployed a new batch of Type-88 surface-to-ship missiles on Miyako-jima in Okinawa, which is 170 km from the Diaoyu Islands, for restraint on China's patrols around the latter and access to the Miyako Strait. In addition, Japan

---

[25] Kazuo Nagata. "The Philippines Agrees to the US Military's Return to Subic Bay for Greater Sense of Presence", in *The Yomiuri Shimbun*, Oct. 30, 2013.

[26] Han Shuo & Li Yuan. "US Troops to Enter a Philippine Base on the Edge of the South China Sea to Watch China's Movements", in *Global Times*, Aug. 17, 2013.

[27] In 2010, the United States not only increased troops in Afghanistan and consolidated its military presence in its Asian allies, but also held a number of military exercises on an unprecedented scale in the Asia-Pacific region. In July, an American sea and air battle group sailed into the waters east of South Korea for the largest US–South Korea military exercise in the past 34 years. In August, an American aircraft carrier sailed into the South China Sea on a high-profile visit to Vietnam. Toward the end of November, the US and South Korea held another military exercise in the Sea of Japan and the Yellow Sea. This was followed by "Japan's largest military operation in peace time", or the US–Japan military exercise, in early December. America sent ten thousand troops, a group of 20 ships headed by the Washington aircraft carrier, and 150 aircraft including the B-52 Stratofortress. Japan contributed over 34,000 troops, 40 ships and 250 aircraft.

[28] Zhi Yuan. "2010 TACOM Report Stresses Importance of Asia-Pacific", http://mil.news.sohu.com/20110110/n278764686.shtml.

[29] Dai Xu. *The C-shaped Besiegement: China's Breakout Despite Internal Trouble and External Threat*. Wenhui Press, 2010, 6–8.

[30] Anonymous. "Exposed: Japan's Trump Card for 'Island Grab Battle'", http://news.xinhuanet.com/mil/2014-02/05/c_126088970.htm.

has decided to establish bases and deploy guarding troops on three islands close to the Diaoyu Islands, namely Miyako-jima, Amami-O-shima, and Ishigaki-jima. It has also planned to concentrate the newly developed SSM surface-to-ship missiles in Kyushu in case China attacks the southwestern islands.[31] Furthermore, Japan has the "technological capability, know-how, and materials for making nuclear weapons within a very short time."[32] As the Japanese navy and air forces grow stronger, Japan may gradually become the main force on the front line of the US–Japan alliance.

Vietnam has become the largest arms importer in Southeast Asia and has surpassed China as the third largest importer of weapons from Russia. In recent years, it has purchased or planned to purchase from Russia and Holland a large number of weapons (e.g., the Bastion antiship missile, the Kilo-class submarine, the Gepard-class frigate, the Sigma-class corvette, the Lightning-class missile boat, Su-30 fighter–bomber, and P-3C antisubmarine patrol aircraft) in order to comprehensively enhance its capability of competing with China in the South China Sea. The Coastal Fleet, which is being organized, is equipped with six Gepard 3.9-class frigates, 12 Lightning-class missile boats, and six Kilo-class submarines as well as Russian-made K-300P Bastion shore-based supersonic antiship missiles. The Vietnamese air force is equipped with 30 Su-27/30, 60 Su-22 M, and nearly 100 Mig-21.

India, which has maintained its position as the world's largest arms importer since 2010, was the fifth country to openly proclaim the capability of building aircraft carriers on its own following the United States, Russia, Britain, and France. Its navy has developed into a marine force with absolute superiority in the Indian Ocean. With three aircraft carriers (Viraat, Vikramaditya, and Vikrant), it ranks at the top in overall strength among the 40 countries around the Indian Ocean. It has the Indian Ocean largely under its control and attempts to enter the Pacific. India also has a considerable capability of developing weapons. Apart from aircraft carriers, it has succeeded in developing its own advanced weapons including nuclear-powered submarines with ballistic missiles, fifth-generation fighters, destroyers with guided missiles, and antiship missiles. Some of these weapons have been issued to its armed forces. India has always seen China and Pakistan as major threats and is highly vigilant to China's entry into the Indian Ocean. It has engaged itself in affairs in China's surrounding sea areas through trade cooperation and joint military exercises. While this is out of consideration for its own interests, it can also be seen as a countermeasure to China's deep penetration into the Indian Ocean.

[31]Anonymous. "Japan Deploys Stream of Missile Defense Against China for Diaoyu Island", http://news.xinhuanet.com/world/2014-06/16/c_126624809.htm.

[32]Zhang Wenmu. "The Significance of America's 'Return to Asia'", in *China Entrepreneur 2011*.

2.5 Military Expenditure and the "China Threat" Theory

Military expenditure, propaganda campaign, and the creation of fait accompli are interrelated issues on three levels. Military expenditure is often used as the ground for the "China threat" theory or the "China danger" theory as hyped by some countries, which will then make a greater noise for the occupation and development of the islands and waters over which they have disputes with China. For instance, on October 12, 2011, India and Vietnam signed an agreement on the development of oil and gas in areas in the South China Sea. Two of these areas involve the waters disputed by China and Vietnam. Unfortunately, this was no isolated case. In the South China Sea, besides the areas disputed by China and Vietnam, great powers outside the region are often seen to support Philippines, Malaysia, Brunei, and Indonesia in areas disputed by China and these countries. The United States, Britain, France, Russia, Japan, Norway, and Australia frequently respond to invitations to bid for oil and gas areas initiated by these countries within China's discontinuous boundary.[33]

The "China threat" theory and the "China danger" theory are untenable in many ways. However, the countries have achieved their goal in view of the initiation and effect of the propaganda campaigns.

Taking advantage of the concern about China's possible ascendancy in the Pacific on the part of Japan, Vietnam, India, Philippines, and other countries, the United States has emerged as their "mainstay" and thrown its weight about on the disputes in the East China Sea and the South China Sea. Thanks to the Japanese people's lack of readiness for a strong China and the advocacy of the right-wing opinions on the Diaoyu Islands issue, the Japanese government has gained legitimate domestic support for military buildup. The Vietnamese government has won wide support for its tough stance against China through propaganda about the detention of Vietnamese fishermen by China and the conflicts at sea between the two countries. Philippines has received free or low-cost assistance from America and Japan due to the grievance and vulnerability it professed during its marine conflict with China. Capitalizing on the discussions about the year-by-year increase of China's military expenditure, Japan has increased its own military expenditure; from 2003 to 2012, Vietnam's military expenditure went up by 130 %. However, for the countries that tend to play up the "China threat" and "China danger," the greatest gain has been the advantage in strategic confrontation and the

---

[33]Zhao Quansheng (the US). 'Analysis of America's Response to the Rise of China", in *Forum for International Issues*, winter issue, 2005; Zhu Feng. "Origins of America's Perceptions of 'the Rise of China' and the 'China Threat'", in *American Studies Quarterly*, 2005 (3); Zhang Jingquan. "A Preliminary Exploration of Japan's Attitudes toward the Maritime Rights and its Maritime Strategy", in *Journal of Contemporary Asia-Pacific Studies*, 2005 (5); Research Group of Japan's Strategies. "Contemporary Japanese Foreign Strategy: Causes, Means and Prospects", in *Contemporary International Relations*, 2006 (12); Li Mingjie & Qiu Jun. "A Brief Summary of Oil Exploitation in the South China Sea by Surrounding Countries", in *Study of Maritime Development Strategies*, 2006 (15).

near-completion of the strategic encirclement of China. Except for Pakistan, China has hardly any friends among its "close neighbors."

Such a state of affairs has put China on the defensive.

Objectively speaking, China's claims to the disputed islands and waters have legitimacy based on historical tradition and are unlikely to be less convincing than those of any other country so far as international legal principles are concerned. However, small countries like Vietnam and Philippines can be difficult to get along with. For instance, the Philippines alleges that China would resort to force though no armed conflict has yet taken place; Vietnam frequently assumes a posture of desperate fight although it knows that it is evenly matched with China in order to give the impression of being bullied. As for the powerful countries like the United States and Japan, they are not only cavalier about any prospect of resorting to force, but also convinced that their allies would certainly be on their side once conflict breaks out. Their assumption of a posture showing they are not to be trifled with has given rise to a mentality among other countries as bystanders who dare not protest against their domineering conduct yet are curious to see which side would win the game—China or them. Thus China finds itself caught in a dilemma between small countries difficult to get along with and great powers which it cannot afford to offend.

China's vexation from military expenditure almost follows the same logic.

China's absolute military expenditure ranks second in the world. However, its percentage in GDP and fiscal revenue or the per capita figure is not quite outstanding, in comparison with countries worldwide and those having stakes in its surrounding waters.

According to the data compiled by Stockholm International Peace Research Institute (SIPRI) (Tables 2.6, 2.7, 2.8 and 2.9), the percentage of China's military expenditure in its GDP has been lower than that of the United States, Russia, the

Table 2.6 Military expenditure of China and countries bordering on the same ocean (2003–2013) (x million USD, at yearly average exchange rate)

Year	China	The US	Russia	Japan	India	Vietnam	The Philippines	The Republic of Korea
2003	34,771	41,5223	16,974	42,725	16,334	842	1301	15,847
2004	40,014	46,4676	20,955	45,585	20,238	915	1243	17,830
2005	46,290	503,353	27,337	44,689	23,072	1026	1373	22,160
2006	56,666	527,660	34,518	42,180	23,952	1287	1607	25,177
2007	71,740	556,961	43,535	41,465	28,254	1785	2014	27,726
2008	91,658	621,131	56,184	46,755	33,002	2138	2271	26,072
2009	11,1785	668,567	51,533	51,464	38,722	2401	2116	24,409
2010	123,338	698,180	58,720	53,796	46,090	2672	2438	27,572
2011	147,268	711,338	70,238	60,452	49,634	2686	2701	30,884
2012	167,712	684,780	81,079	59,564	47,214	3361	2899	31,660
2013	188,460	640,221	87,837	48,604	47,398	3387	3472	33,937

Source SIPRI: http://www.sipri.org/research/armaments/milex/milex_database

Table 2.7 Per capita military expenditure of China and countries bordering on the same ocean (2003–2013) (USD at yearly average exchange rate)

Year	China	The US	Russia	Japan	India	Vietnam	The Philippines	The Republic of Korea
2003	27.0	1431	117	335	14.9	10.5	15.7	331
2004	30.9	1587	146	357	18.2	11.2	14.8	371
2005	35.5	1703	191	350	20.5	12.5	16	460
2006	43.2	1768	242	330	21.0	15.4	18.4	520
2007	54.4	1849	306	325	24.4	21.2	22.7	571
2008	69.2	2043	396	366	28.1	25.1	25.1	533
2009	84.0	2179	363	403	32.5	27.9	23	496
2010	92.2	2257	412	422	38.2	30.7	26.1	558
2011	110	2283	491	473	40.6	30.6	28.4	620
2012	124	2181	565	467	38.2	37.9	30	633
2013	138	2023	621	382	38.1	37.8	35.6	676

Source SIPRI: http://www.sipri.org/research/armaments/milex/milex_database

Table 2.8 Military expenditure of China and countries bordering on the same ocean, as a percentage of GDP (%) (2003–2013)

Year	China (S)	The US	Russia	Japan	India	Vietnam	The Philippines	The Republic of Korea
2003	2.1	3.7	3.9	1	2.8	2.1	1.6	2.5
2004	2.1	3.9	3.5	1	2.8	2	1.4	2.5
2005	2.1	4	3.6	1	2.8	1.9	1.3	2.6
2006	2.1	3.9	3.5	1	2.5	2.1	1.3	2.6
2007	2.1	4	3.4	1	2.3	2.5	1.3	2.6
2008	2	4.3	3.3	1	2.6	2.3	1.3	2.8
2009	2.2	4.8	4.1	1	2.9	2.5	1.3	2.9
2010	2.1	4.8	3.8	1	2.7	2.5	1.2	2.7
2011	2	4.7	3.7	1	2.6	2.2	1.2	2.8
2012	2	4.4	3.9	1	2.5	2.4	1.2	2.8
2013	2	3.8	4.1	1	2.5	2.3	1.3	2.8

Source SIPRI: http://www.sipri.org/research/armaments/milex/milex_database

Republic of Korea, India, and Vietnam since 2007. In 2013, China's GDP ($8.52 trillion) was 51.4 % of that of the United States ($16.57 trillion), but its military expenditure barely accounted for 29.44 % of the latter's. Since 2009, the percentage of China's military expenditure in its public expenditure has been lower than that of the Republic of Korea, the United States, Russia, and India, and has steadily declined. Since 2012, it has become comparable to that of Vietnam. The per capita military expenditure among Chinese citizens has always been lower than that of the United States, the Republic of Korea, Russia, and Japan. In 2013, it

Table 2.9 Military expenditure of China and countries bordering on the same ocean, as a percentage of public spending (%) (2003–2013)

Year	China	The US	Russia	Japan	India	Vietnam	The Philippines	The Republic of Korea
2003	11.4	10.3	12.3	2.8	9.6	7.6	7.3	12.2
2004	11.4	10.9	11.2	2.9	11.0	7.5	6.8	11.7
2005	11.0	11.0	10.9	2.9	10.7	6.8	6.8	12.6
2006	11.1	11.0	11.2	2.8	9.7	7.4	6.9	12.3
2007	10.9	10.8	10.1	2.6	9.0	8.2	7.1	12.1
2008	9.9	11.1	9.9	2.9	9.1	8.0	7.0	12.5
2009	9.6	10.8	10.2	2.6	10.9	7.2	6.3	12.7
2010	9.1	11.4	10.1	2.5	10.1	7.7	6.4	12.9
2011	8.4	11.4	10.3	2.5	9.7	7.0	6.7	12.9
2012	8.2	10.9	10.8	2.4	9.4	7.8	6.2	13.1
2013	8.3	10.0	11.2	2.4	9.0	8.1	6.8	12.8

Source SIPRI: http://www.sipri.org/research/armaments/milex/milex_database

accounted for 6.82, 22.22, 20.41, and 36.13 % of the levels of the United States, the Republic of Korea, Russia, and Japan, respectively.

The overall level of China's military expenditure may be even lower if the following factors are taken into consideration: China has the largest number of people serving in its armed forces; the official figures of China's military expenditure are typically way lower than the SIPRI estimates[34]; China has to make up for historical setbacks in the development of its military[35]; China's military expenditure includes subsidies for ex-service personnel; and China needs to improve the efficiency of its military spending.[36]

[34]For instance, SIPRI estimated that China's military expenditure was $188.460 billion in 2013. However, according to the draft budget reviewed at the first session of the 12th National People's Congress in March 2013, China's military expenditure for the year was 720.168 billion yuan, or approx. $116.284 billion (the average exchange rate between the US dollar and RMB was 6.1932 in 2013).

[35]At the beginning of the reform and opening up, China maintained a very low level of military expenditure in order to invest more of its limited financial resources into economic development. As a result, its military equipment was upgraded very slowly. Armaments were still at the mechanization stage, informationization had just started, and the overall standard was comparable to that of the United States, Japan and other developed countries more than twenty years back. There was a technological gap of one generation, if not two generations, between the Chinese navy and the strong navies in the world. The air force was still in the transition from homeland air defense to integrated air-space operation in terms of equipment and training.

[36]The downfall of senior generals due to corruption (including former vice chairman of the Central Military Commission Xu Caihou and the former deputy chief of the PLA's General Logistics Department Gu Junshan) and the Chinese government's emphasis on the idea that "corruption in the military is the most serious" reflects to some degree serious flaws in the use of China's military expenditure.

To be fair, there may still be a gap between China's military expenditure and its actual needs. This is because China cannot depend on other countries for its security, given its growing external reliance for energy resources and trade. Besides, it would be unrealistic and risky to do so when some countries are restricting China's access to oceans by the strategic passes they seized from China when it was too weak to stop them. It would be impossible for China to change the status quo without the support of adequate military expenditure. So, what should be the proper level of China's military spending? The simplest method of calculation would be to see how much other countries spend on attempts to thwart China's effort to change the situation. We may assume that the United States, while committing 60 % of its military strength to the Pacific, would invest 60 % of its military expenditure. That alone would provide significant justification for the reasonable increase of China's military spending. This is of course coupled with other factors to consider, including hostility from Japan, India, Vietnam, and Philippines, and the need to defend sovereignty and territorial integrity.

Under such circumstances, it is quite thought-provoking why China's prudent decision in military expenditure after considering its historical gaps and financial capacity would draw fierce criticism from some countries. They may have the entrenched belief that China should bow to reality and accept it as reasonable to depend on other countries for development at the expense of its sovereignty. Another reason, which is not quite presentable, is that they do not want to see the gap between China and them in military strength become even narrower. At least they need to find an excuse for investing more in the maintenance of the gap. All these are in the final analysis attributable to the unfair international political order and the inherent mentality of international hegemonism.

2.6 Hidden Risks in Overseas Security

This issue is actually related to the foregoing discussions on the isolation of China in the surrounding waters due to sovereignty disputes and the competition in international interests. The gravest challenge to overseas security is that of sea routes.

It is an appalling truth that the security of Chinese ships sailing from their country may no longer be under the absolute control of China before they go beyond our territorial seas.

China's access to the Pacific has to pass many straits and sea routes. There are three major routes. The northern route has to pass the Korea Strait and the Kuril Islands; the eastern route is made up of the Japanese archipelago, Ryukyu Islands, Diaoyu Islands, and Taiwan; and the southern route goes straight to the Pacific via the Taiwan Straits or the coastal areas of Guangdong and Guangxi, and proceeds to the Indian Ocean across the Pacific (it has to pass the Strait of Malacca in either case).

In other words, China has to bow to Russia, the Republic of Korea and Japan for the northern route, Japan for the eastern route, and Indonesia, Malaysia, Singapore and Thailand for the southern route. Moreover, China has to bow to the United States for all the three routes, because it controls Taiwan, which is allied with Japan and the Republic of Korea, in which it has military bases, and has built or rent military bases in Singapore, Thailand, Malaysia, and Indonesia.[37] Besides, the attitude of Philippines and Vietnam cannot be neglected because Philippines is located in the middle between the eastern route and the southern route, and Vietnam's maritime space is parallel to or overlaps with much of the southern route.

However, among these countries, the United States regards China as a strategic rival; Japan, Vietnam, and Philippines have deteriorating relations with China due to sovereignty disputes over islands and waters; the Republic of Korea has differences with China over the principles on the demarcation of the continental shelf and sovereignty over Suyan Rock; Singapore is closer to America than to China. Once conflict arises between China and other countries, which would result in the cutting of sea routes and attacks on merchant ships, China will soon find it on the defensive, with all the commercial access to the oceans completely blocked.

Furthermore, out of consideration for possible military confrontation, the United States has, in disregard of the natural geographical restrictions on China, prepared three "island chains" against China. The Alieutian Islands, Chiba Islands, Japanese archipelago, Ryukyu Islands, Diaoyu Islands, Taiwan, Philippines, and Indonesian islands constitute the first island chain. Ogasawara Islands, Volcano Islands, Mariana, Guam and Yap Islands, Pelew Islands, Halmahera, New Zealand, and Australia make up the second. The third island chain mainly consists of the military bases on the Hawaiian Islands, which serve both as the strategic rear in support of the American armed forces in Asia-Pacific, but also an outpost for the defense of the American mainland.

Since 2013, the Chinese navy has frequently held military exercises after breaking through the first or second island chain. However, whether it can do so in an actual war situation has yet to be tested.

[37]In 1991, the United States signed an agreement with Malaysia on the lease of the naval base in Lumut to the US Navy for temporary rest, maintenance and replenishment. Malaysia also agreed to the US military's use of its naval base in Butterworth and the naval port at Kota Kinabalu for the refueling of US naval aircrafts. In 1992, the US signed an agreement with Singapore on the use of the naval base at Sembawang as a center for the maintenance and replenishment of US naval ships and the logistics headquarters in the West Pacific. In 2000, the US signed another agreement with Singapore for the use of the naval base at Changi, which can accommodate large US naval ships including aircraft carriers. In 2003, Thailand agreed to lease the land in the vicinity of Sattahip naval base to the US as the site of a military base for logistics supply and the storage of materials and equipment; it allowed the US to rent the naval ports in Bangkok, Phuket and Pattaya for temporary rest, replenishment and maintenance of American naval ships. After the 9/11 attacks, the US military fully restored military cooperation with Indonesia with counter-terrorism as the starting point. Indonesia agreed to the lease of the naval base in Jakarta and the naval port in Surabaya to the US Navy for temporary rest and replenishment.

Even if China manages to break through the island chains and enter the ocean, it will still face a host of challenges. In fact, the adverse situation it finds in offshore sea routes is only one aspect of the lack of security for maritime passages. There is even less self-reliance for the security of ocean passages.

As its ocean routes spread almost all over the world, China is increasingly enjoying the benefit and convenience of global passages. However, such benefit and convenience, like a sandcastle, may vanish overnight.

The Gulf of Alaska, Korea Strait, Makassar Strait, Sunda Strait, Strait of Malacca, Mandab Strait, Suez Canal, Strait of Gibraltar, Skagerrak, Kattegat, Greenland–Iceland–United Kingdom Strait, sea routes south of Africa and those of North America, Strait of Hormuz, Panama Canal, and Straits of Florida[38]—these 16 international straits are universally acknowledged as important lines of transportation. They are also regarded by the United States as strategic junctions essential to the defense of its maritime rights and interests. The Korea Strait and the Strait of Malacca, as the strategic passes for China's access to the oceans, are of self-evident importance. The Mandad Strait, Suez Canal, Strait of Gibraltar, Strait of Hormuz, Panama Canal, and Sunda Strait are also important for China.[39] The Mandad Strait, Suez Canal, Strait of Gibraltar, and Strait of Hormuz are vital links between the European markets and the African markets. The Sunda Strait is deemed the most convenient route from China to West Africa and South Africa. And there is no better sea route than the one through the Panama Canal from China to North America and the western part of South America.

However, all of these maritime lines of transportation are under the control of the United States, typically with American troops stationed in the vicinity. As a result, in terms of sea route security, China has to bow to America not only for the offshore routes, but also for the ocean routes.

This, of course, is only part of the problem. In terms of overseas security, China also faces fierce competition in every respect.

With high external reliance for energy resources and trade, Japan has a great deal of interests overlapping those of China in all the important routes on the Pacific and the Indian Ocean as well as the origins of energy and resources and the destinations of their exports. In the Indian Ocean, such close and all-dimensional competition is joined by a country of growing importance, India. With the steady development of its economy and a population comparable to that of China, India may also have increasing need for foreign trade and international cooperation in energy and resources.

A careful analysis of the rivalry between China, Japan, and India, which will soon reach a climax, would probably show that China has the worst strategic position.

---

[38]Liu Rongzi & Qi Lianming. *A Study of the Value System of Uninhabited Islands in China*. China Ocean Press, 2006, 129.

[39]Sébille-Lopez, Philippe (France). *Géopolitique du pétrole*. Tr. Pan Geming et al. Social Sciences Academic Press, 2008, 247.

Thanks to its geographic location by the Indian Ocean, India enjoys inherent advantage in all respects, including security and savings in transportation costs. Its major weakness lies in an underdeveloped industrial system and inferiority to China and Japan in overseas trade, especially export, which places it at the lower end of the global system of production and division of labor.

For its access to the Indian Ocean via the Strait of Malacca, Japan cannot afford to ignore China. However, thanks to its close alliance with the United States and the latter's control over oceans around the world, this minor disadvantage can be safely neglected. Besides, with a history of industrialization dating back to the late nineteenth century, Japan is superior to China in its familiarity with international rules[40] and popularity in the West. In developing overseas market for its goods, Japan suffers less resistance and unfair treatment.

Things are different for China. It has to cope with keen competition from Japan and India, and be always on guard against America's incessant surveillance, tracking, and deterrence. Additionally, partly because of the economic pressure on countries from the financial crisis in 2008 and partly due to exporting countries' concerns about the very high market share of Chinese goods, China has to face unpredictable restrictions or sanctions in target markets against dumping or unfair competition. Besides, the provenances of its energy and resources include regions in the Middle East, Latin America, and Africa, where conflicts may often arise, resulting in a poor level of security.

These, of course, are only part of the problem. The increase of Chinese projects of foreign investment and engineering cooperation and that of the number of people going abroad for traveling, study, and work also place China under exponentially increasing pressure as to the security of its investments, citizens, and trade abroad.

2.7 Underdeveloped Seas

For sea power and maritime development, internal buildup and upgrading are as important as outward extension and expansion. The latter signifies the height and breadth attainable for a country's sea power and marine undertakings. It is a flexible increase that cannot be totally controlled and will change over time and in different situations. In contrast, internal buildup and upgrading reflect the profundity of a country's sea power and marine undertakings. More inflexible and controllable, it can be considered the reserve of that country's sea power and marine undertakings, and determines the capability and possibility of their extension and expansion.

---

[40]As a member of the G8, an important platform for major industrial countries to meet and discuss policies, Japan has fully participated in the creation of the contemporary rules for international trade. The G8 started as the G6, which was initiated by France and established by France, Germany, Italy, Japan, Britain and the United States in 1975. It became the G7 when Canada joined in 1976 and the G8 when Russia joined in 1997.

As a Chinese saying goes, to forge iron, one must be strong. Considering the complex international situation, the limitation of strength and the shortage of geographic leeway, China will have difficult access to the oceans. For some time to come, it would be reasonable for China to extend and expand its sea power and marine undertakings according to its ability and strength.

However, misguided development of industry and regional economy may have hindered, rather than promoted and accelerated, the natural progress in sea power and marine undertakings. If one does not focus on forging iron or has no interest in it, when will he become a tough ironsmith? When will the buildup and upgrading in sea power and marine undertakings at home provide genuine and adequate support for their extension and expansion abroad?

We may have some idea of how serious the situation is from the low level of China's overall maritime development.

The overall index of China's maritime development is only around 2 %. This is not only lower than the proportion in countries with well-developed marine economy (14–17 %), but also lower than the world average level of 4 %.[41]

The prime example of this is of course the fact that most of our marine industries are characterized by lack of excellent conglomerates, poor international competitiveness, low input–output ratio, and limited technological competence. Emerging industries with high added value, such as marine electric power, marine chemical industry, and marine biomedicine, have either just begun or are still at the stage of extensive operation. With limited scale, their potential has yet to be fully tapped and demonstrated.[42] In 2013, they accounted for only 0.4, 1, and 4 % in the total added value of China's major marine industries.

There is also much room for improvement in areas of common concern including oil and gas prospecting and exploitation at sea and the development of deep sea oil and gas. Offshore oil and gas are under-prospected, with only 26.4 % of the offshore oil reserve and 10.9 % of the offshore natural gas reserve ascertained. This being the case for offshore oil and gas, we can imagine what it is like for deep sea oil and gas. According to the plan of CNOOC, the company would collect 50 million tons of oil in 2010 and produce 25 million tons of oil equivalent in the deep waters of the South China Sea in 2015 and 50 million tons in 2020. In comparison, Shell's oil output was nearly 160 million tons in 2009. In other words, CNOOC's oil output in 2020 will be less than half of Shell's deep sea oil output in 2009. From this we can imagine the gap between China's marine oil and gas companies and their more advanced counterparts in the capability of development.[43]

Even in such pillar marine industries as shipping and fishery, the Chinese mainland lags behind developed countries and regions (including Taiwan) in many

[41]Xu Haocheng. "The Third Wave of Coastal Development", in *Decision-making*, 2007 (3).

[42]Song Pengxia & Yang Qun. "Exploitation of Marine Resources Needs 'Blue Engine' to Catch up with Land Economy", in *Jiefang Daily*, Oct. 28, 2005.

[43]Kong Zhiguo. "One CNOOC Is Not Enough", in *China Economic Weekly*, 2010 (37).

Table 2.10 Exploited proportion of China's marine resources

Oil and gas	Tourism	Placer	Shallow beaches	Offshore fishery
5 %	30 %	5 %	2 %	Over developed

Source Wang Fang and Yang Jinsen (2002)

ways. In terms of fishery, to curb excessive offshore fishing, some developed countries have restructured their fishery industry, highlighting the added value of fishery products and a product differentiation policy. Meanwhile, they have developed deep sea fishery using advanced technologies and equipment. In the Chinese mainland, however, the industry is beset by low refrigerating technology, poor operation, ill-equipped deep sea fishing boats, and lack of technological advances in the deep processing of fishery products. In terms of marine transportation, some of China's ocean-going ships are rather old, having problems in ship management, safety standards, and the quality of crews. Most of the ports, which are fundamental to ocean transportation, have been built in an ill-planned rush. They are in many ways at odds with the global trend toward integrated international logistic centers with functions related to industry, business, and trade.[44]

Moreover, some longstanding problems such as the overdevelopment of offshore fishery (Table 2.10), serious damage to some islands,[45] increasing pollutants from the land, aggravating pollution from mariculture, rapidly expanding reclamation of land from the sea, and prevalent ecological deterioration (Tables 2.11 and 2.12), have not shown any obvious sign of improvement. In fact, some of them tend to get worse. As shown in Table 2.9, reclamation of land from the sea, which has remained at a high level since 2005, has affected ecological and resource indices in the waters in question. After 2004, when the amount of pollutants flowing from major rivers into the sea exceeded 10 million tons for the first time, the number kept rising until 2010. Since then, it has stabilized above the level of 16 million tons (Table 2.13). The increase of pollutants from the land has caused pollution in at least 55 % of China's offshore waters and severe eutrophication in 70 % of such waters, with "death zones" appearing in some neighboring areas. The Bohai Sea, the waters close to the estuary of the Yangtze River, the estuary of the Pearl River, Hangzhou Bay, and the waters of Jiangsu and some large/medium-sized cities have become the most polluted areas. Severe ecological damage has occurred on the East Coast of Hainan, the western Guangdong waters, Beihai City of Guangxi Province, and Beilun Port.[46] In recent years, red tide disasters have

[44]The research project group of the Development Strategy Institute of the State Oceanic Administration. *China's Ocean Development Report*. China Ocean Press, 2007, 125.

[45]Liu Rongzi & Qi Lianming. *A Study of the Value System of Uninhabited Islands in China*. China Ocean Press, 2006, 158-162.

[46]The research project group of the Development Strategy Institute of the State Oceanic Administration. *China's Ocean Development Report*. China Ocean Press, 2007, 186–8.

frequently taken place in Dalian City of Liaoning Province, Bohai Gulf, area outside the estuary of the Yangtze, and central and southern parts of Zhejiang Province.

This shows that, in addition to the low utilization of marine resources, due importance has not been accorded to the sustainable development of marine economy. Its incidental or consequent negative externality, which is at a quite high level, has greatly offset the positive effect of marine economy.

Table 2.11 Areas of Chinese maritime space with water quality lower than the first category in summer (km^2) (2003–2013)

Year	Area of waters with Cat. 2 quality	Area of waters with Cat. 3 quality	Area of waters with Cat. 4 quality	Area of waters with quality lower than Cat. 4	Total
2003	80000	22000	15000	25000	142000
2004	66000	4000	31000	32000	169000
2005	58000	34000	18000	29000	139000
2006	51020	52140	17440	28370	148970
2007	51290	47510	16760	29720	145280
2008	65480	28840	17420	25260	137000
2009	70920	25500	20840	29720	146980
2010	70430	36190	23070	48030	177720
2011	47160	36490	15630	44340	143620
2012	46910	30030	24700	67880	169520
2013	47840	34310	18340	43800	144290

Source State Oceanic Administration. *Communiqué on China's Marine Environment* (*2003–2013*)

Table 2.12 Area of land reclaimed from the sea in China (ha.) (2003–2013)

Year	Area with ascertained rights
2003	2123.00
2004	5352.00
2005	11,662.24
2006	11,293.94
2007	13,425.00
2008	11,000.71
2009	17,888.09
2010	13,598.74
2011	13,594.92
2012	8619.08
2013	13,169.54

Source State Oceanic Administration. *Communiqué on the Use and Management of Maritime Space* (*2003–2013*)

Table 2.13 Amount of pollutants flowing from major Chinese rivers into the sea (×10,000 tons) (2003–2013)

Year	Amount of pollutants entering the sea
2003	619
2004	1145
2005	1071
2006	1382
2007	1407
2008	1149
2009	1367
2010	1751
2011	1820
2012	1705
2013	1672

Source State Oceanic Administration. *Communiqué on China's Marine Environment (2003–2013)*. *Note* Variations in the rivers examined from year to year may affect the comparability of data. However, since the most important rivers (i.e., the Yangtze River, Yellow River, and Pearl River) were always among the samples, the error is not significant and the data are still convincing

2.8 The Harm of Seeking Regional Balance

The policy to address regional imbalance in development has long been popular in China. Yet it also serves as an example of how misguided policies can be an impediment to China's sea power and marine undertakings.

The Chinese government has always seen regional balance in development as an important goal of state governance. To this end, China has introduced a variety of measures to narrow the gap between regions in recent years.

Since the mid-1990s, probably encouraged by the effect of the policy for special economic zones and open coastal cities, China has accorded importance to the revival of the old industrial bases in the northeast, Great Western Development, and the rise of the central region as strategies for national development.

Under the influence of the idea that regional imbalance must be eliminated, the Central Government has treated the eastern regions and the western regions in obviously different ways. At the beginning of "reform and opening up," its support for the coastal areas was policy oriented. In contrast, it has given underdeveloped areas integrated support including favorable policy, financial transfer payment and special subsidies, aid to major projects, and the supply of personnel (e.g., temporary reassignment of cadres from eastern regions and the Central Government, college students serving as volunteer teachers).

The special economic zones and the open coastal cities made it with no support in fund and personnel from the Central Government. Nowadays, apart from policy, the Central Government is capable of providing support in funding, projects, and personnel for particular regions. Thus it seems reasonable to expect those regions to have a better chance to succeed. However, this has not happened. The gap between the coastal regions and the inland provinces has actually widened. In 1978, the GDP of Shanghai (the province-level administrative area with the highest GDP) was 41 times that of Tibet (the province-level administrative area with the lowest GDP); in 2010, the GDP of Guangdong (which had the highest GDP) was 89.6 times that of Tibet (which had the lowest GDP).

Why is it so? Regional imbalance in economic development may not stem from having or not having support from the state, but from inherent regional differences in natural environment and geographic location and local governments' capability of public service.

Thirty years ago, why did China choose the coast rather than the inland as the starting point of reform and opening up?

The reason is that the coast enjoyed more noticeable advantages. As China opened up to the outside world, the coast became not only the frontier of opening up, but also a hub between the domestic market and the world market. After all, the transaction of bulk goods had to be almost entirely conducted across the sea, and the related decisions were merely a product of necessity.

Nowadays, in addition to its geographic advantages, the coast displays an economic agglomeration effect. Research shows that the coastal regions are home to many industrial clusters, which have attracted over 90 % of China's foreign trade and more than 85 % of its high-tech industries. Moreover, in transaction, government is giving way to market, and policy to trade rules. It can be said, therefore, that the coast is way superior to the other regions, especially the west, in terms of the development-supporting elements.

China seems to be entering a period of growing reliance on marine economy. This can be seen from a comparison between the GDP and per capita GDP ranking of the province-level administrative areas in 1978 (Table 2.14) and the ranking in 2010 (Table 1.3). In 1978, the total GDP of the 12 coastal provinces was 190.60 billion yuan, representing 52.6 % of the national GDP of 362.41 billion yuan and the per capita GDP of 379 yuan. In 2010, the total GDP of the same areas was 25,196.44 billion yuan, accounting for 63.3 % of the national GDP of 39,798.3 billion yuan.

Observation of individual cases would yield the same result. In 1978, when Fujian and Yunnan were on roughly the same level in economic development, their GDPs were 6.64 billion yuan and 6.905 billion yuan, and their per capita GDPs were 273 yuan and 226 yuan; Fujian's GDP was 96.1 % of Yunnan's, and its per capita GDP was 120.8 % of Yunnan's. In 2010, their GDPs were 1435.71 billion yuan and 722.01 billion yuan and their per capita GDPs were 37,981.8 yuan and 15,628.0 yuan; the ratio between the former and the latter had increased to 198.8 and 243.0 %, respectively.

Against this background, one would hardly expect the "ice-breaking effect" of preferential policies. People may ask, if the inland has developed like this with strong support by the state, how would it be like without the preferential policies, the investment of trillions of yuan, and other forms of support by the state? What would have been achieved if such funds and policies were given to other regions?

Table 2.14 Provincial rankings in GDP and per capita GDP in 1978

Area	GDP (100 million yuan)	Per capita GDP (yuan)	Area	GDP (100 million yuan)	Per capita GDP (yuan)
Beijing	108.84	1290	Henan	162.92	232
Tianjin	82.65	1160	Hubei	151	332
Hebei	183.06	364	Hunan	146.99	286
Shanxi	88	365	Guangdong	185.85	369
Inner Mongolia	58.04	317	Guangxi	75.85	225
Liaoning	229.2	680	Hainan	16.4	314
Jilin	81.98	381	Sichuan	184.61	262
Heilongjiang	174.78	564	Guizhou	46.62	175
Shanghai	272.81	2498	Yunnan	69.05	226
Jiangsu	249.24	430	Tibet	6.65	375
Zhejiang	123.72	331	Shaanxi	81.07	291
Anhui	113.96	244	Gansu	64.73	348
Fujian	66.37	273	Qinghai	15.54	428
Jiangxi	87	276	Ningxia	13	370
Shandong	225.45	316	Xinjiang	39.07	313

Source State Statistical Bureau's website: http://data.stats.gov.cn/workspace/. *Note* The data for Chongqing is not available because it was not yet a provincial-level administrative area at the time

Some regions are willing and able to raise funds on their own and seek new approaches to development (for instance, the "blue economic zone of the peninsular" Shandong has planned to build with an investment of one trillion yuan, and Haixi Economic Zone in Fujian). In contrast to some places' reliance on financial aid without a clear roadmap of development, is this not more conducive to the country's economic strength and does it not deserve more to be supported by the Central Government? Is it fair to show preference to the backward over the advanced?

Perhaps we need to change our view on regional imbalance in development.

Regional balance in development is generally understood to mean that regions with the same size of land and population should reach the same level of development or be not much different in per capita income and living standard. Anyway, it has much to do with wealth, total, or average.

In the twenty-first century, as global warming, industrial pollution and "urban diseases" become worldwide concerns, people have come to realize that it is problematic to associate the development of an area with nothing but the economic indices. Equal importance should be accorded to environment, health, and the quality of life. However, what is the relationship like between economic indices and the later proposed non-economic ones?

Relevant discussions typically view environmental development and the cure of "urban diseases" as diametrically opposite to economic development. However, considering the difference between individual needs (the satisfaction of which is the so-called sense of happiness), such opinions are more or less assumptive.

In fact, at a given time, different individuals or groups of people may have varying interests in things, while the same individual or group may shift their interests over time. A sound society is able to satisfy myriad wishes in constant change, and offer the possibility for people to satisfy their reasonable wishes through various choices.

Since human society came into existence, transaction, and migration have been principal ways for people to satisfy their reasonable wishes. Therefore, the development of any region can be indicated by the migration of population and the means and scale of transaction. This is also true of environment and the quality of life. Just take a look around: in the past, people were content to have their own apartments; today, many are striding toward big houses and holiday residences. People used to feel proud of living in a factory compound, but now it is fashionable to live in the countryside. Industrialization was once the hallmark of a city; nowadays a city must also be pleasant to live in and eco-friendly… The list may go on.

In this sense, whether different regions have given full play to their advantages and developed in a way that best suits them based on a sensible distribution of resources is a key measure of the balance in development. This is well proven by what has happened since the start of reform and opening up. The massive return of migrant workers from cities to rural areas from 2004 to 2005 indicated individuals' perception of the imbalance in development between the cities and the countryside, the coast and the inland. The nationwide discussion of how to overcome GDP fetishism since 2003 and some inland areas' protection of their environmental resources show how such imbalance has been understood in a new light on the institutional level.

Local governments should detect the gap between their goals of governance and individual perceptions from the state of migration and improve the efficiency of governance accordingly.

Therefore, regional balance or imbalance in development is not a matter of right or wrong. It merely reflects whether the regions have achieved full development under given conditions. Whether regional balance in development can be achieved depends on two points: (1) Each region should promote the free flow of resources as dictated by the law of the market according to the principle of comparative advantage. Then it should share its achievements with other regions through the exchange of its strengths for those of others. (2) As part of the first point and its prerequisite (human is a type of resource and also conducts the transaction of resources), people should be free to migrate, express their will, and voice their opinion on the development of a place by voting with their feet.

In a market economy, if all the regions have distinct characteristics, with not much movement of population between them, one may be sure that balance in development has been achieved.

Why is it that this simple truth is understood by few and pointed out by even fewer?

This is mainly because it has been taken for granted that regional imbalance in development is undesirable.

Fear of such imbalance stems not so much from the gap between regions per se as from the anxiety to lift a small number of regions out of poverty.

Therefore, instead of studying how to bridge the gap, we should discuss how to eliminate poverty in the backward areas as soon as possible while maintaining steady development nationwide.

Poverty may be overcome in either of the two ways: a given amount of resources may be shared by a smaller population, or a greater population may make as much use of a given amount of resources as possible. This can be done by means of processing, marketing, and transaction, which can extend the use of resources almost infinitely and extract more benefit from them.

Anyway, the faster and healthier development of the coastal regions can only be beneficial for China. It would not only be conducive to the increase of national wealth, but it would also benefit underdeveloped areas through increased mobility and the spread of good practices. When people in these areas decide to vote with their feet, they will have more and better places to go; when these areas no longer wait for the first way to eliminate poverty, they will have more examples to follow.

Therefore, when we evaluate the development of the western regions, apart from the state's support, we should never underestimate migrant workers' contribution to the economy of their hometowns in terms of consumption, funds, and ideas. A survey conducted by the Rural Areas Department of the State Statistics Bureau in 2006 shows that 70 % of the migrant workers across the country have chosen to work in the eastern regions, and the number of migrant workers from the western regions was 28.33 million (in Yunnan, 90 % of the labor force aged under 40 worked outside the province in the same year). Their income would eventually be spent on daily necessities for their families, travels, and social activities, with the rest deposited in hometown banks. As regional imbalance in development grows, the regional gap in personal income has not widened; in fact, it has even narrowed to some degree. In 1978, the highest per capita GDP in a province-level administrative area (Shanghai) was 14.3 times as much as the lowest (in Guizhou). In 2010, the former was 6.8 times as much as the latter.

This indicates that the real impediments against regional balance in development are all the factors that are inimical to the free mobility of social resources, such as monopoly, regional protectionism, lack of protection for the rights of market players, and improper control over business by administrative power; these are compounded by outdated mechanism and problems left over from the age of planned economy, notably the household registration policy, urban–rural dual structure, and the under-developed social security system. Such factors also include constraints on the coastal regions due to the wrong concept of regional balance in development; with elements that could have generated more profits in coastal regions invested in other areas, those coastal regions have failed to reach a level of development they could have attained.

To achieve regional balance in development, the Central Government should work harder to address the obstacles and defects. In terms of regional development, it should unequivocally encourage the coastal regions to fulfill their potential to the greatest extent possible, for China's future is on the sea.

The implementation of policies comes at a price. If the government's policy agrees with personal choice, it will contribute to social progress. Disagreement between them will add to the price; moreover, it will reduce the wealth created by society and distort its course of development.[47] Despite its initial purpose, the current Chinese policy for limiting regional imbalance in development is actually at odds with the trend of social development.

Therefore, the government should first of all reexamine the policy to support the development in the central and western regions. Instead of trying to narrow the gap between regions through assumptive intervention in the allocation of resources, the government should facilitate the mobility of resources in keeping with the trend of social development, promote competition between local governments in the provision of services, and encourage regions to highlight their comparative advantages in development. This would be the only way to bring about a state of harmony. The challenge behind regional imbalance is not a matter of which regions the Central Government should provide with preferential policies and financial transfer payment, but how to remove the obstacles against the mobility of people, capital, and resources and eliminate local protectionism.

2.9 The Lack of Strategic Awareness

The low level of comprehensive development of China's marine economy and the hindrance of marine economy and marine undertakings from the pursuit of regional balance reflect a lack of strategic awareness in marine governance. This has not only led to the lack of insight into and prospective study of the evolution of modern sea power, but also marks impracticality in many views on the status quo of sea power and suggestions on how to realize it.

In China, there are three wrong tendencies in the examination of its sea power predicament as follows:

1. Continued indecision about whether China should choose to be a land-oriented or sea-oriented country;
2. Equating controversial sea power with the whole of sea power, equating the protection of maritime sovereignty with the preservation, and development of complete sea power, and furthermore, equating the development of military strength on the sea with the defense of maritime sovereignty;
3. The invariable emphasis on the strategic orientation toward offshore defense in terms of the development of military strength on the sea.

[47]Kong Zhiguo & Zhao Yue. "How to Understand Institutions", in *Economic Journal for Postgraduates of Shandong University*, 2001 (2).

No matter in how eloquent terms these tendencies are expressed, we can hardly cover up their superficiality and narrow mindedness. The reason is simple: those who are affected by such tendencies not only fail to appreciate the whole of sea power based on its change since modern times, but they are also far from grasping the essence of a country's growth into a great maritime nation.

Considering the changes in the forms and contexts of war brought about by information warfare and air and space warfare, land and sea should not be considered as opposite to each other. To a country with both land and sea, the land (as the carrier of the domestic market and resources and the depth of conventional war) and the sea (as linkage to the global market and carrier of international resources) are no longer in an either–or relationship as under the conditions of totally conventional warfare, but bound together in mutual complementation and mutual support. Moreover, with the globe becoming a "flat" village[48] and weapons of mass destruction being an effective deterrence against large-scale wars,[49] the sea is playing a more prominent role as the hub and focus of external connection for a country with sea routes. China is of course no exception.

An understanding of the evolution of sea power would tell us that today's sea power is quite different from what it used to be in the period between the fifteenth century and the mid-twentieth century, when it was about the competition in size and strength, firepower, the sturdiness of ships, and the expanse of colonies. Sea power has become a system in which there are interests besides sovereignty, and rights and obligations apart from power. In addition to gaining profit from the sea, a country must or should pay a price by means of the provision of domestic public products such as maritime governance and global public products such as ecological protection in international waters. Sea power can expand or diminish, sometimes transcending the categories of territorial land, sea, and airspace. Maritime sovereignty is linked to sea power, but they are never the same thing.

A close look at the maritime practices of various countries would reveal a change in the wrestling at sea based on military strength. In terms of naval supremacy, instead of the zero-sum game in which the sea cannot be allowed to be used by any rival or the negative-sum game causing losses to both sides, they are seeking control based on cooperation and positive-sum game through Pareto improvement. Confrontation and opposition at sea in the military sense has totally given way to all-dimensional offensive and defensive postures with little distinction between coastal, mid-distance, and high seas. Even the line between what is sea and what is not has become blurry due to the increasing interpenetration and cooperation between military branches. We may say that the maritime frontier where offense and defense between rivals or potential rivals take place extends as far as national

---

[48]Friedman, Thomas (the US). *The World is Flat: A Brief History of the Twenty-First Century*. Tr. He Fan, Xiao Yingying and Hao Zhengfei. Hunan Science and Technology Press, 2013, 40, 42–154.

[49]Gaddis, John Lewis (the US). *The Cold War*. Trn. Zhai Qiang & Zhang Jing. Social Sciences Academic Press, 2013, 73–4, 92–5.

interests. If we need to emphasize our defensive position, we may use "defense," rather than the inaccurate term of "offshore defense."

Such wrong tendencies have brought negative impact that may not be neglected.

First of all, due to the lack of prospective research into the evolution of modern sea power and that of responsive measures, a national strategy for maritime development has yet to be designed and an effective model of maritime governance has yet to be fully established.

Since the advent of reform and opening up, China has attached increasing importance to the protection and realization of sea power and the development of marine programs. The 17th National Congress of the CPC in October 2007 designated the sea as the orientation of industrial development; the 18th National Congress of the CPC in November 2012 proposed straightforward the goal of "building a strong maritime nation." In October 2013, President Xi Jinping put forward the strategic vision of building a Maritime Silk Road in collaboration with ASEAN.

China has also made remarkable progress in maritime governance. Statistics about the sea have become more scientific and refined, a system of laws and regulations on the sea have taken initial shape, and results have been achieved in the development and protection of islands, the protection of marine environment and biodiversity, the planning and management of maritime spaces, and international maritime exchange and cooperation. The year 2013, in particular, saw the founding of the National Maritime Commission, the restructuring of the State Oceanic Administration, and the Bureau's integration of its former law enforcement duties for maritime surveillance, fishery administration, coast guard, and antismuggling operation. These indicate a new level of integrated coordination and management of maritime development.

However, this does not mean that China already has a clear strategy for the full realization of sea power and the development of marine programs. There are a host of questions yet to be answered–how to implement the decision to "build a strong maritime nation," what role the Maritime Silk Road is to play in it, what an overall strategic framework should include, what approach to maritime rise China should adopt, whether Western models of maritime governance are applicable to China, and so on.

Second, inappropriateness and divergence between end and means are frequent occurrences in maritime governance. Otherwise, there would not be such problems as restricting the development of marine economy and marine programs. Some of them, which are related to many governmental branches with administrative control over the sea, are more difficult to solve. For instance, the development of uninhabited islands was for a time in the doldrums. In fact, the Regulations on the Protection and Utilization of Uninhabited Sea Islands jointly issued by the State Oceanic Administration, the Ministry of Civil Affairs, and the Headquarters of the General Staff went into effect as early as on July 1, 2003. Since then, however, there has been no improvement in the situation where many of such islands lay idle and a very small number are developed in a haphazard way. This is due to the lack of clear demarcation of duties between local governments and the authorities for environmental protection, mineral products, land, maritime administration, and resources.

It has been a prevalent policy to promote regional balance by preferential treatment of the western regions or the inland at the expense of the eastern or coastal regions. Discussions on the predicament of maritime governance have been going on endlessly, with new problems cropping up before old ones are solved.

However, some issues may not be so complicated. For instance, for the increase of investment in marine science and technology and the expansion of marine education, it is essential to clearly define the departments for making it happen with thorough accountability. Such issues may become problematic due to the entrenched disregard of the sea. Some may argue that, since our energy is limited, it is far more important to defend rights and interests related to disputed sovereignty on the sea. This is merely self-deception. Would China shelf its marine programs until the day when all the disputes at sea have been resolved? Definitely not.

The key is resolve and attention. With correct orientation and all-out efforts, the most difficult issues can be readily resolved. For instance, the State Oceanic Administration volunteered to take charge of the protection and development of uninhabited islands. As a result, the situation has improved significantly since the introduction of the so-called "NBO's Ten Rules" (Circular on Improving Service and Support for Increasing Domestic Demand and Fast and Steady Economic Development) in December 2008. In April 2011, the NBO released a list of 176 sea islands in eight provinces (Liaoning, Shandong, Jiangsu, Zhejiang, Fujian, Guangdong, Guangxi and Hainan). These were the first batch of uninhabited sea islands about to be developed and utilized. An initial success was achieved.

Third, sometimes we may lose the best opportunity to secure rights and interests. This can make it easier for great powers to make strategic adjustments and for small countries to mislead the international public opinion, which will add to the pressure on China's rise on the sea.

For instance, as early as in 1996, when there were not yet international sovereignty disputes over Zengmu Reef and Huangyan Island, Zhang Haiwen and other scholars at the National Institute for Marine Strategy called for the state to pay attention to the maritime rights and interests associated with such territories through the assertion of sovereignty and active development.[50]

However, this insightful piece of advice was underestimated and did not translate into state action. As time went by, potential disputes became open troubles. In late February 2009, Philippine congress proclaimed sovereignty over Huangyan Island.[51] Since then, there has been confrontation between China and Philippines over that issue. If the latter wins out, Zengmu Reef will also be in danger.

[50]Zhang Haiwen. "Studies on China's Maritime Rights", in *Study of Maritime Development Strategies*, 1996 (8).

[51]Liu Hua et al. "The Philippines' Deliberate Occupation of China's Huangyan Island", in *International Herald Leader*, March 3, 2009.

Finally, such wrong tendencies may prevent us from examining sea power and marine programs as well as international competition with a broader vision of a higher comparative value.

Obsession with the relationship between sovereignty and sea power would make it difficult to perceive sea power beyond sovereignty, which is probably a very important, if not the most impressive, part of future maritime rights and interests. It is known to few that two-thirds of the world's maritime space is the high seas, which have an international sea bed area of 251.7 million km^2; the high seas also have more renewable and nonrenewable resources than the sovereignty waters of all the countries combined.[52] Therefore, any insightful country would do what they can to expand their interests in the high seas and the international sea bed area. China is entitled to freedom on the high seas according to the international law, including the freedom of navigation and overflight, the laying of cables and pipelines on the sea bed, the construction of artificial islands and other facilities, fishery and scientific research, and the sharing of other resources in the international sea bed area.

So far, however, China has only made considerable use of the freedom of navigation, overflight, and the laying of cables and pipelines on the sea bed due to the increase of foreign trade and international exchange. It has gained exclusive rights to prospect in a 75,000-km^2 area with polymetallic nodules on the sea bed of the Pacific and a 10,000-km^2 area with polymetallic sulfide in the international sea bed area under the southwest Indian Ocean, for which it enjoys priority for exploitation. Apart from these, little has been achieved in the obtainment of maritime rights and interests.

[52]Yang Jinsen. "Building China into a Strong Maritime Nation in the Pacific: Reflections and Suggestions", in *Study of Maritime Development Strategies*, 2000 (1).

Chapter 3
Evolution of International Sea Power: Trend and Influence

China has not done well in following and understanding the evolution of international sea power and maritime development at a strategic level, and it cannot preserve its complete sea power and promote its capacities of maritime development and exploitation in a vacuum environment. This has been the root cause of the challenges and difficulties it faces on the sea.

Consequently, only by forming clear judgments on the ongoing interactions between humanity and the sea, the previous changes, and their impact on people's assessment and perception of sea power on the basis of studying the evolution of the international sea power can we elevate our understanding from a low, empirical level, make it more objective and complete, and be more likely to find out the obstacles to China's rise to an important maritime nation and work out some concrete advice contributing to greater accomplishment in its seaward development.

3.1 Piratical-Style Competition and Mahan's Contribution

Though there are historical records of navies and sea battles as early as 500–400 BC, since sea power is always related to the concept of nation-state, we still believe that sea power originated in the fifteenth century when Europe expanded and nation-states started to emerge.

The race for colonies between Portugal and Spain via the around-the-world voyages was the starting point. Initially, pirates and navies could readily change into each other; sea power was nothing but naval supremacy, i.e., the command of sea. Whether the means for obtaining the command was fair and aboveboard was, more often than not, unimportant.

Spain replaced Portugal; Holland, Spain; and Britain, Holland. Melee broke out among Britain, France, Holland, and Spain at times—all the maritime activities of these countries can be largely seen as piratical activities. This is not only because

Z. Kong, *The Making of a Maritime Power*, Research Series on the Chinese Dream and China's Development Path, DOI 10.1007/978-981-10-1786-5_3

the navies of many countries were fleets of pirates approved by the authorities—which explains why many big-name naval generals, such as Sir John Hawkins, the first English naval commander to enter Spain in the Elizabethan era and Francis Drake, the first English around-the-world voyager knighted by Queen Elizabeth I in person, were also big-name pirates of their time[1]; but also because even regular navies, once out on the sea, could not resist the temptation of pirating—they would, for instance, plunder and attack merchant ships of enemy states or other states.

In the mid and late nineteenth century, things started to change. After Alfred Thayer Mahan presented his sea power theory, with the rise of the United States on the sea, though the importance of the state's naval strength was still stressed, besides the armed force on the sea, the safety of voyage routes, trade, overseas markets, etc., were also included in the category of sea power; moreover, the state's naval operations were gradually distinguished from piracy. Although states at war attacked enemy merchant vessels from time to time, such attacks were no longer seen as a fair and square form of warfare.

As the first strategist in the world to expound on the concept of sea power, Mahan combined sea interest, sea hegemony, sea power, etc., into his concept of sea power and then derived the path to achieving sea power by strengthening the navy.

Influenced by the then-prevalent logic that "might is right," which shaped the international political and economic order,[2] the "lawless" logic promoting the utilization of naval power in a boundless pursuit of state interests permeates Mahan's sea power theory. There is no distinction between legal and illegal wield of naval power. Seeking sea hegemony and defending maritime territory were seen as the same.[3] People of later times who have appreciated, imitated, and followed him have mostly used these violence-advocating strategies, tactics, and methods as a source of their basis, goals, or even examples.[4]

However, many people have overlooked—even Mahan himself might very well neglect—the fact that looking beyond the paradigm of pure maritime armed force building, and the introduction of the cost–benefit approach to the analysis of sea power and the construction of the strategic framework for sea power development have been Mahan's greatest contribution. When he discusses sea power, the weighing of costs and benefits has also (see Table 3.1) become the origin of his theory.

---

[1]Konstam, Angus (2010). *Piracy: The Complete History*. (Yang, Yujie, Zhao, Guomei, et al., trans.) Beijing: People's Liberation Army Press, pp. 38–63.

[2]Wang, Hanling (2006). Trends in International Law of the Sea: Commemorating the 10th Anniversary of China's approval of the United Nations Convention on the Law of the Sea (UNCLOS). *China Ocean News*, May 30.

[3]Such sea power obviously cannot win the approval of people who oppose aggression and hegemony. See Zhang, Wenmu (2003). A Discussion of Sea Power. *World Economics and Politics*, no. 10; Liang, Fang (ed.) (2007). *A Study of Naval History and Future Sea Warfare*, Beijing: China Ocean Press.

[4]*Seapower: A Guide for the Twenty-First Century*, Shanghai: Shanghai People's Publishing House, pp. 64–102.

Table 3.1 Mahan's elements of sea power and their impact on costs and benefits

Elements of sea power	Costs	Benefits
Land area	Land rivals against sea, and land power against sea power	–
Marine resources	–	Increase of wealth
Coastline	The longer the coastline, the greater the pressure on defense and the greater the costs	–
Ports	Vulnerable to attacks from the sea	Beneficial to both domestic and foreign trade
Strategic passes on the sea	–	Beneficial to the layout of global trade
Shipping capacity	–	Conducive to the expansion of the trade network on the sea and the increase of business revenue
Navy	Arms, ships and personnel training	Safeguarding the territory and commercial security
Trade capacity	–	Advantageous position in world trade
Population	–	Supplying troops and sailors
Science and technology	–	Beneficial to navigation and marine defense
Industrial production	–	Supplying ships, equipment, goods, etc.; beneficial to the improvement of ocean navigation, the expansion of trade and the strengthening of the navy
Colonies	–	Expanding overseas markets and increasing trade opportunities
National character	If national character hinders marine programs, efforts to remove the character will be the costs	If national character is beneficial to marine programs, then it will be benefits
Government	If the government does not attach importance to the sea, it will be a hindrance. The greater its mobilization capacity, the higher the costs	If it values the sea, the greater its mobilization capacity, the greater the benefits

Source A.T. Mahan, 2006, Chinese translation. The table is based on Mahan's arguments scattered in his dissertation

When analyzing the advantages and disadvantages of geographical location, he points out that the British Isles are geographically defensible. In this respect, Britain has an advantage. But he also says that the vast colonies were a great burden on Britain in defense—this may be counted as expense. He then proceeds to state that Britain's developed trade increased considerably its capability for covering the expense.[5]

[5]Mahan, A.T. (2006). *The Influence of Sea Power upon History*. (An, Changrong, and Cheng, Zhongqin, trans.) Beijing: People's Liberation Army Press, pp. 64–74.

When assessing the advantages and disadvantages of national characteristics, he stresses that compared with Spain, Portugal, and France, Britain and Holland had more colonies. However, because the later two were more dependent on commerce and trade than the former three and could thus supply various goods to emerging markets, they could have greater trade revenue and thus the return rates of their colonies were higher significantly.[6]

When he lists the six major elements of sea power, i.e., geographical position, physical conformation, extent of territory, number of population, national character, and character of the government, he generally approaches his analysis from the perspective of expense but benefits are his ultimate concern. As he frankly writes, whether the geographical position is defensible or not, whether the physical conformation and extent of territory have a great demand on the navy or not, whether the size and quality of the population promote or hinder the development of the navy, whether the national character is conductive to trade and overseas business of the state, and whether the government holds a positive or negative attitude to the sea and the navy, there is only one purpose—to enunciate that the development of sea power includes "not only the military strength afloat, that rules the sea or any part of it by force of arms, but also the peaceful commerce and shipping from which alone a military fleet naturally and healthfully springs, and on which it securely rests." All these things—"(1) production; (2) shipping; and (3) colonies and markets, in a word…" serve to expand sea power.[7]

He states clearly that the development of sea power includes "not only the military strength afloat, that rules the sea or any part of it by force of arms, but also the peaceful commerce and shipping from which alone a military fleet naturally and healthfully springs, and on which it securely rests."[8] Such an analytical method is identical with that adopted by many contemporary Western economists who observed sea power. As asserted by Adam Smith, Douglass Cecil North, Robert Thomas, et al.,[9] the interplay between the boom of trade and the rise on the sea had an indispensable impact on the rise of the Western world; and to obtain benefits from the sea, the countries concerned had paid corresponding prices in international relations, military, economy and policy.

---

[6]Mahan, A.T. (2006). *The Influence of Sea Power upon History*. (An, Changrong, and Cheng, Zhongqin, trans.) Beijing: People's Liberation Army Press, pp. 38–45.

[7]Mahan, A.T. (2006). *The Influence of Sea Power upon History*. (An, Changrong, and Cheng, Zhongqin, trans.) Beijing: People's Liberation Army Press, p. 91.

[8]Mahan, A.T. (2006). *The Influence of Sea Power upon History*. (An, Changrong, and Cheng, Zhongqin, trans.) Beijing: People's Liberation Army Press, p. 38.

[9]Smith, Adam (1974). *An Inquiry into the Nature and Causes of the Wealth of Nations*. (Guo, Dali, and Wang, Yanan, trans.) Beijing: The Commercial Press, pp. 127–210; North, Douglas and Thomas, Robert P. (1999). *The Rise of the Western World: A New Economic History*. (Li, Yiping, Cai, Lei, et al., trans.) Beijing: Huaxia Publishing House, pp. 117–192; North, Douglass (1995). *Structure and Change in Economic History*. (Chen, Yu, and Luo, Huaping, trans.) Shanghai: Joint Publishing Company and Shanghai People's Publishing House, pp. 162–190; North, Douglass (2008). *Understanding the Process of Economic Change*. (Zhong, Zhengsheng, Xing, Hua, et al., trans.) Beijing: China Renmin University Press, pp. 126–128.

However, a closer look may reveal some slight differences between the economists and Mahan.

An overview of Mahan's sea power system may lead to the discovery that though the domestic significance of a state's sea power—the impact of maritime benefits both on economic and fiscal growth and on the expense of public goods needed in the bid to develop marine programs—can basically be included in his sea power system, it tends to overemphasize benefits but neglect expense and overemphasize short-term gains but neglect long-term benefits. For instance, it is likely to give inadequate consideration to such international expenses as the reactions from enemy or rival states, and overlooks public services such as maintaining the marine order and marine salvage—when it discusses the importance of elements such as straits, sea islands, and marine resources, it tends to see the various benefits but hardly considers what it should do to preserve or utilize the natural conveniences provided by the ocean.

Such unbalanced attention paid to the costs and benefits of sea power is evidently problematic. It shows that, subconsciously, Mahan deems military strength as the ultimate resort, if not the only means. He sees the limitations of the pure pursuit of military power, but fails to find a good way to bring about a virtuous cycle through the interplay between military power and other related factors. The confusion between maritime rights and marine benefits, between sea rights and influence on the sea,[10] sea power, and sea violence has, to some extent a manifestation.

---

[10]I have found three lines vaguely alluding to sea rights:

> "The history of sea power, while embracing in its broad sweep all that tends to make a people great upon the sea or by the sea", "England's rights, or reparation for its wrongs, were demanded by its fleets throughout the world…" and "For two hundred years England has been the great commercial nation of the world…yet of all nations it has ever been most reluctant to concede the immunities of commerce and the rights of neutrals. Regarded not as a matter of right, but of policy…".

The first line arguably supports the right of every country to exploit the ocean legally and reasonably; as for the second line, considering the arrogant and domineering behaviors of English ships in that period, it was inevitable for England to lodge unjustifiable demands, but this does rule out the possibility that under some circumstances some of its demands were justifiable, particularly for individual merchants engaged in free trade; The third line expresses the attitude of England, a power, toward sea power. Though the word "right" is mentioned, Mahan does not make clear his opinion.

Moreover, even such vague statements are mixed into long discourses hyping military strength and hegemony. Adopting the stance of Western maritime powers, Mahan's theory on sea power believes that advantageous military strengths on the sea can help obtain the dominion over the world; the theory is filled with various battle examples and citation supporting this belief.

"*…the history of sea power…is largely a military history.*" The main thread determined by Mahan for his theory perhaps also explains why *power* rather than *rights*, as stressed by law, plays a dominant role in his dissertation.

See Mahan, A.T. (2006), Chinese translation, p. 1 of Preface, p. 77, p. 694, p. 77. See also Zhang, Wenmu (2003b) for reference.

Let us see economists approach similar issues following the same train of thought. When discussing colonies, Adam Smith points out that, though all of them were maritime powers, Britain and France were leaving Spain and Portugal behind. This was determined by whether the mother country provided enough public goods for its colonies so that they could become its peaceful trade bases. The reason why the latter two fell behind was that they had extorted excessive taxes and levies and thus evoked fierce resistance.[11] When exploring the causes of the rise of the Western world, North also points out that what distinguished Britain and Holland, two long-time good performers, from France and Spain, which declined after culminating in strength, were the long-standing driving forces inside the country that fuelled institutional innovation and technological progress, which then gave birth to the driving force giving momentum to sustainable economic growth.[12]

Though North may be suspected of arguing in favor of Western countries[13] and his conclusion that the rise of Britain and Holland can be solely attributed to their own efforts, their defeat of France and Spain on the sea indeed had some bearing on the fact that they transformed their trade with the colonies into a source of revenue whereas their rivals extorted excessive taxes and levies from their colonies in an unreasonable fashion.

3.2 Sovereignty and Sea Rights Do not Come for Free

In a world where the creed for international relations was "there was no permanent friend nor enemy, but only permanent interests," it was a matter of course for countries to favor gains against losses, to be obsessed with "grabbing" and neglect the need to "keep." However, in the game of international relations, such a situation beneficial to only one country other than others either does not exist at all or only exists for a short time.

In history, there were many empires with unrivaled military strengths, which had all been committed to the conquest of the world. However, none of them escaped the fate of fall. Why?

Because sovereignty and interests both come at a price.

If the land, population, wealth, resources, and taxes within the borders of a sovereign state and the various benefits it receives from the international community are seen as "benefits," to ensure that the benefits belong to it and continue to

---

[11]Smith, Adam (1974). *An Inquiry into the Nature and Causes of the Wealth of Nations*. (Guo, Dali, and Wang, Yanan, trans.) Beijing: The Commercial Press, pp. 127–210.

[12]North, Douglass (1995). *Structure and Change in Economic History*. (Chen, Yu, and Luo, Huaping, trans.) Shanghai: Joint Publishing Company and Shanghai People's Publishing House, pp. 162–190; North, Douglass (2008). *Understanding the Process of Economic Change*. (Zhong, Zhengsheng, Xing, Hua, et al., trans.) Beijing: China Renmin University Press, pp. 126–128.

[13]Sheng, Hong (2002). "Free Trade" for the United Kingdom: An Epochal Lie. *Dushu*, no. 12.

grow and that they will not suffer losses because of external interference, the state has to make some efforts—for example, providing public goods such as administration of justice, public security, diplomacy, defense, and property protection. These are not enough, because sovereignty is not only a domestic matter, but, in a sense, defined by its relations with other states. Therefore, the costs and benefits of maintaining sovereignty are not solely dependent on the sovereign state's will and efforts. The international community has to examine the sovereignty it claims by international law and take a certain stance. When the stance is not favorable for the sovereign state and there are, say, charges of aggression, obstruction, provocation, and fulfillment of international responsibilities, the expense for sovereignty will increase.

Therefore, to ensure the integrity of sovereignty, providing good domestic public services and winning international support, or to say the least, maintaining fairly small international opposition, defines the amount of the expense the sovereign state has to pay. In other words, to display and exercise sovereignty, at a definite level of benefits, the government of a state must not only consider offering the best possible domestic services, but also consider how it should compete globally as a competitor.[14]

Therefore, when a sovereign state makes a claim of sovereignty, it has to consider two issues: first, whether the gains are worth the costs that come with them; and second, whether its capacity of paying the costs is equal to, or even higher than, the total of the related costs demanded by the international community (for international responsibilities, aggression, obstruction and provocation) and the necessary expenses on public services. If the paying capacity falls below the costs demanded by the international community and domestic society for the benefits of its sovereignty, the benefits of its sovereignty claim will be substantially compromised. The aggression schemes of Germany, Japan, and Italy during World War II can be seen as sovereignty claims. However, because the expense the international community demanded of them was far beyond their paying capacities,[15] they suffered failures and reverted to the state of sovereignty before the war. The frustration France and Spain experienced as against Britain and Holland in the Western process of modernization in fact arose from their insufficient capacity for providing domestic services.[16]

Therefore, a rational country does not make sovereignty claims too liberally. When it exercises its sovereignty, it will do two things well correspondingly: first, it

[14]North, Douglass (2008). *Understanding the Process of Economic Change*. (Zhong, Zhengsheng, Xing, Hua, et al., trans.) Beijing: China Renmin University Press, p. 27.

[15]The governments' and peoples' charge of, opposition to and fight against aggression were all expenses they demanded of these fascist countries based on their consideration of long-term or practical interests.

[16]North, Douglass (2008). *Understanding the Process of Economic Change*. (Zhong, Zhengsheng, Xing, Hua, et al., trans.) Beijing: China Renmin University Press, pp. 163–177.

tries its best, through a series of institutional arrangements, to improve the benefits-acquiring efficiency and increase the total of benefits acquired within the bounds of its sovereignty claims, because greater sovereignty returns typically means a higher capacity for paying sovereignty expenses; second, it tries every possible means to avoid extreme situations where it is required by the international community and domestic society to pay unreasonable expenses. As for the second, the more legitimate (by international and domestic law) and more compliant with custom (by customary law), the less possible it is for such extreme situations to arise.

The fact that territorial sea is also called "blue territory," and sea power-related practices in history have all proven that though sea power is sometimes distinguished from sovereignty, it is part of sovereignty when discussed in the sense of territorial integrity. In this case, treatises on the bounds of sovereignty also apply to sea power. The costs and benefits of sea power in Mahan's theoretical context, because of his disregard of "law" and "custom" and over-confidence in the military strength safeguarding benefits, cannot truthfully and comprehensively reflect a state's costs of sea power, or the real bounds of its sea power benefits.

When a state safeguards and practices sea power, it should give due consideration to the cost–benefit system of sea power, to how to improve the system by increasing benefits and lowering costs, and how to defend its complete sea power by improving its expense-paying capacity.

If it considers only external ostensible benefits but does not pay attention to making efforts to improve productive efficiency and increase national wealth via legitimate means; or if it focuses on wielding military strength to neutralize all hostile forces and other interested parties but ignores potential antagonistic sentiments and the increased costs of frequent use of armed forces, the state has overestimated the value of the benefits and underestimated the costs it has to pay; its acts and logic are not essentially different from those of pirates. In this way it increases the expense of international trade and encroaches on rather than contributes to the total social wealth.

With expense underestimated and benefits manipulated, it is inevitable that such logic of sea power will incur the following consequences: in situations where the regulatory rules backed by a justice-safeguarding global force are absent, the practices of sea power worldwide tend to be mired into a vicious cycle characterized by military determinism, supremacy of benefit, rampant piratical behavior and "meeting violence with violence." To maintain competitive advantage or overcome disadvantages in the vicious cycle, those who exercise sovereignty tend to increase their arsenal and develop the navy at an expense exceeding their paying capacity; not only may this overburden the state with constantly increasing expense to such an extent that the state declines, but the expense is more likely to grow as external expense increases exponentially. In the end humankind will suffer severely. In the context of modern warfare, the destruction of the entire human race may be caused.

3.3 The Rise of Peaceful Competition on the Sea

The destruction of the human race is naturally an end any rational person does not wish to see. Thus Mahan's concept of sea power must be discarded or modified.

This is probably why the signatories to the United Nations Convention on the Law of the Sea (UNCLOS) have continued increasing and the non-signatories acquiesce to it despite its many weaknesses, because jurisprudentially UNCLOS overcomes many faults for which Mahan's concept has incurred criticism.

The UNCLOS not only prescribes transnational public services ignored by Mahan—including maintaining the maritime order, salvaging, preventing, and reducing environmental pollution and jointly repressing piracy, etc.—as obligations for signatory states and stipulates the reparatory measures[17] for the expense of negative external effect, but also encourages people to exploit the sea "peacefully"[18] and try their best to stay out of an arms race. Therefore, the expense for sea power calculated by the signatory states in this way is closer to the real expense for the exercise of sea power.

It believes that sea power first of all falls into the category of sovereignty. In the expense system of sea power, the sovereign state must pay the "expense for sovereignty" in the universal sense and provide what are known as "domestic public services"; besides, some components of sea power, as an extension of sovereignty, are beyond sovereignty. Rights such as "innocent passage," "transit passage," the laying of submarine cables or pipelines, and authorization of activities in the Area[19] all belong to the type of rights. The expense the party which exercises

---

[17]See the *United Nations Convention on the Law of the Sea*: Article 24, "Duties of the coastal State"; Article 44, "Duties of States bordering straits"; Article 56, "Rights, jurisdiction and duties of the coastal State in the exclusive economic zone"; Article 58, "Rights and duties of other States in the exclusive economic zone"; Article 61, "Conservation of the living resources"; Article 98, "Duty to render assistance"; Article 99, "Prohibition of the transport of slaves"; Article 100, "Duty to cooperate in the repression of piracy"; Articles 117–119, "Duty of States to adopt with respect to their nationals measures for the conservation of the living resources of the high seas," "Cooperation of States in the conservation and management of living resources", "Conservation of the living resources of the high seas"; Article 139, "Responsibility to ensure compliance and liability for damage"; Article 145, "Protection of the marine environment"; Article 146, "Protection of human life"; Article 194, "Measures to prevent, reduce and control pollution of the marine environment"; Article 195, "Duty not to transfer damage or hazards or transform one type of pollution into another."

[18]See the *United Nations Convention on the Law of the Sea*: *Preamble*; Article 136, "Common heritage of mankind"; Article 140, "Benefit of mankind"; Article 141, "Use of the Area exclusively for peaceful purposes"; Article 237, "Obligations under other conventions on the protection and preservation of the marine environment"; Article 248, " Duty to provide information to the coastal States"; Article 249, "Duty to comply with certain conditions"; Article 263, "Responsibility and liability"; Article 279, "Obligation to settle disputes by peaceful means"; Article 280, "Settlement of disputes by any peaceful means chosen by the parties"; Article 301, "Peaceful uses of the seas"; Article 304, "Responsibility and liability for damage."

[19]The activities in the Area refers to resource surveying and exploring activities conducted by the state on the seabed and ocean floor and in the soil there outside the state's scope of jurisdiction.

sea power (not necessarily a state)[20] pays is that it needs to comply with the UNCLOS, fulfill international responsibilities, and adopt effective measures to handle the relationships between mankind and the sea, between the state and the neighboring states, between the state and the other states whose water it crosses, between the state and the other states whose waters its ships navigate across—or in other words, it is obliged to fulfill international responsibilities or "provide international public services."

Though under the UNCLOS the costs of sea power increase considerably, so do the benefits. Because every signatory is entitled to full rights only on the premise that it must follow the prescribed rules and offer conveniences to other signatories, cooperation, mutual help, and good faith now underlie sea power. In this framework, all the benefits the sovereign state can obtain from outside are based on the consensuses reached on the United Nations law of the sea. The idea is basically "to do good and invite good"—that is, to exercise sea power properly on the basis of a comprehensive cost–benefit analysis. Therefore, the chances of the suicidal vicious cycle of sea power, highly probably in Mahan's context, become lower and lower.

However, it is problematic to hold the simplistic opinion that maritime rights and interests are all the benefits the state can obtain from sea power and everything is okay if it complies with the UNCLOS. Some interests are likely to have nothing to do with sovereignty and rights. For instance, the interests that come with scientific research in the Arctic Ocean and Antarctica have not been covered by international or domestic law. Do they count as the benefits of sea power[21]? Some issues regarding maritime interests are yet to be resolved. For example, the disputes over maritime borders of some countries need to be settled through negotiation or by judicial decisions. Before that the regulatory role of international and domestic law stays negligible. Can benefits from the sea of each party involved in the disputes count as benefits of sea power? This paper tends to give a positive answer, because they are essentially different from illegal maritime interests gained from hegemonic and piratical acts, and agree in spirit with the peaceful, legitimate use of the sea promoted by the UNCLOS and the jurisprudent principle, nullum crimen sine lege.

Facts have shown that the costs and benefits of sea power are very flexible. After the promulgation of the UNCLOS, the state's capacity of acquiring benefits from the sea is key to truly exercising sea power and maximizing its effect in the framework of international law. For a state with inadequate means and abilities for obtaining benefits from the sea, if it has a limited extent of territory, one more water area is merely one more area of water, and nothing more. Sometimes, it may even become a liability. After all, the state needs to invest human power and financial resources on public facilities for security, environmental conservation, and disaster relief, etc., over a vast area of waters. Misadministration may lead to rampant piracy

---

[20]When disputes arise, the agent of sea power has always been the government of the nation-state. The reason why an enterprise or individual of a state has certain rights is essentially that their state is a signatory to the United Nations Convention on the Law of the Sea.

[21]Kang, Juan and Tian, Hui. Russia Plants Underwater Flag to Claim Arctic Seafloor. http://www.news365.com.cn/yw/200708/t20070803_1519228.htm.

and smuggling on the sea and thus incur infamy and affect its trade and exchanges with other countries. The loss outweighs the gain.

This is also what the UNCLOS has repeatedly stressed. It believes not only that the costs and benefits of sea power are variable, but that a state's capacity for obtaining benefits from the sea determines its final achievements in maritime competition. It explicitly encourages the signatories to engage in peaceful competition in the exploitation of the sea and acknowledges that as the influence of a state increases on the sea, it should shoulder more international responsibilities and make more contributions to the accumulation of the human race's common maritime wealth. However, this is based on more advanced maritime technology, stronger capacity of obtaining wealth from the sea, and greater extent of maritime shipping, which of course implies that the state can obtain more benefits from the sea directly or indirectly.

After the promulgation of the UNCLOS, the most profound change to the world sea power landscape is not that the cost–benefit system fits better with sea power practices, but that costs and benefits become variable and that the association of sea power with the state's capacity of peacefully conquering and exploiting the ocean becomes a consensus. In brief, the Convention encourages the signatory states to compete against each other on the sea in the form of "production competition."

3.4 Comparable Elements of Sea Power

The progresses represented by the UNCLOS tell us that we should define sea power as well as its benefits and costs comprehensively in a longer term from a wider perspective. The rise on the sea involves not only military, but also politics, economy, technology, and international relations; in a given time and space, it may be a static issue, but it may become a dynamic issue if the time and space change. In a well-grounded framework of sea power, rights are more important than power. To utilize marine resources and obtain wealth in a peaceful, legal, and fair fashion while striving to provide the domestic and international public goods needed is far better than short-sighted, purely predatory actions ignoring the improvement of productive and trade capacities. By constantly improving the overall capacity of exploiting marine resources, every state is likely to obtain benefits continuously and form a virtuous cycle; while maintaining the complete sea power, it can ensure that the total benefits from the sea and its influence on the sea both grow continuously.

However, the UNCLOS has failed to take it further and tell people how to improve the capacity of obtaining resources from the sea and how to accomplish and expand the state's sea power in a comprehensive way. Except technology, exploration, maritime economy, maritime shipping, and natural structure of sea power, the UNCLOS does not touch upon other factors influencing a state's ratio of costs and benefits of sea power; nor does it elaborate on how the factors touched upon influence the development of a state's sea power.

Perhaps we can accomplish that on the basis of Mahan's work and the UNCLOS.

Mahan provides us with a fairly good framework of analysis. As mentioned above, his theoretical framework contains a cost–benefit analysis of the elements influencing sea power (as reflected in Table 3.1, which the author has presented). He believes that through this analysis, every state can form a picture of their situation, find out their weaknesses and the ways to tackle them, and formulate a feasible plan to strengthen the sea power as he terms it.

Though we do not entirely agree to Mahan's concept of sea power, we can obviously derive a similar table on the cost–benefit analysis of the elements of sea power (see Table 3.2) integrating our arguments by assimilating the advancements of the UNCLOS in the perception of sea power, drawing upon the new features and trends of contemporary maritime development of different states and making necessary adjustments to some factors and conditions mentioned by Mahan. It is our hope that this table can serve as reference for states engaged in modern maritime competition in which "production competition" is more important than military competition.

A comparison between Tables 3.1 and 3.2 shows that, since the term "colony" in Mahan's theory has been outdated and has a direct bearing on overseas markets, it is changed directly into "overseas market."

Considering that the concept, "extent of territory," now includes both land and sea, and that the government's major operations mainly include providing domestic and international services and participating in international competition, Mahan's concepts of land area and government are no longer valid. Therefore, the two elements are modified and further divided so as to stress the interdependence between land and sea in the category of the extent of territory and the coordination between giving priority to sea, mobilization, guidance, and strategic vision in government.

Mahan's concepts of national character, population, and marine resources are too sketchy—for instance, marine resources include both renewable and nonrenewable resources, and this was something unknown in Mahan's time. The distinctions regarding national character, namely being warlike, commercially minded, adventurous and innovative, evidently are more closely associated with different aspects of sea power. Though Mahan mentions them, he confuses the relations between the four and sees the generality but fails to see their differences. The population and personnel structure influence different aspects of sea power, so it is of course not right to confuse them. Given the fact that different components of these elements are differently oriented, for the convenience of discussion and analysis, we have separately listed those which can influence sea power fairly independently.

As for the maritime industry, education and population training, air force, strategic missile force and information warfare force, and world sea power, they are products of modern society or have been neglected by Mahan. However, since they are indispensable to a state's sea power, they have been factored in as elements of sea power.

Table 3.2 The modified 22 sea power elements and their influence on sea power cost and benefit

Elements		Costs	Benefits	Nature
Government	Importance attached to the sea	Correct policy; other programs may be affected by restrictions	Maritime development and strengthening of the navy	Variable
	Capacity for mobilization	Government centralization	Achieving anticipated maritime development within a certain period	
	Guidance of views	Correct view of sea power; ability to use, and create publicity	Guiding people to care for and get close to the sea	
	Strategic vision	Focusing on key factors and achieving development by legal, diplomatic, and peaceful means	Approaching maximum benefit from the sea	
Education and personnel training		Priority given to education and an efficient educational system	The provision of personnel needed by various programs, including excellent mariners, navy soldiers and officers, and other personnel	Variable
Science and technology		Personnel training, science and technology policy, financial support	Conducive to the development of shipping and maritime defense	Variable
Industrial production		Industrial personnel, industrial policy, development of science and technology	The provision of shipbuilding, machinery and products, which can help enhance ocean-going capability, expand the scope of trade, and strengthen the navy	Variable
Trade capacity		Personnel support, trade policy, and business sense	Favorable position in world trade	Variable
Shipping capacity		Industrial development, navigation technology, excellent mariners	Conducive to expanding the maritime trade network and increasing business income	Variable
Overseas markets		Legal support, guarantee of safety, domestic market and products	Increasing trade opportunities	Variable

(continued)

Table 3.2 (continued)

Elements		Costs	Benefits	Nature
Population	Size	Governance and the provision of products and services	Provision of soldiers and domestic market	Variable over time
	Composition	Population engaged in land economy	Population engaged in maritime economy	Variable over time
	Personnel structure	Clear goal and support for personnel development	Navigation personnel and personnel necessary for each link of maritime economy	Variable
Maritime trade		Capability of trade and transportation	Increasing fiscal revenue	Variable
Development of marine resources		Ability to obtain marine resources	Obtainment of marine resources	Variable
Maritime industry		Support in government policy, personnel and technology	Increasing maritime income as well as the government's and individuals' reliance on the sea	Variable
Navy		Armaments, ships, strategic assistance forces, soldiers and various specialists	The protection of territorial security, the development and utilization of marine resources, and oceanic trade	Variable
National character	Martial spirit	Possibly excessive reliance on force	The development of military strength	Variable over time
	Commercially minded	Need for the state's legal and diplomatic protection	Development of domestic and foreign trade and increase of income	
	Adventurous	Going beyond the limits of national and international law	Development of overseas trade	
	Innovative	Personnel training and guidance by the government	Technological development	
Air force		Armaments, combat aircraft, and personnel training	Making up for the navy's deficiency and strengthening coastal defense	Variable
Strategic missile force		Armaments and personnel training	Making up for the navy's deficiency and strengthening coastal defense	Variable

(continued)

Table 3.2 (continued)

Elements		Costs	Benefits	Nature
Information warfare force		Armaments and personnel training	Making up for the navy's deficiency and strengthening coastal defense	Variable
Coastline		The longer it is, the greater the pressure and cost	Unlikely to be long occupied by an enemy; the addition of an area with concentrated maritime economy	Invariable
Ports		Vulnerable to attacks from the sea	Conducive to domestic and overseas trade	Invariable
Strategic passes on the sea		Security service and navigation route service	Conducive to the layout of global trade and maritime security of the nation	Invariable
Marine resources	Renewable resources	Technology for sustainable use and maintenance; definition of rights	Adding to the wealth of a nation	Variable over time
	Nonrenewable resources	Efficiency of use and extraction technology; definition of rights	Adding to the wealth of a nation	Invariable
Extent of territory	Land	Land rivals against sea and land power against sea power	Support for maritime development and the defense of sea power	Invariable
	Sea	Competition with the land, need for protection by the navy and maritime development	Foundation for maritime development and support for economic development	
World sea power		Altering the relative position of a country's sea power in the world	Inspirational effect that encourages a country to change its sea power strategy	Variable over time

Note Among the modified 22 sea power elements that may influence sea power cost and benefit, some are the revised or elaborated version of a few of the sea power elements identified by Mahan. Comparison may shed more light on the significance of the elements to sea power

Of these elements, some are natural conditions (invariable) or generally constant (variable over time). In a short term, they are similar to invariable elements as termed in economics, such as the extent of territory, the length of the coastline, ports, islands, straits, size of population, composition of population and national character; others are variable conditions, such as personnel structure, industrial production, trade capacity, shipping capacity, government thinking, science and technology and colonies, which are similar to variable elements as termed in economics. Some are not only costs but also benefits, depending essentially on the perspective and circumstances. For example, the extent of territory and the length of coastline not only determine, in a certain degree, the costs of defense, but also are related to the costs an enemy state has to pay in an attempt to destroy its sea power. So if viewed from this perspective, they are not only costs but also benefits. Ports, islands, and straits may be beneficial to a state in that they can help maintain its sea power or reduce the costs for maintaining it—this of course falls into the category of benefits; but on the other hand, if they are controlled by an enemy state, they may be beneficial in the same way to the enemy state.

Besides, both variable and invariable conditions are relative. Among variable conditions, government, science, and technology and the personnel structure of the population are easier to change than other variable conditions; among invariable conditions, the nonrenewable resources, extent of territory, length of coastline, ports, islands, and straits are harder to change than other invariable conditions. However, in the utility function of a state's sea power, their relative importance compared with that of all the other elements are likely to change.

3.5 "Spoon-Shaped Chain" of Sea Power

According to the specific features of each element and their likely changes when exterior conditions alter, now we attempt to describe different features regarding the benefits and costs in the cost–benefit system of sea power.

In Table 3.2, it is not hard to find that there are certain connections between these elements of sea power.

Some elements are in a competitive relationship with another or some other elements. However, the benefits brought about by the latter can directly support the development of the former—though the latter cannot cover all of the expense for the former, they can win space and time for the former to accumulate resources to cover the expense. The relationships of the air force, strategic missile force, and information warfare force with the navy are like this. Even if the war is not on home soil, the former three can, to a certain extent, ease the dire pressure on the navy in maintaining sea power.[22]

[22]Guo, Shizhen and Pei, Meicheng (2007). *A History of Military Equipment*. Beijing: People's Liberation Army Press, pp. 1158–1176.

There are other elements whose improvement in the cost–benefit ratio, more often than not, means the increase of benefits or the rise of benefit-obtaining possibilities. Take the relationship between the sea and land within the extent of territory for example. Apart from their interdependence in military defense, they also support each other in economic development. Generally speaking, it is universally known that a great proportion of goods produced on the land is transported to their places of sales by sea, whereas foods, marine, and energy resources from the sea are eventually sold on the land; but people have rarely noticed that for a state whose development on the land and sea are imbalanced, whichever of the two develops first will usually become the provider of initial capital, human resources and materials for the other.

In terms of government, the relationships between attaching importance to the sea, mobilization capacity, guidance, and strategic vision are also similar. In the process of advancing maritime development, only if it has the right strategic vision can the government formulate right strategies and measures, guide the entire society to establish the right perception of the ocean, utilizing the resources available very efficiently to implement the strategies, measures, and concepts, and eventually achieve balanced development on the land and waters within the extent of territory. As a result, all land and marine resources can be optimally deployed. This will, in turn, influence how much importance the government attaches to the sea, its strategy of maritime development and the techniques of employing various means in the implementation of the strategy.

As for some other elements, the benefits are the premise for the state to obtain benefits from another element or other elements. That is to say, the benefits of the former are the costs of the latter. For instance, the development of science and technology can only achieved with policy support, good education, and personnel training. The development of the maritime industry and maritime trade and the exploitation of marine resources are the combined effect of government, education and personnel training, science and technology, industrial production, shipping capacity and trade capacity.

From the relationship of the elements of sea power which serve as each other's costs and benefits, it can be inferred that in the spoon-shaped chain of sea power—from the extent of territory and world sea power to government, to education and personnel training, to science and technology, to industry production, trade capacity and shipping capacity, to maritime trade, marine resource development and maritime industry, to the navy, and to marine resources, ports, coastline and strategic passes on the sea—maritime trade, marine resource development, maritime industry, navy, marine resources, ports, coastline and strategic passes on the sea make up the spoon-shaped chain, whereas overseas markets, the national character, population, air force, and strategic missile force, which, as indispensable elements, should have been included in the chain, but can only serve as auxiliary parts of the spoon-shaped structure of sea power because they function one-directionally or cannot exert their influence within a short term. From the relationships we can derive a chain structure based on the relationships between the elements of sea power (see Fig. 3.1).

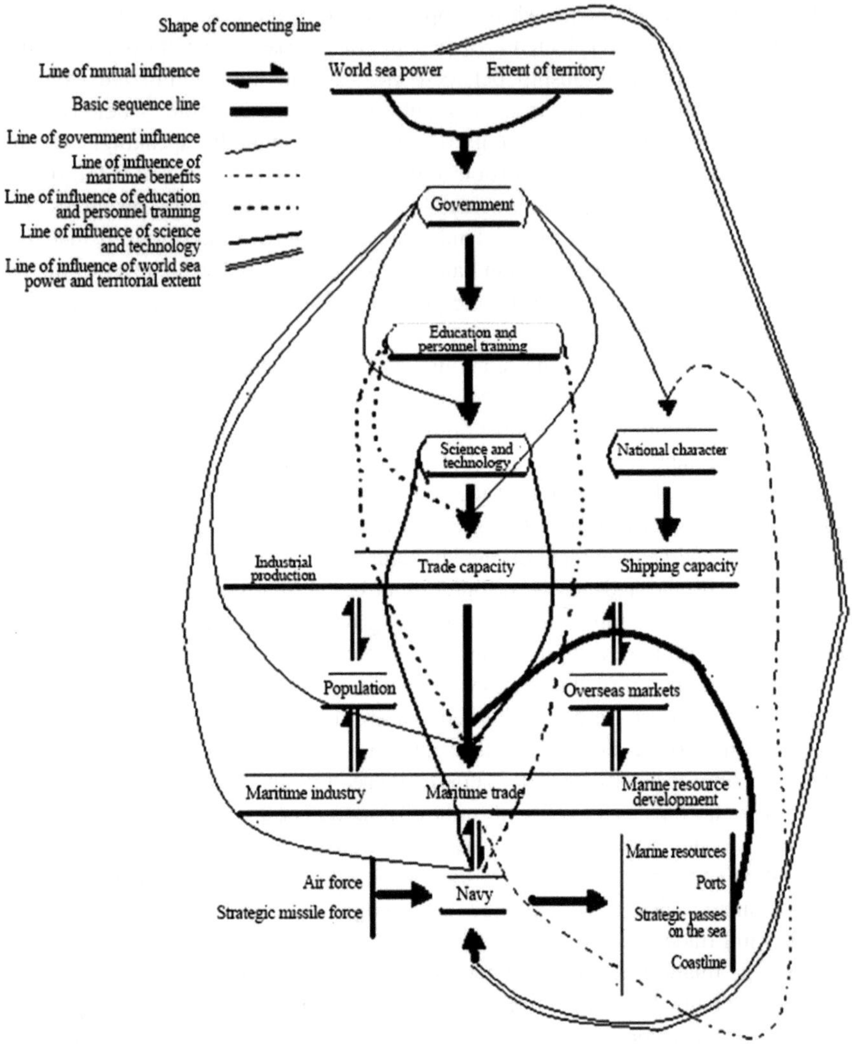

Fig. 3.1 Relationships between elements of sea power. *Note* In this diagram, the relationships between the elements of sea power are evident. We can instantly see that government, education, and personnel training, as well as science and technology are the fundamental conditions for the development of sea power, whereas a state's industrial production, trade capacity, shipping capacity, and navy are the premises for the development of its maritime economy. Though the national character, the development of world sea power and the proportion of sea to land within a state's territory may influence its practices of sea power, the government may harness the negative factors through policies

In this spoon-shaped chain structure, government, education and personnel training, and science and technology make up the spoon handle, which determines or influences the development of many other elements. Government is related to nearly all the other elements; the personnel needed in all links of sea power nearly invariably depends on what type of personnel a state's education and personnel training system can produce and how the personnel is organized. Wherever management, appliances, skills, and organization are needed, there is science and technology, whose importance cannot be overemphasized. Therefore, they can be seen as primary elements of sea power.

Industrial production, trade capacity, and shipping capacity can be seen as capacity magnifiers of the spoon. Their level of development determines the scale of maritime trade, marine resource development and the maritime industry and the role of marine resources, ports, coastline, and strategic passes on the sea. This proves that sea power is flexible. Though some elements are invariable or invariable over a long period of time, the overall cost–benefit structure of sea power can be changed. As long as the industrial production, trade capacity, and shipping capacity improve continuously, the effect and benefits of the invariable elements will reach their peaks, and so will the effect and benefits of the variable elements.

Here we must talk about the navy in specific. As a component of the spoon, the navy may not be seen as benefit of sea power like the other components. However, it determines whether or not the state can obtain these benefits. In this sense, it is like the safety valve at the bottom of the spoon. If the valve is not properly shut, the spoon will hold nothing; if it is, the spoon can be filled. Therefore, it, together with industrial production, trade capacity, and shipping capacity, constitutes the premise for the state's benefits of sea power.

To sum up, none of the elements of sea power exist or function in an isolated fashion. The change of one element invariably evokes the change of another or even many elements. Even if the amount and state of some elements are constant, their significance and role will change as other elements above or below them vary. If a state wishes to change the status of sea power, unless there are some unexpected circumstances, the most important thing to do is to change those variable elements of sea power, improve those elements conducive to the increase of sea power benefits and thus improve the system of sea power benefits.

3.6 In Search of Equilibrium

The analysis above can lead to the following understanding of sea power: the realization of sea power means cost as well as benefit and has an intrinsic cost–benefit system. Since both the cost and benefit of sea power are generally changeable, it is possible to optimize the system by changing certain elements of sea power.

However, since sea power is part of sovereignty, there is no absolute symmetry between the cost paid by a country and its benefit from sea power. In other words, the equilibrium between the marginal cost of sea power and the marginal benefit from it does not always occur in reality.

In fact, when paying the price of sea power, a country may sometimes largely disregard the benefit from it. When damage to sea power affects sovereignty and

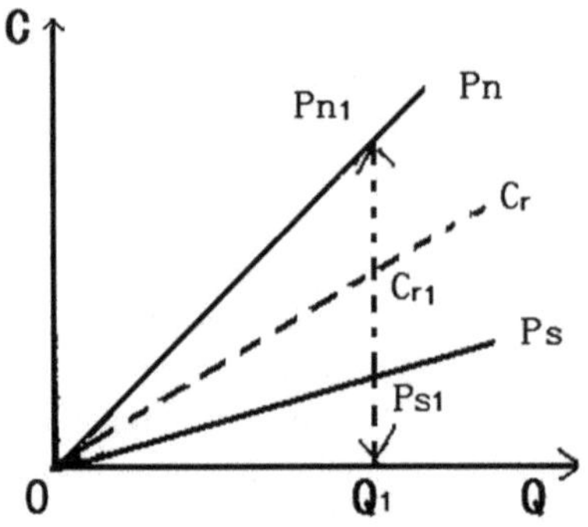

Fig. 3.2 Variation of the cost of sea power. *Comment* In reality, some countries tend to disregard the relationship between the cost of sea power and the benefit from it. The cost it pays for its sea power varies between zero and all the wealth it can assemble. In this diagram, Pn is a country's overall wealth, Cr is the actual cost of sea power it pays, and Ps refers to its benefit from sea power. While Pn and Ps are relatively stable, Cr is variable. At Q1, Cr1 can be either Pn1 or Ps1, or zero. Generally speaking, however, Cr will vary between Pn and Ps. *Note Horizontal axis* Q means benefit from sea power, and *vertical axis* C means the cost of sea power

territorial integrity, the whole nation will be mobilized to defend the dignity of sea power and sovereignty if both the government and the people feel that they have been humiliated and bullied. During the Ming Dynasty, the government spent far more on fighting Japanese pirates than it benefited from the sea after the ban on maritime trade was imposed.[23] When a country is under no external pressure for its sea power, which does not involve sovereignty or territorial integrity, and when it values development on land, it may pay no or just a little cost, and it can gain almost pure benefit from the sea. In other words, the cost a country pays for its sea power can either be nearly zero or all the resources it can mobilize (Fig. 3.2).

Following the lift of the ban on maritime trade in 1567 (in the reign of Emperor Muzong of the Ming Dynasty), the Ming government gained enormous benefit from Yue Port in Zhangzhou, Fujian Province. The cost it paid consisted of the expenses of establishing counties along with the local bureaucracy and maintaining the Trade Tax Bureau.[24] Such costs were almost negligible in view of the expenditures on the local administration of the southern provinces during the Ming Dynasty.[25]

However, this only illustrates how greatly the cost of sea power can vary within a short period. In the long run, how much a country will pay for sea power mainly depends on the magnitude of the benefit it gains from the sea and its expectations of

[23]Wang, Yuquan (ed.) (2007). *A General History of Chinese Economy: The Ming Dynasty*. Beijing: China Social Sciences Press, p. 510.

[24]Chao, Zhongchen (2005). *Overseas Trade and the Ban on Maritime Trade during the Ming Dynasty*. Beijing: People's Publishing House, p. 212.

[25]Huang, Renyu (1997). *China: A Macro History*. Beijing: SDX Joint Publishing Company, pp. 232–239.

such profit. The divorce between cost and benefit cannot last for long. If cost is much higher than benefit, when a certain sea power problem has been resolved, the cost of sea power will be greatly reduced and sometimes may even affect the necessary expenditure on the maintenance of sea power. The fight between the Ming Empire and the Japanese pirates "involved millions of troops and an innumerable amount of money. The population was decimated and wealth squandered like dirt." After the war, not only the economy in southeast China fell into depression, but the central government was plunged in a deep financial crisis with sharply reduced revenues. In contrast, if the benefit from sea power is much higher than the cost, it would give rise to difficulties calling for the government to spend more on sea power and provide policies and services accordingly. This is a reasonable explanation for the fact that the discovery of the American continent by Christopher Columbus led the Western powers to contend for control over the sea in the name of nations, establish colonies, and join the competition of foreign trade. The lift of the ban on maritime trade during the mid and late Ming Dynasty was due to the observation that "pirates would turn into merchants if the market is open and merchants would become pirates if the market is banned." The ban on maritime trade, as a policy in which the government paid little for sea power, seriously hindered the further expansion of maritime benefit.[26]

The most desirable approach, therefore, is to determine the cost to pay for sea power according to the benefit from it without too much discrepancy between them.

However, it is certainly a challenge to measure the benefit from sea power and, furthermore, to determine the cost to pay for such benefit. First of all, this is because the sea power's cost–benefit system, as discussed before, is subject to change along with the variation of sea power elements. It is also because the benefit from sea power depends on how much a country relies on sea power for its economy as well as the benefit for the enterprises and individuals involved in sea-related lines of work. It is almost a mission impossible to combine dispersed decisions derived from different cost–benefit frameworks for analysis.

However, the following approach may be of some help.

Practice has shown that the success of an institution is closely related to the degree to which it is understood and supported because this dictates the ratio between its marginal cost and marginal benefit. The same is true of sea power-related practice. The quest for the cost a country should pay for the benefit from its sea power is to seek equality between marginal cost and marginal benefit. Theoretically speaking, at the point where cost and benefit meet, the benefit gained by the country equals the cost it pays for sea power (Fig. 3.3).

[26]The Ming government's lift of the ban on maritime trade in 1567 was related to the thriving of business and the massive inflow of silver that resulted from such trade. On the one hand, the enormous income from maritime trade prompted major sea merchants headed by Wang Zhi and Xu Hai to pressure or appeal to the government. On the other hand, officials like Lin Fu, Xu Zemin and Xu Guangqi called for lifting the ban for social stability and the increase of revenues for local governments. See Chao, Zhongchen (2005). *Overseas Trade and the Ban on Maritime Trade during the Ming Dynasty*. Beijing: People's Publishing House, pp. 170–243.

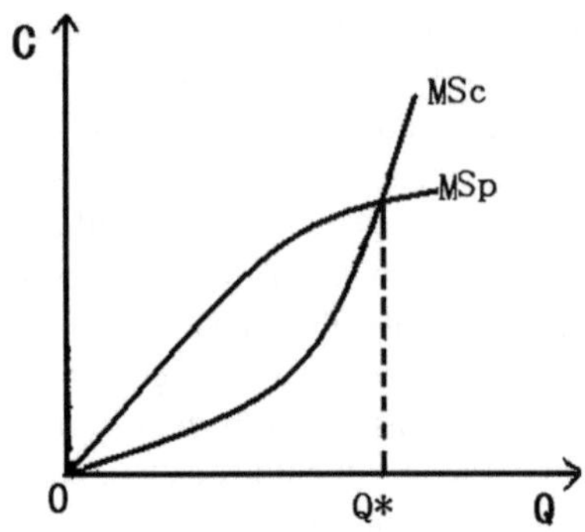

Fig. 3.3 The optimal point for the payment of the cost for sea power. *Comment* In this diagram, Q* is the point where MSc (the marginal cost curve) meets MSp (the marginal benefit curve). Theoretically speaking, at the point where the cost of a country's sea power meets the benefit from it, the benefit gained by the country equals the cost it pays for sea power. In reality, this point is reflected by the choice made by individuals or enterprises to live and work in inland or coastal regions. *Note Horizontal axis* Q means the benefit from sea power, and *vertical axis* C means the cost of sea power

In any country, the existence of more individuals and enterprises involved in sea-related industries and a greater scale of marine economy indicate more benefit gained from the sea. If so, the country should pay the cost to support the development of marine programs accordingly. Yet this is not an absolute rule.

We should, according to the marginal principle, leave out the part where the total annual volume of import and export trade overlaps with marine economy, add the remainder to the total volume of marine economy, and constantly compare the result with the change of the cost of sea power to see whether each monetary unit of increase in such cost has brought greater benefit from sea power. If the answer is affirmative, more should be invested in sea power; if not, it means that we have paid too much for sea power and should start to cut back; if cost and benefit are found to be equal, it means that we have reached the optimal point and can stay there for a short while. There is an easier approach, which is to observe the flow from human resources and capital to sea-related industries. If such flow ceases or even starts to reverse, any increase in the cost of sea power would be unwise; if such flow keeps accelerating, increase in the cost of sea power will be worthwhile at all events.

3.7 Cost–Benefit Analysis of China's Sea Power

By analyzing the necessity and certainty of China's rise on the sea as well as the challenges against its sea power, with reference to the table of "The modified 22 sea power elements and their influence on sea power cost and benefit" based on Mahan's studies in the first chapter, we can develop a table that generally reflects the situation of China's sea power (Table 3.3).

Table 3.3 The modified 22 sea power elements and China's performance

Element		Costs	Benefits	Status quo in China	Nature	Evaluation
Government	Importance attached to the sea	Correct policy; other programs may be affected by restrictions	Maritime development and strengthening of the navy	Improving from insufficient recognition	Variable	Average
	Capacity for mobilization	Government centralization	Achieving anticipated maritime development within a certain period	The government has gathered powerful resources, but development has yet to reach the anticipated level		
	Guidance of views	Correct view of sea power; ability to use and create publicity	Guiding people to care for and get close to the sea	A sound view of sea power has yet to form		
	Strategic vision	Grasping key factors that can create favorable conditions for development by legal, diplomatic and peaceful means	Approaching maximum benefit from the sea	Initial strategic awareness has been developed, but a clear strategy is lacking		
Education and personnel training		Priority given to education and an efficient educational system	The provision of personnel needed by various programs, including excellent mariners, navy soldiers and officers, and other personnel	Backwardness in specialized education	Variable	Poor
Science and technology		Personnel training, science and technology policy, financial support	Conducive to the development of shipping and maritime defense	Technological breakthroughs have been achieved, but the upgrading of equipment is slow	Variable	Average

(continued)

Table 3.3 (continued)

Element	Costs	Benefits	Status quo in China	Nature	Evaluation
Industrial production	Industrial personnel, industrial policy, development of science and technology	The provision of shipbuilding, machinery and products, which can help enhance ocean-going capability, expand the scope of trade, and strengthen the navy	A relatively well-developed industrial system with significant potential for production	Variable	Excellent
Trade capacity	Personnel support, trade policy, and business sense	Favorable position in world trade	Well-developed trade network and high reliance on import/export trade	Variable	Excellent
Shipping capacity	Industrial development, navigation technology, excellent mariners	Conducive to expanding the maritime trade network and increasing business income	Already capable of reaching most ports in the world	Variable	Excellent
Overseas markets	Legal support, guarantee of safety, domestic market and products	Increasing trade opportunities	Upgrading needed for products, increased overseas investment, high probability of meeting trade barriers in the markets of developed countries, and high risk in some markets in Africa and South America	Variable	Average

(continued)

Table 3.3 (continued)

Element		Costs	Benefits	Status quo in China	Nature	Evaluation
Population	Size	Governance and the provision of products and services	Provision of soldiers and domestic market	A large population with mobility restricted by family culture and the household registration system	Variable over time	Average
	Composition	Population engaged in land economy	Population engaged in maritime economy	Concentration of population in coastal regions	Variable over time	
	Personnel structure	Clear goal and support for personnel development	Navigation personnel and personnel necessary for each link of maritime economy	Fewer outstanding persons in specialized organizations than peripheral support organizations	Variable	
Maritime trade		Capability of trade and transportation	Increasing fiscal revenue	The vast majority of import and export trade is conducted on the sea	Variable	Excellent
Development of marine resources		Ability to obtain marine resources	Obtainment of marine resources	Small-scale, backward management and poor equipment	Variable	Poor
Maritime industry		Support in government policy, personnel and technology	Increasing maritime income as well as the government's and individuals' reliance on the sea	Improvement is going on steadily, but industries with advanced technology are lacking in scale	Variable	Average
Navy		Armaments, ships, strategic assistance forces, soldiers and various specialists	The protection of territorial security, the development and utilization of marine resources, and oceanic trade	The navy has abundant ships but has yet to be tested in the modernization of armaments and the capability of ocean-going operation	Variable	Average

(continued)

Table 3.3 (continued)

Element		Costs	Benefits	Status quo in China	Nature	Evaluation
National character	Martial spirit	Possibly excessive reliance on force	The development of military strength	Lack of martial spirit	Variable over time	Average
	Commercially minded	Need for the state's legal and diplomatic protection	Development of domestic and foreign trade and increase of income	Significantly enhanced business sense		
	Adventurous	Going beyond the limits of national and international law	Development of overseas trade	Lack of a tradition of adventure		
	Innovative	Personnel training and guidance by the government	Technological development	Lack of originality and independent innovation		
Air force		Armaments, combat aircraft, and personnel training	Making up for the navy's deficiency and strengthening coastal defense	China lags behind the US and Russia for one or two generations in the modernization of armaments	Variable	Average
Strategic missile force		Armaments and personnel training	Making up for the navy's deficiency and strengthening coastal defense	The strategic missile force is capable of deterrence to some degree	Variable	Excellent
Information warfare force		Armaments and personnel training	Making up for the navy's deficiency and strengthening coastal defense	Still at the initial stage, yet to translate into real capability of the armies	Variable	Poor
Coastline		The longer it is, the greater the pressure and cost	Unlikely to be long occupied by an enemy; the addition of an area with concentrated maritime economy	A long coastline	Invariable	Poor
Ports		Vulnerable to attacks from the sea	Conducive to domestic and overseas trade	Narrow waters and ports that are vulnerable to attacks	Invariable	Poor

(continued)

Table 3.3 (continued)

Element		Costs	Benefits	Status quo in China	Nature	Evaluation
Strategic passes on the sea		Security service and navigation route service	Conducive to the layout of global trade and maritime security of the nation	Few strategic passes and even fewer under control	Invariable	Poor
Marine resources	Renewable resources	Technology for sustainable use and maintenance; definition of rights	Adding to the wealth of a nation	Over-development	Variable over time	Average
	Nonrenewable resources	Efficiency of use and extraction technology; definition of rights	Adding to the wealth of a nation	Abundant but disputed	Invariable	
Extent of territory	Land	In competition with the sea, fueling competition between land power and sea power	Support for maritime development and the defense of sea power	A vast land that can provide strategic depth, more complementary to than competitive with the sea	Invariable	Average
	Sea	Competition with the land, need for protection by the navy and maritime development	Foundation for maritime development and support for economic development	The existence of extensive areas of disputed waters and many neighboring maritime countries having sovereignty disputes with China		
World sea power		Altering the relative position of a country's sea power in the world	Inspirational effect that encourages a country to change its sea power strategy	Besieged regional sea power; rights to prospect in two international seabed areas; navigation rights	Variable over time	Poor

Note Among the modified 22 sea power elements that may influence sea power cost and benefit, some are the revised or elaborated version of a few of the sea power elements identified by Mahan. Comparison may shed more light on the significance of the elements to sea power

For any sea power element, we would make a simple description of its influence on China's sea power from a cost–benefit perspective and, based on this, make an evaluation of such performance. If cost and benefit are largely equal or difficult to compare, it would be average; if cost is greater than benefit, it would be poor; it benefit is greater than cost, it would be excellent.

According to Table 3.3, among the 22 sea power elements, there are 10 for which benefit and cost are difficult to compare, 5 for which cost is greater than benefit, and 7 for which cost is less than benefit. On the whole, not only certain basic conditions already exist for China's maritime rise, but the capacity magnifier in the "spoon-shaped chain" also perform very well. The size of its market, the relatively well-developed industrial system, and its tremendous influence on international trade provide vast opportunities and the primordial impetus for China's rapid rise as an important maritime nation.

However, we should also be aware of the downside: the overall performance of the sea-related sea power elements can hardly compare with that of the supporting non-sea power elements (in particular, the "safety valve" of the "spoon-shaped chain" is capable of limited safety); this is compounded by the geographic conditions unfavorable to China's access to the oceans and the complicated international relations in the surrounding regions. In light of this, if China wants to realize complete sea power and help its marine programs to develop faster, it must make every effort to reform its mechanisms, ideas and capabilities. It is imperative to rapidly improve the provision of public goods including governance, national defense, and oceanographic research as well as the quality of social services.

Some of these may be relatively easy to change, such as the government's view and related laws and regulations. Some may be more difficult, such as the increase of military strength, for apart from armaments, tactical skills, training, and the quality of fighters cannot be improved very quickly. The same is true of oceanographic research: besides the availability of funds, it takes time to train and develop the personnel.

However, there is good news: except for world sea power, which can hardly be changed by China alone, and the land-sea composition and nonrenewable resources, which are subject to natural endowment, all the sea power elements for which cost is greater than benefit or for which cost and benefit are roughly equal or difficult to compare can be changed. It is fully possible for China to change them through its own effort.

Chapter 4
Peaceful Growth: Dilemma and Prerequisites

From the preceding discussions, beyond the challenges, limitations, and suppression faced by China as it moves towards the oceans, we can see that first of all, the fundamental truth that the dream of great renewal of the Chinese nation is being limited by the sea. The oceans can turn at any time from a key pillar of development to our Achilles heel in terms of security and the springboard for damaging action by competing nations. Hence, the oceans are crucial to China's transition from "nation on the rise" to world power and will determine China's eventual role on the international scene as it seeks to establish the image of world power for itself. Finally, the oceans will also determine the degree to which internal and external reforms would be implemented. To a certain degree, this shows how important a maritime rise is to China.

However, the challenges, limitations, and suppression faced by China as it moves toward the oceans also highlight the possible gap between dreams and reality. Although China has, at the 18th National Congress of the Communist Party of China (CPC), stated its determination to protect its sea power and set itself the goal of "establishing itself as an important maritime nation," the forcefulness of its stated ambition itself is an indication of the challenges that lie ahead. This is because as a relative latecomer to the maritime power game, China needs to participate in the process of globalization as well as complete its ongoing processes of attitude transformation, and industry and system reforms in order to truly possess the capabilities needed for a great maritime nation to access, develop, and exploit marine resources and to ensure its rise on the seas.

4.1 Growing Pains

The tasks of transformation, reforms and reorientation have determined the challenges, limitations and suppression faced by China as it moves towards the oceans. The first characteristic of these challenges can be summarized as "growing pains."

Z. Kong, *The Making of a Maritime Power*, Research Series on the Chinese Dream and China's Development Path, DOI 10.1007/978-981-10-1786-5_4

Why do we say that?

Not only has a true maritime nation withstood the test of time and possessed a culture that has had intimate maritime exchanges, it also has a keen sense of survival and developmental attitude that is firmly rooted in the seas. A true maritime nation is also determined to become more familiar with the oceans no matter how many setbacks it has faced, possess significant and continued experience in oceanic navigation, and have a viable security plan in place.

For China, a country does not feature a culture that has had intimate maritime exchanges, the move towards the oceans is not optional. It is a move that is driven by survival considerations rather than the desire for risk. Although the country has just begun to accumulate significant and continued experience in oceanic navigation and to put a viable security plan in place, we should continue to examine the general attitudes of Chinese citizens vis-à-vis the oceans.

Generally speaking, China is but an adolescent in the maritime world. Although the youth of the nation are slowly but surely maturing in terms of their social position, capabilities, and influence, theirknowledge of the oceans needs to be further reinforced and embedded in his psyche. Further, in terms of his interactions with the oceans, he would still need to conduct further explorations and to figure out his future trajectory while considering the pros and cons of various possible actions. All this is a process of balance and adjustment.

Therefore, the need to further improve China' maritime management capabilities and ability to access marine resources, and the need to proactively optimize its decision-making process when it comes to the pros and cons of defending its sea power are factors that have led to both internal pressures and motivations. In turn, the impact on international society by the development outcome and potential generated from such efforts as well as the judgment and reactions of global players vis-à-vis their interests are factors that create external pressures and motivations. The former indicates the initiative made by China as it seeks to become a mature maritime nation, while the latter provides China with a frame of reference and tests, inadvertent or intentional, in its eventual role.

This means that China cannot simply shut its doors, exert pressure on itself and work towards being an important maritime nation all by itself. What is needed for China is to truly integrate itself into the maritime world, and realize its objective of growth on the seas through interactions with the oceans and all maritime nations and a continual process of learning through practice. As such, it is critical that we fully apprise ourselves of China's position in the context of global maritime politics.

4.2 Promoting an Evolution in International Rules Through Self-development

When analyzing in detail the challenges, limitations and suppression faced by China as it moves towards the oceans, we can already see the contours of China's relationships with other nations in the maritime world. A suitable metaphor would be that of the relationship between a Johnny-come-lately and other residents within a village setting.

We should note that this young man is polite, genteel, kind, generous, hard-working, humble, and low-key. All in all, these are positive traits. This young man has begun to establish business relationships with others in the village after accruing some wealth through hard work. He has also earned everyone's goodwill thanks to his generosity and good temper.

It would appear that this young man is set on the path to a blissful life. However, the peace would soon be broken.

It turns out that this young man has come from a pretty good family background himself: one of his ancestors had been the village head for a long time. The current village head becomes a little worried. Although the genial young man has already declared that he is not at all interested in the post of village head, his star is truly on the ascendant. What if he were to change his mind some day, or what if a faction were to develop around him in the village? The village head would clearly be in trouble then. So, seeing that this young man is on the up-and-up, the village head feels a pang in his insides, and fears the day the young man would steal his thunder. So he tries ways and means to create trouble for the young man and besmirch his reputation, telling the world of the young man's arrogance, of his failure to play by the rules, and of the fearsome consequences if the young man were to be put in charge of the village in the footsteps of his ancestor. He even terms the entire set of shenanigans as the "Theory of the Fearsome Youth."

And then, there are a couple of families that had trampled on the youth's family as it went into decline, and had robbed the family of some land. Although these families differ in terms of their individual wealth, they are pretty much the same in terms of personality: belligerent in the way they talk and handle matters, dismissive of possible consequences, selfish and extreme. Now, in their minds, the land that they had robbed clearly belongs to them. Therefore, whenever the youth knocks on their doors to request the return of his family lands, an argument would ensue. These families do not shy from conflict, telling the young man, "Why, is your name on a land marker somewhere? How is it then, that I am working the land now, huh?" They are highly unwilling to see the young man advance, and cannot wait to see him vanish off the face of the earth as they know that their past will eventually come back to haunt them as long as the youth continues to have the intention and accumulate resources. "The Theory of the Fearsome Youth" has come just in time for them. They gather round the banner of the current village head and trip over themselves to provoke the youth in numbers.

Finally, a couple of peers of the youth who happen to have done quite well for themselves too see that this young man, who really is not much better than them, moves up in life, acquires a car and home, and even engages in investments and charitable activities everywhere. Clearly, he is setting himself up to be the head of his generation. These peers become a little jealous, and these feelings fester over time. No longer are these young men all in the same boat together. These feelings, of course, they keep to themselves at this point. However, they look out for opportunities to trip up the young man so as to slow down his advance, or better yet, halt his advance entirely. To them, the "Theory of the Fearsome Youth" undoubtedly provides an excellent opportunity. As such, they join in the cacophony against the youth.

The first group is powerful and influential, while the second group likes to get up to shady maneuvers while protesting their innocence. These two groups of people are analogous to armed village reactionaries, while the third group of people, who are competitive only in spirit but not in terms of true capabilities are essentially fence-sitters. The youth becomes very alone in the face of these three groups of troublemakers. This is because other villagers who are sympathetic would typically choose to stay silent and stand on the sidelines due to the domineering stance of the first group, the hooliganism of the second group, and the pettiness of the third group.

This way, what was originally a straightforward narrative of individual growth has become a matter of international conflict as an adjustment in interests is hardly avoidable. It has also become a matter of ensuring that the rules of play are changed so that the development of latecomers would not be impeded. Whether the youth can successfully surmount the barriers and challenges put up by these three groups of people would have a strong bearing on his growth on the seas as well as obtaining the support and recognition of his detractors. Equally important is the question of whether reasonable, equal and fair competition will prevail on the seas, or if brute power and tyranny will determine the future of maritime affairs.

4.3 Head-on Conflict, Full-on Engagement

Therefore, the youth faces an array of deep challenges if he wishes to achieve a healthy and stable progress towards his goals.

The competitive relationship between the youth and the aforementioned three groups of people clearly indicates this point.

It is probably already clear to the readers that in this allegory, the youth's predicament is similar to the challenges that China faces on the seas. The first group of detractors refers to the US; the second group, Japan, Vietnam, the Philippines, etc.; and the third group, nations such as India and Australia. The economic and political interactions between the youth and these nations can be summarized as "head-on conflict, full-on engagement". This complex relationship consists of both cooperative and competitive aspects in all areas: political, military and economic.

American policy of deterrence, the competition and policy of impedance put up by Japan and India, the worry and efforts to catch-up by Vietnam, the Philippines, etc., in response to China's global political influence, form the general backdrop to the political relationships between China and these nations.

Among the aforementioned nations, the attitude of the US is the most vexing. Although the US has stated that it welcomes China's peaceful rise, after the Cold War it has regarded China as its imaginary strategic rival. Following the 2008 financial crisis in Europe and the US, thanks to its three decades of swift development, certain academic organizations began to position China as an integral "pole" in a new multi polar world that would replace the unipolar world dominated by the US. They have even gone as far as to discuss at several international fora the replacement of the US by China as leader of the international arena. Clearly, the US is not very willing to see this scenario take place. The US, which was still in a morass in Iraq, quickly declared a "return to Asia" in order to limit China to the Pacific, and if this was not possible, to the Indian Ocean at the very limit, by exploiting the complex international situation around China and building up its maritime power.

In 2010, when Barack Obama declared himself to be the first US President to be a "Pacific President," the US also made two political moves, of which the political intent is clear. The first was the repeated expression of its hopes that the current international order in the Asia-Pacific would remain unchanged. Second, the US began to reach out to various countries along the Indian Ocean littoral and those that had disputes with China to strengthen relations with these countries. Particularly in the area of military cooperation, efforts were made to station troops at Darwin in Australia. It was also in this period that the US expressed its support for Vietnam with regard to the South China Sea issue.

What does "no change to the status quo in the Asia-Pacific international order" mean? It means that Taiwan would continue to be separated from the Chinese mainland, and that countries like Japan, Vietnam and the Philippines would not drop their claims to disputed islands and seas because of the pressure from China.

What does "strengthening cooperation with China's competitors" mean? The logic is simple: my enemy's enemy is my friend.

What is the significance of the increasing focus of the US on the Indian Ocean? This move is mainly aimed at sending a message to China: China's rise must not go beyond the control of the US and must be in a way that is acceptable to, and recognized by, the US. Even if China becomes the most powerful nation in Asia, it may not be the regional leader without the assent of the US. This is not the case only in the Asia-Pacific. The potential for China to be thwarted is very real in many places around the world, such as in the Indian Ocean.

On the other hand, China's relationships with Japan and India are far easier to understand: both nations recognized as economic powers and working towards being political and military powers as well, regard China as a competitor.

From their perspectives, not only do they have land or maritime disputes with China, they have also been in competition with China for regional leadership and the right to speak on the global stage for quite some time. To a certain degree, China has become the obstacle to, and cast a shadow on, these two nation's ascent to world power. Japan would never become a key political power as long as China continues to demand its culpability for its invasion during World War II. In 1962, China was able to defeat India in the Sino-Indian War thanks to its greater overall national strength, and even today the two nations continue to have differences on the issue of sovereignty in southern Tibet. Subconsciously, the Indians have always believed that even if they have become a world power, as long as China is ahead of India its worth as a world power would be greatly undermined.

With efforts of the US to impede China's advance and its unrivaled global propaganda capabilities, Japan has followed suit to vilify China in order to cast off its historical burden while India sees an opportunity to catch-up as China's momentum is being slowed down.

We should also note the actions of Vietnam and the Philippines, two countries which we can regard as opportunists. The power differential between themselves and China has also led these two nations to realize that they would be on the losing end in maritime territorial disputes where they have little legal or historical ground if China were to become the key power in the Asia-Pacific. Naturally, as the US is taking the lead in making waves, and is joined enthusiastically by Japan and India, Vietnam and the Philippines are happy to join them. This is, in fact, a political move.

However, there are also differences between the Vietnam and Philippines situations. In terms of bilateral relations, while Vietnam and China have had military conflicts in the 1970s and 1980s, the two countries share similar ideologies and social systems. China had also rendered significant assistance to the Vietcong during the Vietnam War. Therefore, the relationship between China and Vietnam is actually a love–hate relationship. However, there has not been significant political conflict between the Philippines and China in recent memory.

Vietnam and Philippines cases also differ in terms of the degree of determination shown in maritime disputes. From the 1974 Battle of the Xisha Islands to the Sino-Vietnamese War fought between 1979 and 1985, as well as the 1988 Battle of the Nansha Islands, it is clear that Vietnam is belligerent, and when it loses in a battle it walks away sore and begins to bide its time for the next opportune moment; these are the similarities it shares with Japan. On the other hand, the Philippines is a country that is lacking in principles and consistency in its dealings with foreign nations. Its current hardline attitude towards China is but the posturing of a paper tiger supported by the Americans. Filipino Presidents at various times, for instance Joseph Estrada, Gloria Macapagal-Arroyo and Benigno Aquino III have shown varying attitudes towards the dispute centered on the Huangyan Island. This aside, more critically current President Aquino has vacillated over the years, stating his desire to "make a counterattack" on the Huangyan Island at one point and to "open fire" upon Chinese fighter jets at one point, and then claiming that his country would not go to war with China over the Huangyan Island in another. Therefore, the Philippines would have engaged in a political dispute with China anyway, with or without the involvement of the US, Japan, India, etc. Hence, we see that firstly in political terms China faces a political "encirclement" led and organized by the US, with other nations such as Japan, India, Vietnam and the Philippines also involved for various reasons.

The political "encirclement" by nations such as the US and Japan has led to a vicious cycle for China to develop military relationships. Since the interests and political stance of China are different from those of countries like the US, Japan, and other countries involved, and since these countries have made use of their military cooperation schemes to effect military encirclement, China has no reason to turn a blind eye and "outsource" matters such as trade security and overseas development—matters that have an import on the country's future development—to the US and its allies of various levels. The solution for China is to continue to develop its military strength by increasing its investment in, and commitment to, the development of weapons and the modernization of its forces so that it would be capable of taking full control of its trade interests worldwide.

However, such a move by China would further provoke jealousy and anxiety on the part of the US, Japan, India, Vietnam, etc., and lead to a military encirclement on top of the current political encirclement. In fact, this may even be the beginning of an economic encirclement.

In recent years, countries like the US, Japan, Australia, Vietnam, Philippines have quite coincidentally spoken out against China in strong terms as the latter's military become more established. The US, Japan, India, Australia, Vietnam, Philippines, etc., have also strengthened their military cooperation while Japan, India, Australia, Vietnam, Philippines, etc., have focused more energies on weapon manufacture as well as acquired more weapons from the US. Clearly, these are signs of an impending arms race in the Asia-Pacific region.

Around the same time, in what is another dimension of pressure for China, countries such as the US and Japan have also sought ways to "encircle" China in economic terms despite their economic ties with China. America had invited various Asia-Pacific nations to join in negotiations for the Trans-Pacific Partnership Agreement (TPP) with China the sole country neglected. At the end of 2013, the number of Japanese-owned enterprises in India (based on legal-representative registrations) has grown nearly 100 % from 550 at the end of 2008 to 1072. While Japan has signed free-trade agreements with India, Vietnam, Australia, and Philippines none of which has signed a bilateral free-trade agreement with China.

However, it must be said that the threefold political, military and economic encirclement of China led by the US, and involving other countries such as Japan and India will be but one part of China's relations with these countries.

China's cooperation is critical to the US in many areas, such as with the common threat of international terrorism and in major international incidents such as Russia's annexation of Crimea in March 2014. Since 2005, China has held six rounds of Strategic Dialogues with the US and six rounds of Strategic and Economic Dialogues. Since 2010, the two nations have held five rounds of high-level cultural consultations and exchanges. The US has even invited China to participate in Exercise RIMPAC in 2004. All these are important signs that the US is willing to work with China.

The situation is similar with other nations. China–Japan relations have been on a trajectory of decline following Ryutaro Hashimoto's appointment as Prime Minister of Japan in January 1996, with a new low reached following Shinzo Abe's second term as Prime Minister at the end of 2012. Normal exchanges have more or less ceased between the leaders of both nations as the relationship became frosty. The term "cold politics and hot economy" often used to describe China–Japan relations is gradually becoming "double cold." However, channels such as grassroots exchanges and visits by leaders of various political parties have kept communications between the two countries open. Although the mood on economic cooperation has been dampened by political differences, the impact on trade numbers has not been significant. It is the same story with the relationship between Vietnam and China: although the two nations have had a series of run-ins, high-level exchanges have continued to occur. As of June 2013, two countries have held 15 joint patrols in disputed seas, and following anti-China protests in June 2014 Chinese enterprises have also received compensation for damage caused.

In addition, if we look past the superficial signs, we will see that currently China is the number one trading partner of the United States, Japan, India, Australia and Vietnam, and is likely to stay this way for some time. Trade relations are the true pillar of China's relations with these countries.

To summarize the relationship between China and other nations: "full-on engagement, head-on conflict," while the phrase order with countries such as America and Japan should be reversed to read "head-on conflict, full-on engagement" to differentiate the degree of conflict versus agreement due to respective interests. The government's primary focus should be on the attempt to contain and encircle China by countries such as the US, and Japan. On one hand, full-on engagement, driven by grassroots interactions and the power of the market, is inevitable; for other countries, mutually beneficial full-on engagement with China driven by an open market is the key thrust of their relations with China. However, given the varying cultures and interests of each country, conflicts during contact are also unavoidable from time to time.

The story of China's integration into the global market in early modern times provides great insight into how conflict can come alongside contact. In the mid-19th century, China was a passive player as its market was opened by the West. This was the beginning of industrial and financial development based on foreign knowhow and it took place at approximately the same time as the competition between domestic and foreign textiles. In the 1970s, China once again opened up its market to the West, this time proactively. With this move came the Western lifestyle, high-tech goods and the advent of China as "the world's factory" in what was the international division of labor. In addition, Chinese enterprises had had to play catch-up with their foreign counterparts while at the same time international brands were dislodging domestic brands from their leading market positions. In the twenty-first century, Chinese enterprises grew from strength to strength and became more familiar with the competition rules of the international marketplace, gaining the wherewithal to compete effectively with globally renowned peers in a number of industries including telecommunications, information technology, household appliances, equipment manufacturing, energy and aviation. A growing number of Chinese enterprises and capital are also looking beyond China's borders for more opportunities. China has, while various nations are enjoying the spoils of the Chinese market, managed to elevate itself to the mid to high range of the international value chain by promoting industry upgrading and restructuring. However, this process has also led to a situation with more trade disputes and greater market pressures.

Of course, today, China's interactions with many countries have long gone beyond the economic sphere, with cooperation and exchanges in all areas. This of course can also be understood as the beginning of full-on competition. Under such circumstances, overt and covert competition rooted in commercial and national interests can be said to be all-encompassing. Such competition may take place within China's borders, or overseas; it can take the form of economic competition, or the form of political competition; this competition may involve businesses or industries, or take place in the cultural sphere. When such competition emerges in the area of sea power, apart from disputes centered on sovereign sea power there would also be rights disputes centered on the development and exploitation of marine resources. There will be an increasing number of territorial disputes not only in surrounding waters and islands but also in farther waters. Events such as the 1993 Yinhe Incident and the pressures faced by the China National Petroleum Corporation (CNPC) in the course of developing oil resources in Iraq[1] are all signs of future concerns to come.

As China enters a new age of cooperation with various countries—especially powers—around the world and as cooperation continues to grow both in terms of scale and scope, we can expect to see a growing number of disputes and conflicts with "cooperation amidst competition, competition amidst cooperation." Further, given that strategic confrontation, controversy, and conflict vis-à-vis the US, Japan, etc., may also intensify in scale in the future; we must commence our analysis and preparation in advance.

First, we should examine the factors that work for, and against China, both within the country and overseas. This would allow us to make the necessary preparation to deal with potential challenges rationally and objectively, instead of being overly optimistic or pessimistic, or seeking immediate success or backing off easily in face of setbacks.

Second, we must work to maintain the trajectory and strength of our development, and focus on safeguarding our interests in the face of complex internal and external environments. We would need wisdom and determination in order not to be swayed from the course.

Next, we must have the courage and confidence to face all resistance and pressures, particularly resistance and provocation in the international arena. We must not act upon pique or belligerence; however, we should not shy away from conflict when necessary. We must interact and engage with our counterparts in a reasonable and fact-based manner.

Finally, China must have the courage to try and break free the unreasonable rules and situations, and emphasize reasonable, peaceful and effective harnessing of marine resources and promote the establishment of an international maritime order that is fair and equal. This would require a long-term perspective and strategy.

---

[1]Kang, Dexi (2008). CNPC Facing Competitive Pressure from the West in Iraq. *International Herald Leader*, 21 April.

4.4 Issues and Tensions

The multiplicity of issues, limitations and challenges faced by China in all areas is also a key shaping factor in China's all-round growth. China is growing in terms of both its "hard power" and "soft power." In addition, not only is it working to improve itself, it is also seeking to improve the international maritime, politics and economy. China's efforts do not merely include contact and competition with the relevant countries but also the rectification and re-construction of international maritime rules.

However, the array of goals and effects sought also foreground the complexity of the situation, and the challenging choices that China has to make, as it seeks to safeguard comprehensive sea power. That the international relations on the seas encompass both full-on engagement and head-on conflict already shows that a simple, one-dimensional understanding of the challenges and opportunities brought by the oceans and sea power would not do. However, we need not doubt that for China, a country with little awareness of the seas, which lacks a strong maritime tradition and history, which is dealing with a number of longstanding problems, which is situated in a challenging geopolitical environment and which has few factors going for it in terms of maritime development, the situation is truly daunting with a number of issues and Catch-22s requiring resolution.

First of all, there is the challenge of both the existing "stock" problems and the "incremental" problems.

To summarize the plethora of internal and external issues, limitations and challenges faced by China: a new problem arises before the old one is solved.

Existing problems faced by China as it seeks to extend its development to the seas include: the lack of experience in maritime management and administrative finesse as well as an awareness of the sea and a strong maritime tradition. Further, China is also not in possession of complete "sovereign" sea power for reasons of historical legacy and the current international set-up.

However, together two trends tend to exacerbate the problems.

The first trend is, with the passage of time the number of existing problems increases, with problems also snowballing into bigger ones and generating additional ones in the process.

For example, in the area of maritime management: structural changes to maritime industries are but perfunctory at the moment. On the other hand, there is little efficiency and focus in technological innovation. As a result, China's hands continued to be tied in terms of improving the system of accountability for environmental protection. This has led to stagnation in China's ability to derive benefits from maritime management while its costs continue to rise.

In addition, in terms of disputed islands and maritime disputes, the level of such disputes could have been limited to the bilateral level if they are solved as soon as possible. If they are not solved in time, those countries with maritime disputes with China may join the alliance made up of countries such as the US and Japan, elevating what was originally a bilateral issue to a multilateral issue. The dispute with Vietnam is a case in point.

The second trend is certain "incremental" problems which require some time to resolve can take on an even larger "stock" scale in the meantime. For example, with the expansion of business cooperation, the state will be increasingly called upon to provide for security needs on this growing scale. Another example would be the open opportunity for the development and exploitation of marine resources given by the United Nations Convention on the Law of the Sea (UNCLOS) and related international laws as well as other nations, such as for the exploitation and development of mineral and gas resources within "areas" and resource-producing countries (regions).

Second, there is the intersection of the "hard" or the "necessary" and the "soft" or the "flexible" in problem resolution.

The "hard" or the "necessary" and the "soft" or "flexible" aspects of issues are often intertwined.

For example, while the return of Taiwan and the recovery of disputed islands and waters are "hard" problems, just how to resolve these issues is a "soft" problem as there are multiple options available. The enhancement of China's marine resource development and exploitation capabilities is a "soft" problem although the sheer necessity of this move is "rigid" or "hard".

From the perspective of a democratic nation, the Taiwan question alongside island and maritime territorial disputes all have to do with national sovereignty and territorial integrity. Hence, they are the "bottom line" for China in the area of sea power and the need to resolve them is non-negotiable. Hence, this is a "hard" problem. Under special circumstances, China may draw on all of what it possesses to defend its sovereign sea power. However, as to when Taiwan and the mainland will be unified, how the unification would look like, and what steps China would take to recover surrounding islands and maritime territory, the possibilities are endless.

As the costs of navigating and managing the oceans and the benefits derived from the oceans will grow or shrink depending on China's capabilities for exploiting marine resources, coastal defense and ensuring the security of blue-water shipping, compared to the issue of sea power (one inextricably tinged with the matter of national sovereignty) the enhancement of one's marine resource development and exploitation capabilities is undoubtedly a "soft" problem. However, as a growing maritime nation, China's enhancement of its marine resource development and exploitation capabilities is critical to its relationship and interaction with the seas, and is necessary if it wishes to become an internationally recognized maritime nation. Hence, this is also a problem of "rigidity" or necessity.

Certain "soft" problems can turn into "hard" problems at a certain scale. The most salient example would be that of pollution in coastal waters. Kept within certain levels, such pollution is allowed or taken as benign and ignored. However, high levels of pollution in coastal waters will cause a negative impact on both the marine environment and the lives of local residents, and at this stage, it has become a social problem that must be resolved.

Third, there are disputes where both national sovereignty and property rights are at stake.

The issue of sea power involves both domestic law and international law. Hence, with sea power China must first lead the activity to define its sovereignty before economists can talk about including property rights into various institutions and mechanisms within the state. A country's sea power must be underscored by sovereignty before property rights can be discussed.

This has reflected the complexity of certain island and maritime territorial disputes faced by China, as property rights become contested between nations as a result of sovereign competition.

On the subject of sea power, both China and its competitors have touted "lawful and reasonable bases" for their claims. This is true in most cases, as their claims are supported by domestic laws and compatible with the spirit of international law. However, there are cases where "lawful and reasonable bases" touted by separate nations are hardly lawful or reasonable when viewed from their counterparts' domestic legal perspective. Contradictions in legal terms together with the gap between historical and current possession have exacerbated China's difficulties in turning around the current situation of other parties' actual possession of the disputed islands and waters, and pressing territorial and subsequent property rights claims. The outcome will be determined by the game between China and other relevant countries.[2]

Regardless of whether this game is carried out peacefully or through armed conflict it does not appear that the disputes at hand can be resolved quickly. In the interim, each disputing party can lay and act on property rights claims to the disputed territory. However, until a property rights solution amenable to both parties has been crafted, neither party would have effective means of putting a stop to its counterpart's property rights claims and related moves. Actually, this is the case with gas exploration and exploitation in the South China Sea vis-à-vis Vietnam and Philippines. The competition for sovereign rights—and property rights—is on.

Fourth, while driven by motivations, China also faces pressures as it seeks to take its development to the seas.

The pressures that China faces as it seeks to take its development to the oceans include suppression by stronger nations and intrusions by smaller neighbors. In addition, the country also lacks experience with the seas. On the other hand, the motivations that drive China include a prosperous maritime economy, the development of its coastal regions, overseas trade, etc. These pressures and motivations come from both within and outside of China.

However, no matter where these pressures and motivations come from, shrewd handling can turn pressures into motivations and even the catalyst for China's growth on the seas. Conversely, poor handling can turn motivations into pressures and create trouble or even barriers for China's maritime development.

---

[2]Kong, Zhiguo (2011). *Maritime Rights, Property Rights Competition and the Tunhai Policy*. Social Sciences Academic Press, pp. 92–95.

Therefore, we should not worry unduly about the return of the US, to the Asia-Pacific region and its leadership of a political, military and economic encirclement of China joined by Japan, India, Vietnam and the rest. Furthermore, the possibility of China breaking through the barricades put up by multiple countries to freedom on the seas is significant. As long as China is able to catch-up with the US, it can be regarded as a true maritime nation even if it suffers a minor setback every now and then.

Of course, though China has already chalked up some achievements in its drive to take its development to the seas, and domestic calls for China to protect its sea power are growing by the day, we should not be overly optimistic. Without adequate understanding and strategic guidance, complacency can cause China to underestimate the challenges and pressures involved, while extreme nationalist sentiments that accompany calls for the protection of the country's sea power can lead to poor decision-making by the state. The "overreaching" seen with China's effort to ensure even economic development between regions is the best anecdotal example of this point.

Fifth, the necessity of China's maritime rise is intertwined with its goal of a peaceful rise.

While China's future development relies more on the oceans, it is currently "being held by the throat" in terms of its access to the seas. In time to come, the pain of seeing marine resources being divvied up among other nations will be more acute. The need to resolve this situation as soon as possible is growing by the day. Today, China seeks to establish itself as a responsible power. Hence, it can no longer ignore the oceans, and must work to enhance its marine resource development and exploitation abilities, clarify its sea power and seek to possess complete sea power.

However, in order to achieve this China must be able to rival the likes of the US, Japan and other Asia-Pacific maritime nations or otherwise possess an effective deterrent against them. Therefore, the impetus to enhance China's naval power is one that arises naturally. This would appear to be in tension with the concept of a peaceful rise on the seas by China, a concept that has been much emphasized by China and which other members of the international community have hoped for.

However, the two are actually part of the same whole. To achieve peace, we need common understanding and cooperation between various parties. Similarly, China's "peaceful rise" is predicated not only on China's efforts but also the understanding and support of the international community. In a situation where there is deliberate and even malicious encirclement of China, building up effective military deterrence is necessary for China. It not only helps China work through impedances put up by other nations in the name of peace yet with a belligerent manner, but also adds ballast to China's peaceful rise, and creates the greatest room possible for China to achieve maritime development and complete sea power.

Therefore, China must not buy into a simplistic explanation of what a "peaceful rise" entails and fall into an over-reliance on the cultivation of a peaceful image on the international stage. Instead, it should ensure that it is prepared to tackle any unexpected development that may take place. At the same time, in the event China encounters a counterpart that is unwilling to resolve a dispute through peaceful means, we must not become a passive player that gives way at every turn in the development of our sea power (or of the nation) simply because of the fantasy of peace. The issue should be resolved as soon as possible when the time is right and the necessary conditions are in place.

Sometimes, peace cannot be obtained simply by wishing for it to happen. We may have to fight in order to obtain peace.

Sixth: with opportunity comes risk, and vice versa.

This problem is centered on the tension between the necessity of China's maritime rise and its goal of a peaceful rise.

On one hand, the thinking on sea power has seen significant changes internationally. For instance, the United Nations Convention on the Law of the Sea (UNCLOS) sets out expectations for "peaceful competition" and emphasizes a balance between responsibility and duty. The UNCLOS also lays out guidelines for the establishment of a series of dispute resolution mechanisms. The deepening of globalization thanks to advances in telecommunications and travel technologies has also strengthened and enhanced exchanges between peoples of various nations, regions and ethnic groups and has undoubtedly created an environment that is more than amenable than ever for a peaceful maritime rise by China. This is, without doubt, an excellent opportunity for China as it seeks to extend its development to the oceans.

On the other hand, with opportunity also comes risk. The standards set out by the UNCLOS for the definition of exclusive economic zones and continental shelves are ambiguous. For a country like China which shares limited maritime space with neighboring countries in a region where exclusive economic zones or continental shelves declared by various nations overlap, maritime conflict with its neighbors may be on the cards. In addition, the binding power of the UNCLOS on member nations is insignificant compared to the hold of national interests over the leaders of various nations. Here, the "law of the jungle" which features "survival of the fittest" is the predominant narrative on the seas. Several nations have made significant investments into the enhancement of their capability to wage war on the seas as well as on long-range weapons, which means that armed conflict continues to be a possible option for the resolution of these disputes. The dispute resolution mechanisms mandated in UNCLOS are at risk of being left dormant, with the emphasis on peaceful resolution upended by power and force.

Of course, opportunity may also accompany risk. If China is able to resolve disputes in as peaceful a manner as possible and break through the barricades put up by the US, Japan, etc., to emerge victoriously into the oceans, we would be writing a new chapter in the history of man, a chapter on a peaceful maritime rise for the good of mankind.

Seventh: the problem of tactical conservatism versus strategic offense.

China has already decided that it would take its development all the way to the blue water and that it would seek control of key oceans around the world in either a passive or active fashion. This, together with China's economic strength and influence, makes it abundantly clear that China is posturing itself as a future important maritime nation. Thus, there is a strong element of the "offensive" in China's bid to extend its development to the oceans.

This is in strong contrast to the position of tactical defense that China has claimed for a long time. Although the Chinese navy is currently transitioning from a focus on coastal defense to "coastal and blue-water defense" and claims that the latter is but a more proactive form of defense, fundamentally the basic stance of "defense" has remained unchanged.

Tactical conservatism means that in strategic terms, China will tend to opt for a path that is a departure from the traditional "zero-sum" or even "negative-sum" approach used for a nation's ascent to the status of an important maritime nation.

Historically, the possession of overseas colonies, an overseas sphere of influence and the ability to conquer others by force has served nations such as Portugal, Spain, Holland, Britain, the US, Germany and Russia well in their respective quests to become maritime powers. However, today China does not even have a formal ally to speak of, let alone colonies and overseas sphere of influence. In addition, China is a relative latecomer to the maritime powers game and has yet to achieve territorial integrity. In military terms, its strength has yet to match that of the US (and its allies). Hence, it is not possible for China to follow the steps of Spain (versus Portugal), Holland (versus Spain), Britain (versus Holland) and the US (versus Britain).

In this sense, China's move to extend to its development to the seas is one that is strategically conservative. However, conversely, this also means that China may need to revise its conservative position in terms of tactics. If China sticks stubbornly to "defense" it will face extraordinary security challenges. Successful "self-defense" in special circumstances requires the ability to defeat one's enemies convincingly, and without doubt China does not possess this ability at the moment. China should align its tactics for greater compatibility with its offensive strategy of taking its development to the seas. As such, its tactics must also take on a more offensive nature. Even when tactics call for defense, such defensive must take on a more offensive approach.

Eighth: China must pave the way to a new order while inheriting the existing order at the same time.

The contradiction between China's conservative tactics and offensive strategy as it seeks to take its development to the seas means that China cannot simply "play catch-up" with existing maritime powers in terms of its marine resource development and exploitation capabilities. Instead, China must also realize a complete set of sea power and explore new ways to boost maritime development. This is predicated on its ability to (to quote Sun Tzu) "subdue the enemy without fighting."

In terms of China's marine resource development and exploitation capabilities, "playing catch-up" with existing maritime powers is the best option for China under the rules of the current global maritime order. Adherence to these existing rules also serves to qualify China as a member of the maritime powers club.

The realization of complete sea power for China and the exploration of new ways to boost maritime development would help China realize its dream of becoming an important maritime nation chiefly through means such as equal exchange with other nations around the world and taking on more responsibilities. Not only would move such as these help to avoid or reduce damage or negative impact caused to the world as a result of conflict as countries such as Britain, and the US, achieved similar results, they would also be helpful in establishing a new maritime philosophy centered on equality, mutual benefit and an emphasis on responsibilities over rights and interests. This implies moving beyond the current maritime order and rules.

The principle of "to subdue the enemy without fighting" will be the link between the old and new world orders in the maritime dimension, as well as between the old rules and the new ones. To accomplish the objective of the principle "to subdue the enemy without fighting" against the interference and limitations placed on China by the "law of the jungle" within the old orders and rules, substantial strength and superior capabilities are needed as a firm guarantee. The spirit of "to subdue the enemy without fighting" is about convincing one's counterparts with the use of "propriety" and "reason." In the new order, "propriety" means adhering to the rules as much as possible without hurting one's own interests, while "reason" encompasses an emphasis on harmony and the possibility of tit for tat, but only when provoked.

Simply put: *China must ensure that it does not end up at the bottom of the totem pole in an old maritime order determined by military force. Instead, it should work hard to become a winner in a new maritime order that has its basis in fair and equal competition.*

4.5 Necessary Conditions for Future Development

Now that we have conducted a detailed analysis of the issues, limitations and challenges that China faces as it seeks to take its development to the oceans, a key task for us now is to look at how these issues, limitations and challenges may be surmounted. In other words, let us now look at how China can be put on the path to its maritime rise.

Determining just how this task can be accomplished exactly is a job for a later time. It is difficult to speak on the specifics at this point in time. However, we can already see the outlines of what this road may look like, or rather, what conditions are needed.

First, the road to China's maritime rise should not be limited to the regional scale, and nor should it take the form of a conservative approach. Instead, what is needed is an open and expansive approach.

The center of the world's economy has shifted to the Asia-Pacific region, and so has the strategic focus of the US. Clearly, an Asia-Pacific maritime power is a global maritime power. The fact that the oceans are the bedrock of the global economy also means that for a large country like China that wishes to become an important maritime nation, such "importance" cannot be limited to a regional projection as its influence on the seas extends to wherever its international trade, cultural and political reach extends to.

Therefore, the road to China's maritime rise cannot simply be based on a conservative approach—despite the attraction of such an approach—and nor can it be limited to the regional scale. The approach must be of a full-on open and expansive nature. In other words, "openness" entails cooperation wherever possible, with partners near or far, while "expansiveness" refers to the growth of one's influence over another as cultural and economic ties deepen.

Second, we must maximize China's comparative advantages: its sizable market and a peace-loving culture to facilitate China's maritime rise. Doing so would allow us to take hold of more opportunities and give us more room to hit back at voices of suspicion and criticism.

China's greatest advantage as it seeks to become an important maritime nation lies in its market of nearly 1.4 billion consumers, a market that is full of economic vitality. This is China's calling card—and strongest card—as it seeks to forge strong relationships with foreign nations. China should play this advantage to the hilt as it works to gain international support, grow its overseas markets and lower trade barriers in overseas markets, etc. This will help more nations and regions realize the centrality of a mutually beneficial, win–win partnership in international maritime interactions today and that engaging and doing business in China generally leads to a win–win situation.

In addition, China must be able to clearly articulate its tradition of peace with countries that may be concerned about China's dominance following its ascendancy to an important maritime nation, concerns that may have arisen as a result of ideology, a difference in systems and/or customs or erroneous discourse. China does not have a tradition of imposing hegemony over others. In the time of Zheng He's far-flung voyages, China's maritime strength was clearly superior compared to the various places he had visited. However, China's position was to behave with propriety and respect local customs and choices.[3] Moreover, the issue here is not whether China can become the dominant power in the region. The true question is, can China concentrate on its own development as it enhances the marine resource development and exploitations capabilities as quickly as possible while achieving for itself complete sovereign sea power and thus to maximize the benefits and resources derived for the sake of national development?

Third, China's maritime rise is the process of the country becoming a naval power. As such, the development of China's naval strength should point towards the realization of the strategy of offensive defense and the ability to defend the nation's interests on a global scale.

Parts of China's maritime territory and islands are currently being occupied, while Taiwan is still separated from the mainland. There is also a political,

---

[3]Levathes, Louise (2004). *When China Ruled the Seas.* (Qiu, Zhonglin, trans.) Guilin: Guangxi Normal University Press, pp. 72–215; Sun, Guangqi (2005). *A History of Sea Navigation in Ancient China.* Beijing: China Ocean Press, pp. 419–421.

economic and military "encirclement" of China led by the US, and involving other countries such as Japan, India and Vietnam. As such, China must be autonomous, self-reliant, and able to protect and defend its own interests. It must change the current situation of asymmetry in terms of strength of the maritime forces, which means that it must work to enhance its military power.

The increasing numbers of Chinese people traveling to all corners of the globe, as well as growing Chinese investment and trade overseas have also raised expectations of the provision of substantial and effective protection for life and property by the government. Further, internally China also needs to enhance its naval strength in order to contain the activities of the navies of surrounding nations. As such, China should have a military presence or engage in military partnership in as many places around the world as possible.

However, the enhancement of China's military strength, the augmentation of its troop presence and the establishment of a global strategy are really about building up effective deterrence for security's sake and to meet the development needs of the nation's modern sea power. Hence, generally speaking, from the perspective of pitting military strength versus military strength China's defensive stance remains unchanged. Nevertheless, to underscore its determination to realize complete sea power and to enable its maritime rise, China should also emphasize the offensive aspect of its defense to create a compelling deterrent.

Fourth, China's maritime rise is rooted in peace, and peace is also the chief means by which China can achieve its maritime rise.

China's ascendancy as an important maritime nation does not change its trajectory of a peaceful rise. It actually serves as a guarantee. Modern warfare typically results in widespread damage and/or fatalities. Hence, the stronger China is in military terms, the smaller the possibility that other nations—especially the great powers—would engage with China militarily. This means that China's chances of a peaceful maritime rise are greater as a result. This has absolutely no impact on China's hopes of a peaceful rise on the seas.

In addition, as peaceful competition between nations on the seas intensifies, the implication that the world does not need an arrogant superpower that constantly flexes its muscles (i.e., the US) and dictates the actions of other nations. What China can do here is to establish a positive example of a peaceful rise and show the world that it can do better than any other country, that it can better access the resources needed to boost its economic development, and that it can live in harmony with countries that bear no malice. Further, China can only be widely regarded as an important maritime nation when it voluntarily and consciously offers international public goods and public services, which are not in exchange for interference in the affairs of other nations.

Finally, China's maritime rise cannot be achieved in a single day, and there may be ups and downs during the process. Hence, China must be prepared to work over the long term.

China's maritime rise project is a systematic, long-term endeavor that involves investments in institutions, industries, trade, maritime awareness, education, technologies, etc. At the same time, it is also the result of cooperation between various parties both within and outside of China. China's maritime rise can be affected by maritime competition between various nations, the putting up of obstructions and stumbling blocks by external forces, and changes in the world political and economic patterns. Given the multitude of dimensions and hence challenges involved, the possibility of "ups and downs" in China's quest to become an important maritime nation is also significant. Therefore, we should not expect the objective to be achieved overnight and should instead gird ourselves for a long-term battle.

Looking back at our history, we must learn to critically examine the key factors that would have an impact on China's maritime rise. What kind of a "maritime China" would stand the test of time? Are there any historical scenarios or experiences that we can learn from?

Chapter 5
Learning from *Tuntian* of Western Han

The core sea power issue that confronts China is this: how to ensure the country's maritime security within the modern environment, and how to keep a balance between maintaining effective military deterrence and the maximization of benefits gained from the seas. While doing so, China also needs to develop an identification with, and passion for, the seas among its people. That is to say, how can China ensure security in its surrounding seas and embrace leapfrog development brought on by the maritime economy in an environment where the supply of the relevant public goods from the government is inadequate and where the nation's maritime development and exploitation capabilities are still lacking?

This situation is similar to the challenges that had confronted the people of the Western Han Dynasty over two thousand years ago on terra firma.

5.1 Why Learn from the Western Han?

The core sea power issue that confronts China is this: how to ensure the country's maritime security within the modern sea power environment, and how to keep a balance between maintaining effective military deterrence and the maximization of benefits gained from the seas. While doing so, China also needs to develop an identification with, and passion for, the seas among its people. That is to say, how can China ensure security in its surrounding seas and embrace leapfrog development brought on by the maritime economy in an environment where the supply of the relevant public goods from the government is inadequate and where the nation's maritime development and exploitation capabilities are still lacking?

This situation is similar to the challenges that had confronted the people of the Western Han Dynasty over 2000 years ago on terra firma.

During the early Western Han Dynasty, the rulers and people were united in their reflection on and weariness of war. Development was regarded as the foremost task of the day, with policies targeted at rest and recovery of the nation alongside

Z. Kong, *The Making of a Maritime Power*, Research Series on the Chinese Dream and China's Development Path, DOI 10.1007/978-981-10-1786-5_5

Confucian teachings. However, the quest for stable development was constantly threatened by the invasions and harassment of the Xiongnu in border areas. This scenario is similar to what we are seeing today: a contemporary China that is seeking further development and advocating peaceful co-existence is yet being encircled, harassed and robbed on the seas.

The importance of disputed territories. Today, maritime territories are being disputed due to the vast amount of resources present as well as the strategic value of these seas. The larger the maritime territory, the higher the chance of exploiting both existing and potential resources. Therefore, larger maritime territories are also more likely to hold greater strategic value. Back then, if a territory is suitable for agricultural development or pastoral use, or if it could be used as a natural defensive barrier or passage route, it would become the subject of dispute. Between two disputing parties, the party with the larger territory has a better chance of exploiting land resources through its mode of production. The party that controls a natural strategic defensive barrier and key passageway will gain the upper hand in the event of a sudden outbreak of conflict.

The disputing parties. Today, the central government is embroiled in maritime disputes with both stronger nations and weaker nations. In addition, it also has to contend with domestic political forces and institutional shackles. It was also the case during the Western Han period: the dynasty had to deal with the powerful Xiongnu, who were adept at lightning-quick invasions on land, as well as smaller kingdoms that numbered in the thousands, such as Yelang.

The geographic distribution of disputed territories. Today, China's maritime border crises come from the east, southeast and south, with the latter two areas particularly concerning. During the Western Han Dynasty, border issues were present in the west, northwest, north, northeast, southwest and southeast, with issues on the northwestern and northern borders especially salient. Some disputed areas were more significant than others.

The make-up of a nation's maritime and land rights. A nation's sea power consists of its maritime territory and various rights as stipulated in the United Nations Convention on the Law of the Sea (UNCLOS). These rights are chiefly concerned with the exploitation and development of marine resources by the sovereign country. The realization of complete sea power for China is necessary for China's development and a political goal of the central government. Land rights in the time of the Western Han included land territory and the ability to develop such territory. At the same time, the realization of a complete set of land rights meant a unified, peaceful, and prosperous order under the rule of the Han people. Such realization was necessary and required from both the perspective of the Western Han court and for the sake of social and economic development.

The power needed to support a nation's maritime and land rights. Today, the maritime power and rights needed for China to realize its sea power include military power and the ability to obtain maritime economic resources. For the Western Han rulers, apart from military strength, they also needed the corresponding land development and exploitation capabilities in order to achieve a complete set of land rights. However, regrettably just like China today lacks the ability to pay the cost for complete sea power, at one point the rulers of the Western Han were also short of the strength required to realize a full set of land rights. Their troops were no match for the Xiongnu, who had spent their entire lives on horseback and were highly adept at archery. Although the Western Han military was able to secure the Central Plain, it was comparatively weak at the borders, and faced challenges in terms of dispute resolution and the building up of effective deterrence as neighboring peoples continued to harass, invade and cause damage to the Western Han Empire. Further, there was also a need at the time to improve the existing agricultural technologies. The people of the Western Han had little experience and confidence in the promotion of agriculture in border regions. Without sufficient capabilities to develop the border regions, effective control by the central government in those regions was not possible. In addition, the strategically vital area was held in the hands of the opponent, which meant that the Western Han Empire was in a passive position in matters such as strategic offense, defense and trade.

Hence, the passive position of the Western Han in the border regions is almost exactly the same as China's maritime predicament today. In both cases, the state's strength falls short of what is needed, with the state working on the development and enhancement of this supporting strength while working to realize full sovereignty and rights at the same time in order to forge a safe and peaceful environment for economic development.

This was something that was successfully achieved during the Western Han. The *tuntian* approach worked against the Xiongnu and helped to mitigate the Western Han's border crises by allowing the Western Han to transform risk into opportunity and achieve a quantum leap and reversal of position in terms of its comparative strength in the border regions. Eventually, the Western Han was able to realize a full set of land rights, establishing a strong foundation for the later prosperity of Western Han. What lessons can we draw from the Western Han example?

Of course, there are differences between sea and land, and the means by which exploitation and development of resources can be achieved also differ between the two. The realization of a nation's land and maritime rights and interests hence also require different approaches and methods. For instance, the defense and development of territorial waters are far more challenging and complex compared to similar efforts on land. While the focus on land is on agriculture, fisheries are the mainstay of the maritime economy. The climate on land tends to be largely stable and amenable to long-term human habitation while the climate on the seas is much rougher, creating far harsher conditions than what is experienced on land. The defense of land territory is largely centered on the ground while the defense of maritime territory involves not only the defense of islands, airspace and water surface but also thousands of meters underwater all the way to the seabed. It is far more challenging to defend maritime territory than to defend land territory. In addition, the nature of military power has also changed. In ancient times, troops that were posted to border regions were mostly infantry soldiers, whose vocations then did not require a high level of professionalism. As such, they were able to discharge both agricultural and border defense tasks adequately. However, the personnel of modern navies are required to perform at a much higher professional and technical level. Moreover, the size of Chinese navy and naval assets is not up to the task of patrolling the vast seas. Hence, it would be much more difficult for Chinese naval personnel to discharge both economic and defense tasks at the same time.

However, the value of the take-home lesson from the Western Han empire's ability to realize a full set of land rights and interests for China's predicament on the seas today should not be discounted.

5.2 About the *Tuntian* Policy During the Western Han

In *A History of the Qin and Han Dynasties*, Qian Mu writes that "When the Han Dynasty was just founded, the prominent problems were the reduction of the number of households and economic difficulty."[1] This has also been recorded multiple times in the *Records of the Grand Historian* and the *Book of Han.*[2,3]

The founding of the Han Dynasty was at a time of significant livelihood and financial pressures. As such, the newly minted dynasty had to turn its focus to the promotion of the economy. This meant that for a long time the court was unwilling to embroil itself in military conflict unless absolutely necessary.

This was because first of all, it is difficult to support any large-scale conflict on the basis of a weak economy. Second, after five and a half centuries of conflict since the Spring and Autumn period, people were looking forward to safety and stability in their lives more than ever. Moreover, long-term unrest had led to a decrease in

---

[1]Qian, Mu (2005). *A History of the Qin and Han Dynasties*. Beijing: SDX Joint Publishing Company, p. 47.

[2]That the population was sparse during the founding of the Western Han Dynasty is illustrated by an experience of the founding emperor Liu Bang. According to the *Records of the Grand Historian*: *The Family Records of Prime Minister Chen*: "Emperor Gaozu, passing by Quni (in what is the southeastern part of Wanxian County in Hebei today) on his way southwards, ascended its city walls and saw that it had houses of significant size. He exclaimed, 'The wonders of this county! I have traveled widely, and the only other place I know that matches this in magnificence is the city of Luoyang.' He then asked the local censor: 'How many households are there in Quni?' The censor responded, 'Over 30,000 households were here during the early Qin. Repeated unrests since then have caused many to die or flee. Today, we have 5000 households left.' Liu Bang, despite his travels all over his empire, was impressed by a city comprising merely 5000 households."

[3]The empire slid into severe economic depression and financial difficulty. As recorded in *Book of Han: Treatise on Food and Money* (*Part 1*), "Han rose and inherited the depression of Qin. Men served in military and the old and weak transported military provisions. There was heavy conscript labor but a lack of financial resources. Even the emperor could not find four horses of the same color to draw his carriage. Some generals and ministers traveled in ox-drawn carts. Common people had neither shelter nor clothing. Therefore…law and decrees were simplified. Lawless people pursuing benefits hoarded and profiteered. Prices soared to such an extent that one *dan* of rice was sold for 10,000 coins and one horse for 100 jin (ingots)." "People lost their livelihood and suffered from severe famine. The price of rice soared to 5000 coins per *dan*. People fed on each other and the population dropped by over a half."

population, making it challenging for the state to mobilize enough manpower for the military. This is best illustrated by the fact that during the Rebellion of the Seven States, the Emperor Jing of Han chose to sacrifice his trusted official Chao Cuo to avoid having to go to war with the rebelling nobles led by Liu Bi.

However, this was not the case with their adversary, the Xiongnu. They were a belligerent people, for they were able to obtain benefits from engaging in military conflict.

First of all, this was because the Xiongnu were originally a nomadic people whose lifestyle practices[4] meant that compared to the Han people; they were not as sensitive and concerned about the prospect of being uprooted as a result of war.

Second, like other nomadic peoples, the Xiongnu spent their lives either on the grasslands or in the forests,[5] spending much time with the beasts. This made them especially adept at skills such as horse riding and archery, skills that gave them a mobile edge in the so-called "cold weapon era."[6]

Moreover, the Xiongnu believe that military strength was primary to survival, and had become used to military conflict between various nomadic peoples.[7] Moreover, the early years of the Han Dynasty also coincided with the beginning of the Xiongnu Empire's ascendancy. At that time, the Xiongnu had enjoyed the gains from several military conflicts. Having conquered various peoples in the Western regions, the Xiongnu established commanderies that collected taxes from the conquered peoples[8]; other conquered peoples like the Donghu and the Loulan were

---

[4]According to research done by Han Maoli, the nomadic peoples moved frequently for reasons of pastoral conservation, seasonal change and depending on the breeds of animals they were rearing at various times. See Han, Maoli (2003). A Preliminary Exploration of the Nomadic Lifestyle of the Grassland Peoples in History. *Researchesin Chinese Economic History*, no. 4 (2003). However, Han had neglected another key factor, that of war. For instance, Xiongnu migration northwards during Qin times and subsequent westwards migration, as well as the westwards migration of the Yuezhi, were all fundamentally the result of defeat in wars.

[5]Tang, Xiaofeng (2006). The Significance of Mountainous Terrain to the Xiongnu. In Hou, Renzhi (ed.) (2006). *Studies in Environmental Changes in the Arid and Semi-Arid Regions of Northern China*. Beijing: The Commercial Press, pp. 281–293. This paper by Tang is significant as it looks at an oft-neglected subject: although the mountains may not have been as important to the nomadic peoples as the grasslands, they were still very important. The majority of Asian scholars have only paid attention to the importance of the grasslands to nomadic peoples. In my opinion, this article is an innovative and insightful contribution to the relevant fields.

[6]According to the *Records of the Grand Historian: The Xiongnu*: "(Among the Xiongnu), the children are able to ride goats and shoot birds and rats using a bow and arrow, while their adolescents shoot foxes and rabbits for food. Their warriors are able to draw a bow and arrow and ride with ease. In terms of their lifestyles, in good times they follow the beasts and hunt for sustenance. In straitened times, they make war and invade the territory of others. Such is their nature."

[7]The conquering of the Xiongnu by other nomadic tribes and the Chinese, as well as their conquering of these tribes and breaching of China's borders also imply Xiongnu's involvement in repeated rounds of military conflict.

[8]Li, Dingyi (1997). *A Brief History of China*. Beijing: Peking University Press, p. 105.

assimilated into the Xiongnu polity.[9] The Xiongnu were thus driven by both the prospect of material gains and the possibility of political gains[10] in their predilection for conflict.[11]

It is easy to see how the Western Han would be placed in a disadvantaged position in a conflict between the two parties.

Not only did the Xiongnu murder and pillage during their repeated invasions, they also had the upper hand in diplomatic dealings with the Han people. This was achieved by relying on Hans who had surrendered to them to craft even more practical strategies that were also more effective at tackling the Western Han,[12] such as the strategy of "coercing peace through battle." Due to military coercion by the Xiongnu, the Han people had to resort to measures such as arranged marriages between Han nobles and the Xiongnu, gifting[13] and the setting up of trading cities in border areas (*tongguanshi*) to keep the peace. In the 70-odd years before Emperor Wu decided to commence a military counterattack against the Xiongnu in 129 BCE, the powers-that-be during the Western Han simply found themselves powerless against the absolute military superiority of the Xiongnu.

---

[9]Zhou, Xishan (2004). *The Four-Thousand-Year War between the Han and the Xiongnu.* Shanghai: Shanghai Pictorial Publishing House, pp. 26–27.

[10]Currently the most northerly Xiongnu site found by archaeologists is located in Transbaikalia in Russia, while the most northwesterly site found thus far is located in Ulaangom in Mongolia. The eastern spread of the Xiongnu reached the Shilka, Argun, Kherlen, Yalu and Liao Rivers, while their Western spread has been detected as far as Ili River in Xinjiang, and the Semirechye region. In the south, the Xiongnu presence has reached Qinghai, Ningxia, northern Shaanxi, Ordos in Inner Mongolia and Shuozhou in Shanxi. Although these may not be indicative of the peak of the Xiongnu empire, they give us a good idea of the strength and influence of the Xiongnu. See Ma, Liqing (2005). *The Original Xiongnu and the Xiongnu: Archaeological Explorations in History and Culture.* Hohhot: Inner Mongolia University Press, p. 43.

[11]In 174 BCE, the Xiongnu sent a letter to Emperor Xiaowen of the Northern Wei which read: "The Kroraina, Wusun, Hujie and 26 other surrounding peoples have become slaves of the Xiongnu. The people of the bow have been united under one family, and the contours of the northern lands have been settled."

[12]For instance, King Xin of Han and Zhonghang Yue were of great help in the crafting of battle and diplomatic strategy. The relevant information can be found in the *Book of Han: Traditions of the Xiongnu* (no. 50), the *Book of Han: Traditions of the Xiongnu* (no. 64 part 1), *Records of the Grand Historian: Annals of Gaozu* and *Book of Han: Annals of Emperor Gaozu* (no. 1 part 2).

[13]In 177 BCE, a letter from the Emperor Wen to Modu Chanyu of the Xiongnu read: "The Han became sworn brothers with the Xiongnu in the hope that you would not violate the border. To this end we have lavished on you an abundance of gifts." The gifts given at one time were recorded in the following list: lined coat with embroideries, a long jacket and a brocade robe, a *bishu* (comb-shaped headdress), an ornamental belt with gold decorations, a gold belt hook, ten bolts of embroidered silk fabric, twenty bolts of brocade, forty bolts of red thick silk fabric and forty bolts of green silk fabric. See the *Book of Han: Traditions of the Xiongnu* (no. 64 part 1).

Apart from the close shave suffered by Gaozu at Pingcheng[14] and the efforts expended in vain during the encirclement of Mayi,[15] various Han nobles, military commanders and officials including the King Xin of Han, King Lu Wan of Yan, Zhonghang Yue, and King Liu Sui of Zhao also either surrendered to, or worked secretly with, the Xiongnu. (See *Book of Han: Traditions of the Xiongnu*, no. 64 part 1.) The Hans found themselves unable to retaliate against the Xiongnu during a dozen or so invasions of various scales.[16] One better-known example is the Battle of Xiao Pass in 166 BCE[17] during which the Xiongnu attempted a large-scale

[14]In 200 BCE, the Emperor Gaozu was surrounded by the Xiongnu at Pingcheng, and was left without food for days. Eventually, he managed to emerge from the crisis by bribing the wife of Modu Chanyu to put in a good word for him. Hence there was a folk song that went: "It was truly difficult in Pingcheng, and the defenders were unable to draw their bows and arrows after seven days of no food." See the *Book of Han: Traditions of the Xiongnu* (no. 64 part 1).

[15]In 133 BCE, the Emperor Wudi—acting on the advice of a local man in Mayi named Nie Yi—attempted to lure the Xiongnu Chanyu into a trap. However, the plot was discovered by the Chanyu. See the *Book of Han: Annals of Emperor Wudi* (no. 6).

[16]For this period, more than ten significant conflicts or battles with the Xiongnu can be found in records in the *Book of Han* and the *Records of the Grand Historian* on the reigns of the Emperors Gaozu, Hui, Wen, Jing, Wu and of the Empress LüZhi: In the ninth lunar month in 200 BCE, "King Xin of Han, was besieged by the Xiongnu at Mayi and surrendered to them." In the 12th lunar month in 181 BCE, "The Xiongnu invaded Didao and captured over 2000 people." In the fifth lunar month of 177 BCE, "The Xiongnu invaded Beidi and Henan for banditry." In the winter of 166 BCE, "The Xiongnu plundered border regions and killed Commander Mao of Beidi." From 166–154 BCE, "The Xiongnu … crossed the border each year to kill and capture large numbers of people, especially in Yunzhong and Liaodong, with over 10,000 people killed in either of them." In the winter of 158 BCE, "Thirty thousand Xiongnu cavalrymen invaded Shang Commandery and another thirty thousand invaded Yunzhong." In the second lunar month in 148 BCE, "The Xiongnu invaded Yan." In the spring of 144 BCE, "The Xiongnu entered Yanmen all the way to Wuquan, entered Shang Commandery and pillaged the horses, killing two thousand soldiers in battle." In the spring of 141 BCE, "The Xiongnu invaded Yanmen and Prefect Feng Jing died in a battle of resistance." See: *Records of the Grand Historian: Annals of Gaozu* (no. 8), *Records of the Grand Historian: Annals of Empress Dowager Lü* (no. 9), *Records of the Grand Historian: Annals of the Xiaowen Emperor* (no. 10), *Records of the Grand Historian: Annals of the Xiaojing Emperor* (no. 11), *Records of the Grand Historian: Annals of the Xiaowu Emperor* (no. 12), and the *Book of Han: Annals of Emperor Gaozu* (no. 1), the *Book of Han: Annals of Emperor Hui* (no. 2), the *Book of Han: Annals of Empress Lü Zhi* (no. 3), the *Book of Han: Annals of Emperor Wen* (no. 4), the *Book of Han: Annals of Emperor Jing* (no. 5) and the *Book of Han: Annals of Emperor Wu* (no. 6).

[17]In the *Book of Han: Traditions of the Xiongnu* (no. 64 part 1), it is written: "In the 14th year in the reign of Emperor Xiaowen, the Xiongnu Chanyu led 140,000 cavalrymen into Zhunuo and Xiaoguan. They killed Commander Mao of Beidi and captured a large number of people and livestock. They advanced to Pengyang and had their cavalrymen break into the palace at Huizhong and burn it. The mounted scouts advanced to Ganquan Palace in Yong. Thereupon Emperor Wen appointed Zhou She, Capital Garrison Commander, and Zhang Wu, Chamberlain for Attendants to command an army of 1000 chariots and 10,000 horsemen stationed by Chang'an. The emperor also made Marquis of Chang (Lu Qing) General of Shang Commandery, Marquis of Ning (Wei Xiu) General of Beidi, Marquis of Longlü (Zhou Zao) General of Longxi, Marquis of Dongyang (Zhang Xiangru) a grand general, and Marquis of Cheng (Dong Chi) a general. These generals led a mighty army with a great number of chariots and cavalrymen into a fight with the Xiongnu. By

invasion with 140,000 men. The Emperor Wen responded by sending five senior military commanders to "lead a mighty army with a great number of chariots and cavalrymen into a fight with the Xiongnu." However, "The Chanyu had stayed within the Great Wall for more than a month, but the Han troops… didn't inflict any casualties." Although the historians record that "As soon as they chased the enemy beyond the Great Wall, the Han troops returned," the failure to kill even one Xiongnu in a month of war makes it clear that it was not so much that the Xiongnu had been driven out as they were indeed dictating the ebbs and flows of the conflict.

When put together, these facts imply a terrible consequence: "peace" is not a problem, since it is gained by giving way again and again. However, if one party is being bullied to the point of losing all patience, what happens then?

At this point, the opinions of Chao Cuo began to gain traction in the Western Han central government.

In his opinion, only military offense against the Xiongnu would serve as an effective deterrent against Xiongnu attacks. "To fight battle with battle" was considered to be the only way out. His viewpoints are mostly reflected in three memorials he made to the court on the matters of military reform and the enhancement of Han defense capabilities. (*Book of Han: Yuan Ang and Chao Cuo*, no. 19.)

In his first memorial, Chao Cuo focused on proposing military reform in the areas of terrain, weaponry, tactics, command, etc., based on the respective strengths and specific characteristics of the Western Han and Xiongnu armies. However, he might have felt that his proposed solution would not immediately mitigate issues of defense on the northern borders, the Xiongnu's incessant breaching of Han borders and the problem of agriculture.[18] Hence, in his second and third memorials to the throne he further proposed the measures of moving Han people to border regions as

(Footnote 17 continued)

then the chief of the Xiongnu had stayed within the Great Wall for more than a month. As soon as they chased the enemy beyond the Great Wall, the Han troops returned without inflicting any casualties. As a result, the Xiongnu grew even more arrogant and presumptuous. They crossed the border each year to kill and capture large numbers of people, especially in Yunzhong and Liaodong, with over 10,000 people killed in either of them. Deeply concerned about the situation, the Han Empire sent a letter to the Xiongnu through an envoy, and the chief of the Xiongnu sent his representative to return the compliment. The issue of heqin (peace through marriage ties) was brought up again between the two sides." A similar account can be found in *Records of the Grand Historian: The Xiongnu* (no. 50).

[18]"Now the Xiongnu migrate from place to place, grazing and hunting crossing the border, either in Yan and Dai, or in Shang Commandery, Beidi and Longxi. If soldiers garrisoning a fortress are short in number, they will cross the border. Sire, if you do not send a force to their rescue, people in the border areas will despair and consider surrender an option; if you send a small rescue force, the strength remains short; if you mobilize and send a larger one from faraway counties, before it arrives, the Xiongnu will have fled. If you do not disband the force, the expenses will be great; if you do, the Xiongnu will invade again." See the *Book of Han: Yuan Ang and Chao Cuo* (no. 19).

a way of securing these regions, encouraging defense by civilians and the establishment of settlements in close proximity to each other. On the subject of populating border regions with migrants as a means to secure the frontiers, he emphasized the need to improve public services and the provision of benefits including the granting of local titles, the possibility for the redemption of servants, the granting of assistance for migrants to establish their households, the granting of property and money, the granting of means of production and accommodation to attract "long-term residents" who would replace posted troops who were relieved once a year. In terms of encouraging civilians in these regions to take up defense, he recommended the establishment of a strong and financially well-endowed local force that would be familiarized with life in the border regions, the skills of horse riding and archery, and the appropriate battle environments. It was also suggested that local residents be encouraged to extend help to each other in times of emergency. As for the dense construction of towns, it was required that every town "should consist of no less than 1000 households" so that they and sentry posts could support each other to make it less likely for the Xiongnu to enter the Han territory and increase the difficulty of their aggression. These three measures became part of what was subsequently termed as the concept of "*tuntian.*"

Chao Cuo's suggestions were adopted by the central government. According to the Book of Han, after Chao's second memorial on the Xiongnu issue to the court, the Emperor Wen decided to accept his suggestion and began the policy of "recruiting migrants to the frontiers" in 169 BCE.[19] In the time of the Emperor Wu, *tuntian* was further implemented on a large scale as a means of defending against and even conquering the Xiongnu and other peoples of the Western regions. At least three rounds of large-scale *tuntian* were implemented: in summer 127 BCE, "100,000 migrants were sent to Shuofang, with another more than three million sent to Maoling"; in 119 BCE, "a total of 725,000 impoverished persons of Guandong were moved to Longxi, Beidi, Xihe, Shang Commandery and Kuaiji".[20] In 111 BCE, "A total of 600,000 officials and troops were posted to Zhangye, Jiuquan, Shang Commandery, Shuofang, Xihe and Hexi to defend the local lands."[21]

Later on, the concept of *tuntian* was further developed into variants such as juntun, mintun and fantun, measures which were also adopted by subsequent dynasties in China for defensive purposes. The establishment of the Xinjiang Production and Construction Corps in October 1954 and the Heilongjiang Production and Construction Corps in August 1968 following the founding of the People's Republic of China in 1949 can be regarded as modern applications of the concept of *tuntian*.

---

[19]*Book of Han: Chao Cuo.*

[20]*Book of Han: Annals of Emperor Wudi* (no. 6).

[21]*Book of Han: Treatise on Food and Money.*

5.3 Military and Tax Substitution

The Western Han found itself in a much improved position in terms of its ability to tackle threats on its land border following the implementation of the strategy of *tuntian*.

As expected, as *tuntian* took place in earnest in border regions in the north, northwest, southwest and southeast such as Shuofang, Xihe, Jiuquan, and Maoling, the Western Han military also underwent a fundamental change in terms of its position vis-à-vis both the Xiongnu and other external threats.

Records show that between 133 BCE and 92 BCE the Western Han engaged in significant combat with the Xiongnu, Korea, as well as Western kingdoms such as the Western Qiang and the Dayuan on a total of 17 occasions.[22] The Han either

[22]In the sixth month of 133 BCE, it was summer. "Censor-in-Chief Han Anguo was made Army-Protecting Commandant; Palace Garrison Chamberlain Li Guang, Commandant of Courageous Cavalry; Chamberlain for the Palace Stables Gongsun He, Commandant of Light Chariots;Minister of Ethnic Affairs Wang Hui, Commander of Garrison Troops; and Superior Grand Master of the Palace Li Xi, Commandant of Reserve Troops. Together, they commanded an army of over 300,000 stationed in Mayi Valley, lured the Chanyu and attempted to ambush him. He crossed the border but sensed their scheme. Thus he fled away."

In 129 BCE, Wei Qing led the first-ever Western Han military victory over the Xiongnu, pursuing them "all the way to Longcheng and killing some 700 Xiongnu."

In 128 BCE, "General Wei Qing was sent out of Yanmen Pass, while General Li Xi was dispatched out of Dai Commandery. A few thousand Xiongnu were killed."

In 127 BCE, "Generals Wei Qing and Li Xi were dispatched from Yunzhong to Gaoque. The troops then moved on to Fuli, where they killed several thousand Xiongnu."

In 124 BCE, "Great General Wei Qing led six generals and over 100,000 troops to Shuofang and Gaoque, killing five thousand enemies."

In 123 BCE, "in the second month of spring, Great General Wei Qing rode out to Dingxiang with six generals and over 100,000 troops, killing over three thousand of the enemy." A month later, Wei Qing led the same troops to a "massive victory" during which "19 thousand Xiongnu were killed".

In the spring of 121 BCE, "(Emperor Wudi) sent Huo Qubing, Commandant of Courageous Cavalry, to lead a force out of Longxi. In Gaolan, it harvested more than 8000 enemy heads." In the summer, "Huo Qubing and Gongsun Ao led a force more than 2000 *li* north. They went beyond Juyan and brought back over 30,000 enemy heads." In the autumn, "King Kunye of the Xiongnu killed King Xiutu and surrendered with his followers, totaling over 40,000. (Emperor Wudi) relocated them in five vassal states located in the Prefectures of Wuwei and Jiuquan."

In the winter of 119 BCE, "General-in-Chief Wei Qing, assisted by four generals, went out by way of Dingxiang. General Huo Qubing marched out by way of Dai. Each commanded a force of 50,000 horsemen. They were followed by hundreds of thousands of footmen. Wei Qing surrounded the Chanyu in Mubei and harvested 19,000 enemy heads. He did not return until his force reached the Tianyan Mountains. Huo Qubing engaged the Left Virtuous Kingand cut off and brought back over 70,000 enemy heads. He returned after he offered sacrifices to Heaven in the Langjuxu Mountains. The two forces suffered tens of thousands of deaths."

In 111 BCE, "(Emperor Wudi) sent an army of 100,000 combining horsemen from Longxi, Tianshui and Anding and footmen from Zhongwei, Henan and Henei commanded by General Li Xi and Chamberlain for Attendants Xu Ziwei to launch an expedition against Western Qiang and conquered it."

walked away with nothing or very little from four conflicts that occurred prior to 127 BCE. However, following the implementation of *tuntian*, a significant change occurred in terms of the number of enemies killed, with the number climbing easily into the tens of thousands.

Furthermore, after the implementation of *tuntian* the Han's superiority in military mobilization and frequency of battle also began to emerge. Prior to 133 BCE, the Western Han was essentially passive players when engaged in conflict with the Xiongnu, often caught helpless when attacked by the Xiongnu as they had difficulty mobilizing enough troops to exert pressure on the enemy. Such attempted mobilizations tended to hurt the economy, with troops mobilized returning without much gain or glory and disbanded after a short period of time.[23] However, after 124 BCE, i.e., 3 years after the large-scale implementation of the *tuntian* policy, the situation changed completely for the Han. Not only were they able to mobilize hundreds of thousands of troops at one go, they were also able to put larger armies to conflicts at

(Footnote 22 continued)

In 110 BCE, "(Emperor Wudi) sent Yang Pu, Commandant of Storied Ships, and Xun Zhi, Left Commandant, to command a force of recruited offenders to attack Korea. Then he sent General Guo Chang and Commandant of Court Gentlemen Wei Guang on an expedition against Ba and Shu. They subdued those disobedient in the wild Southwest. Then he established Yizhou Prefecture."

In 104 BCE, "(Emperor Wudi) sent General Li Guangli to command a force of guilty men to conquer Dawan in the west."

In 100 BCE, in spring "Li Guangli, General of Er Shi, cut off the King of Dawan's head and brought back "blood-sweating" horses as spoils."

In 99 BCE, "In the 5th month, it was summer. The General of Er Shi led a force of 30,000 horsemen to march out by way of Jiuquan and engaged the Right Virtuous King in the Tianshan Mountains. He harvested over 10,000 enemy heads. Then the emperor sent the General of Yinyu to go beyond Xihe and Commandant of Cavalry Li Ling to go north of Juyan with a force of 5000 under his command. They engaged the Chanyu and inflicted over 10,000 deaths on the enemy."

In the spring of 97 BCE, (Emperor Wudi) accepted the tributes from the feudatory princes in Ganquan Palace. "(He) sent Li Guangli, General of Er Shi, to lead a force of 60,000 horsemen and 70,000 footmen out of Shuofang; Gongsun Ao, General of Yinyu, to lead a force of 10,000 horsemen and 30,000 footmen out of Yanmen; Han Yue, General of Mobile Corps, to lead a force of 30,000 footmen out of Wuyuan; and Lu Bode, Commandant of Strong Archers, to lead a force of over 10,000 footmen to join forces with the General of Er Shi."

In the 3rd month of 90 BCE, it was spring. "(Emperor Wudi) sent Li Guangli, General of Er Shi, to command a force of 70,000 out of Wuyuan; Shang Qiucheng, Censor-in-Chief, to command a force of 20,000 out of Xihe; and Ma Tong, Marquis of Chonghe, to command a force of 40,000 horsemen out of Jiuquan. Shang Qiucheng engaged the enemy in the Junji Mountains and killed a lot of enemies."

See the *Book of Han: Annals of Emperor Wudi* (no. 6).

[23]After 133 BCE all the way to 127 BCE, although the Han army under the leadership of famed commander Wei Qing had tried to make the transition from a wholly defensive position to a defense strategy that is centered on offense, from the numbers of Xiongnu killed or captured (hundreds to thousands) we can see that this was a preliminary stage in the Western Han state's efforts. We can surmise that the Western Han troops were not of a significant size and were yet unable to truly put on a deadly offense against the Xiongnu. See the *Book of Han: Annals of Emperor Wudi* (no. 6).

a frequency that exceeded any other prior period during the Western Han. Generally speaking, not only did the Western Han troops perform increasingly well against the Xiongnu, they also turned in spectacular performances in terms of border defense conflicts, ushering a new age in the history of China.

While the spectacular improvement in military performance was certainly closely related to the cumulative effects of economic and financial policies under successive early Western Han rulers, we cannot neglect the impact of the policy of *tuntian* in terms of "military substitution." Just how significant was the effect of such substitution? We can obtain a good idea by answering the following two questions.

The first question is why did the Western Han army perform badly against the Xiongnu prior to the implementation of *tuntian* although large-scale troop mobilization had also been conducted? The second question is: why was the Western Han army unable to engage in sustained battle with invaders or against threats prior to the implementation of large-scale *tuntian*?

We cannot answer these questions simply from the perspective of economic strength. This is because compared to the early Western Han period, during the reigns of the Emperors Wen and Jing (180–141 BCE) the state's financial position had improved greatly. Although economically speaking the situation was not like in the time of the Emperor Wu (141–87 BCE) when "the people had enough to feed on and families were well supported, granaries both in the capital and in remote areas were filled, and there were surpluses in government warehouses"; and when "in the capital, so much money was hoarded that coin strings rot away and its amount could not be verified, fresh grain was put into granaries on grain from previous years every year that it overflew and was exposed to open air until it became rotten and inedible. Common people had their own horses, which could be seen in streets, and even more horses were roaming between field paths. Those who went to a gathering on a mare were turned away. Gatekeepers could afford to eat millet and meat,"[24] Ban Gu's description that "such a drastic change of customs and people's reversion to simplicity within 5–6 decades could only be found during the reigns of King Cheng and King Kang of the Zhou Dynasty and of Emperors Wen and Jing in the Han Dynasty"[25] can be regarded as realistic.

The answer can only be found in the fact that large-scale *tuntian* had indeed enhanced the strength of the Western Han military. This can be seen from the following:

First of all, the policy of *tuntian* had provided an endless stream of personnel for border defense forces. Even if scholars differ in opinion on the scale to which *tuntian* exerted an impact during the Western Han, almost all work on *tuntian* and

[24] *Records of the Grand Historian: Pinghuai* (no. 8).

[25] *Book of Han: Annals of Emperor Jingdi* (no. 5).

which involves the issue of Western Han defenses recognize the significance of the policy.[26]

Further, the fact that *tuntian* personnel were an important component of border defenses also means that their presence contributed to a significant enhancement in the Hans' battle capability. Compared to their predecessors, these battle personnel were more familiar with the frontier environment as well as fighting on horseback and in mountainous terrain. Moreover, as their families were settled in the border regions, they also fought with added courage and energy since protecting the country meant protecting their homes, and vice versa. "Protecting the country" for them was a far less abstract concept compared to troops from elsewhere whose homesickness typically undermined their fighting spirit. Hence, there was a significant difference both in terms of the level of fighting spirit and battle capability exhibited between the *tuntian* settlers and their predecessors who were posted from faraway lands.

Finally, with the *tuntian* policy border defenses forces could be rested as well as access ration supplies more quickly. Following the implementation of the *tuntian* policy, as *tuntian* settlers were often also soldiers, defense forces could be rested and access ration supplies as soon as they returned from the battleground to *tuntian* settlements. This was in contrast to previous arrangements, where troops had to return to their respective originating garrisons (many of which were deep inside the Central Plain)[27] for rest. Sometimes, a great part of the troops had to be relieved,[28] and then march back and forth between the battleground and their originating garrisons in a process that would take 1 year or more in total. Undoubtedly, the implementation of the *tuntian* policy effectively shortened the troop relief cycle and the distances traveled for such a purpose.

Between Wei Qing's chain of attacks against the Xiongnu in spring 123 BCE and Huo Qubing's stream of offenses against the Xiongnu in the spring and summer of 121 BCE was an extremely short period of troop rest that was unimaginable prior to the large-scale implementation of *tuntian.* Prior to the implementation of the policy of *tuntian*, typically a number of years were needed for any large-scale mobilization of troops. This was true even when Wei Qing began to lead offenses of

---

[26]Chen, Xiaoming (2003). A Comparison of Defence at the Northern Borderduring the Eastern and Western Han Periods. *China's Borderland History and Geography Studies*, no. 3; Huang, Jinyan and Chen, Xiaoming (1997). The Scale of Border Troop Deployment and Maintenance Costs during the Han Dynasty. *Researchesin Chinese Economic History*, no. 1; Lin, Chaomin (2005). Han Migrants and the Unification of Yunnan. *Journal of Yunnan Minzu University*, no. 3 (2005); Ma, Dazheng (2005). A Few Issues in the Study of the History of Xinjiang. *Shi Yuan*, no. 4 (2005); Qian, Mu (2005). *A History of the Qin and Han Dynasties*. Beijing: SDX Joint Publishing Company, pp. 152–161.

[27]During the early Western Han period, the troops deployed against the Xiongnu were regular soldiers whose originating garrisons were typically located deep within the empire.

[28]The typical border defense posting during the early Han was for a period of one year.

a limited scale against the Xiongnu: a period of almost 1 year separates each offense.

In addition, although evidence is scanty on this front we can still infer that *tuntian* settlers who had not been formally integrated into the defense formers also formed a sizable civilian militia that on one hand was able to withstand small-scale border attacks and hence relieve some pressure on the regular troops, while on the other hand providing support to regular troops during large-scale conflicts such as landing a hand in defense efforts, transporting rations to the troops, acting as guides for the troops, providing medical assistance, etc.

Apart from direct military substitution, the policy of *tuntian* also played a significant substitutive role in the area of taxation.

Given Chao Cuo's recommendations for *tuntian* and the actual benefits and support for *tuntian* settlers granted by the state, we can infer that the effect of tax substitution was an unintended effect of the *tuntian* policy, which at its infancy was only designed with border defense and not "profits" in mind.

However, with sustained implementation the financial benefits of the *tuntian* policy also became apparent, with the most salient benefit being the reduction in logistics costs.

During the Western Han, the cost of shipping one *dan* of rations to workers building the road to the southwest regions was a whopping 64 *dan*.[29] Given the heightened risks associated with the transport of military rations, the cost of moving rations for troops along the same distance would probably be even higher. In a memorial to the Emperor Wu, court official Zhufu Yan noted, "The cost of transporting rations was one *dan* per thirty *zhong*," meaning that the cost of shipping one *dan* of military rations to the northern borders during Qin times was 192 times that of the cost of the rations. (*Book of Han: Yan Zhu, Zhu Maichen, Wuqiu Shouwang, Zhufu Yan, Xu Yue, Yan An, Zhong Jun, Wang Bao and Jia Juanzhi*, no. 34 part 1.)

A conservative estimate by Huang Jinyan and Chen Xiaoming (1997) places the number of Western Han border defense troops at 300,000. Even if half of all military rations needed could be obtained locally the state would still have to arrange for the transport of four million *dan* of rations from elsewhere within the empire. After we factor in the distances to various border regions and account for terrain differences, using the transport rate of 64 *dan* for every *dan* of rations, the total cost of rations for the border troops and their families alone would be 25,600 *dan* or nearly five times the grain tax of 55,136,900 *dan* as calculated by Huang and Chen. That is to say, using the transport rate of 10 *dan* for every *dan* of rations transported as calculated by Huang and Chen, the total cost of military rations would come up to 79.8 % of the state's annual grain tax collection.

Since the number of border defense troops would be over 300,000 annually given the frequency of border conflicts, and considering the increase in rations

[29]In the Western Dynasty when "the road to the wild Southwest was opened up", "tens of thousands were conscripted to carry rations across hundreds of miles. Generally speaking, only 1 *dan* out of over 10 *zhong* (64 *dan*) could reach the destination." See *Records of the Grand Historian: Pinghuai* (no. 8).

required for cavalry horses, the rations needed for border troops each year would certainly exceed the eight million *dan* figure calculated by Huang and Chen. Hence, military rations would take up all of the state's grain tax collection. However, this is fundamentally impossible. These calculations would also make claims of 800,000–900,000-strong Western Han border defense troops even more implausible.

Hence, the grain tax collection calculated by Huang and Chen could not possibly have provided adequate support for repeated conflicts. However, records of military conflict are aplenty, and the Western Han Empire did, indeed, have border troops numbering 800,000–900,000 at its peak. Then, there are only four likely reasons for this discrepancy: (i) Huang and Chen overestimate the number of troops; (ii) they overestimate the food rations; (iii) they underestimate the grain tax figures, or (iv) estimates of the proportion of locally met ration needs are off.

When we look at studies of population changes as well as of military rations and taxation in the Western Han dynasty, we see that Huang and Chen had underestimated troop numbers and the amount the rations needed[30]; on the other hand, their estimates of grain tax collection are too high.[31] Hence, the first three explanations are not valid. Only the last explanation is possible. In other words, Huang and Chen had underestimated the extent to which the *tuntian* policy had contributed in terms of the rations and supplies needed by border defense troops, which was more than half as stated by the duo.

During the reign of the Emperor Wu of Han, the Western Han Empire moved several million settlers to the borders with the policy of *tuntian*. According to studies conducted by Xu Zhuoyun, these pioneers contributed around 40 % of the total rents. Based on this statistic, the rents turned into the army or the state by *tuntian* settlers together with the proceeds of occasional *tuntian* work by regular

[30]Huang Jinyan and Chen Xiaoming (1997) may have jumped to conclusions with their statement that Zhufu Yan had been exaggerated. Though Jia Yi's description supports Sima Qian's and Zhufu Yan's, this does not proves that the latter two exaggerate the difficulty of grain transport, because when Jia says that "it is hard to transport goods by sea even with money ten times of their worth spent", he is talking about sea transportation. It is common knowledge that the cost of sea transportation was lower than that of land transportation. Thus Huang and Chen's assertion that ten percent of the grains could reach the designated destination is questionable. Moreover, the "hire money" they mentioned was merely the spending on human labor. The wear and tear of vehicles and the consumption of cattle and horses have not been factored. Therefore, they have obviously underestimated the costs of transportation. In addition, in their estimates of border troop numbers during the Western Han period, Huang and Chen had omitted the southwestern and southeastern commanderies in their calculations. See Xin, Deyong (2005). Research on the Mass Migration to Kuaiji in the Reign of Emperor Wudi of Han. *Historical Research*, no. 1; Chen, Xiaoming (2002). Commentary of Economic Development in Border Commanderies in China's North and Southwest during the Han Period. *Jiangxi Social Sciences*, no. 11. Refer to Lei Haizong's study of the period of Emperor Wudi's reign in: Lei, Haizong (2001). *The Culture and Soldiers of China*. Beijing: The Commercial Press, pp. 28–32.

[31]During the reign of the Emperor Yuandi of Han, both population numbers and land development area numbers had vastly outstripped those of earlier periods.

troops and the grain tax collection from existing residents was probably sufficient to provide for a regular army of 300,000 to a million persons.

Over the years, Western Han moved from a tentative moving of small numbers of migrants to the borders to moving hundreds of thousands of *tuntian* settlers at a go (as many as 600,000) and then finally towards a policy of military *tuntian*. Apart from the relief on border defense this policy had brought, another key reason for the state's increasing reliance on *tuntian* was probably its success in providing rations for troops at the borders.

Zhao Chongguo's experiences in temporary *tuntian* at Huangzhong clearly illustrate this point.[32] In a memorial to the Emperor Xuan to request for *tuntian*, Zhao stated that "the grain consumed by my troops and their horses and cattle amounted to 199,630 *hu* monthly," while "the grain transferred from the Agricultural Directorate was sufficient to feed 10,000 persons for a year." Hence, he believed that the practice of *tuntian* would help to mitigate the problem of supplies for his troops and also "lead to surpluses and great savings."

The policy of *tuntian* was one that had helped the state save on military ration expenses as well as on the costs of shipping rations and other supplies to border regions.

From the perspective of public management, these costs would have been borne by all citizens of the country—in the form of tax collection—since they have arisen from the management of public goods.[33] Certainly, the policy of *tuntian* had helped the state to save on expenses that would have been otherwise drawn from tax collection: hence, it served as an effective means of tax substitution.

The military and tax substitutive effect of the policy of *tuntian* gave the Western Han Empire the wherewithal to effectively resist the harassment and threats from powers of other political persuasions outside of its borders and to create a peaceful and stable domestic environment for further economic development.

Although the practice of *tuntian* as well as sustained border troop postings had once stretched the Western Han budget to an impossible point, following decisive victories over the Xiongnu and the peoples of the Western regions, the southwest, the eastern Yue and Korea, the Western Han economy recovered swiftly alongside population numbers as peace was regained. As a result, "by the reign of Emperor Zhao, refugees had returned, more fields were being worked, and slight surpluses were being created. After Emperor Xuan had ascended the throne… the people were settled and secure, with rich harvests for years bringing the cost of grain to five *qian* per *dan*."[34] Thus, Qian Mu was right in saying that the policy of *tuntian* "showed significant impact from the time of Emperors Zhao and Xuan."

---

[32]*Book of Han: Zhao Chongguo and Xin Qingji* (no. 39).

[33]Although the military was compensated by the state for rations generated through its *tuntian* efforts, the policy of *tuntian* had contributed significantly to the savings in tax collection by reducing the cost of shipping rations and other supplies to border regions.

[34]*Book of Han: Treatise on Food and Money* (no. 4 part 1).

5.4 The Formation of Assimilation, Deterrence and Borders

As the policy of *tuntian* was largely carried out in the border regions where the existing population was sparse, the Western Han policy of *tuntian* was a key factor in the development of border regions such as Xinjiang, Gansu and Ningxia.

First of all, the policy of *tuntian* brought knowledge of agricultural practices to border regions. Plant seeds, agricultural tools, and agricultural methods from the Central Plain were imported and used widely. Irrigation works were also conducted.[35] According to Zhang Zexian, the policy of *tuntian* was a key factor in promoting agricultural development in the northwestern border regions during the Han period.[36] Studies on economic history in Xinjiang also show that the policy of *tuntian* during the Western Han and other periods had contributed to the development of much disused land.[37] The policy of *tuntian* had also led to more vibrant economies, with trade growing in both scale and scope. As the economy became more stable, regular market gatherings also began to appear.

Trade and agricultural development led to greater prosperity in the border regions. To take the northern regions of the Ulan Buh Desert as an example: these were originally sparsely populated spots, however, after Emperor Wu had established the Shuofang Commandery and particularly after the Xiongnu had been completely conquered during the reigns of Emperors Zhao and Xuan, "For generations, no beacon fire could be seen. People multiplied and cattle and horses overran the fields." "...border fortresses were securely shut. Cattle and horses overran the fields. For three generations, no alarm of dog barks could be heard and the people were free of military duty and conscript labor."[38] This was how successful the development of the border regions then was.

With development in the border regions, different peoples began to assimilate and China's traditional northwestern borders began to coalesce.

The rulers of Western Han had established the basic model for the policy of *tuntian* in border regions that future dynasties would also employ, i.e., the moving of troops or settlers toward border regions where they would live together with the local people.

The foremost advantage that the policy of *tuntian* had brought to military affairs was building up effective deterrence. On one hand, the strong influence of the state required various border peoples, especially those who were historically weaker, to accept the *tuntian* settlers and their families and to work and live together with the

[35]Wang, Yong (2005). The Promotion of Winter Wheat in the Guanzhong Plain during the Mid to Late Western Han Dynasty. *Journal of Chinese Historical Geography*, no. 3.

[36]Zhang, Zexian (1998). Description of Agricultural Production in the Hexi Corridor in the Han and Tang Dynasties. *Journal of Chinese Historical Studies*, no. 1.

[37]Qi, Qingshun and Tian, Weijiang (2006). *Xinjiang in History*. Urumqi: Xinjiang People's Publishing House.

[38]*Book of Han: Traditions of the Xiongnu*.

newcomers and to facilitate their quick assimilation; on the other hand, *tuntian* settlers also served as a deterrent to local peoples with their presence, giving them cause to think twice as the cost of any disorder or resistance on the part of local people had been raised with increased settler presence.

But because this kind of deterrence was of a righteous nature and founded on the principles of zero slavery, exploitation and oppression, with the goal of promoting tolerance, equality and harmony among the various peoples, there were no bitter disputes between the locals and the newcomers; instead, the policy had brought greater understanding of the state and *tuntian* settlers among the locals. Following the implementation of the policy of *tuntian* during the Western Han, there have also been instances where certain weaker peoples of the Western regions actually requested for *tuntian* to be implemented by the central government in their lands.

When a group of "outsiders" settle in a village, they may invite either suspicion or curiosity and friendliness on the part of the locals. Over time, with contact, communication, interaction, and mutual influence, both groups will naturally look on each other as neighbors and partners. Moreover, in the case of *tuntian*, its righteous implementation had also helped in converting the locals. Hence, eventually, as history shows, the various border peoples assimilated with each other, learning from each other and improving their lives in the processes.

The assimilation of different peoples in border regions was effectively also the process of integrating Huaxia civilization (chiefly in the form of agricultural civilization at that point) with cultures of the places where *tuntian* was implemented (chiefly in the form of nomadic civilization). It was also the process of integrating these regions into China. If Huaxia civilization could coexist with those cultures, and if the local cultures triumphed over Huaxia civilization in the course of competition, leading to effective resistance to, elimination of, or consolidation of the former, then China's borders would effectively stop at this point. This was the reason for ancient China's failure to absorb or conquer what is Korea today as well as Vietnam on several occasions. Hence, the assimilation of various peoples in border regions played an indirect role in propagating Chinese civilization and extending China's borders.

5.5 Border Regions and the Creation of Property Rights

As Owen Lattimore has pointed out, in places where the Western Han had implemented the *tuntian* policy, that is, areas where agricultural and nomadic practices as well as the Han and minority peoples intersected, property rights were in constant flux for a significant period of time due to contestation between the power of the Central Plain and the grassland tribes. Examples of such contests include the Qin and Han empires' struggle against the Xiongnu for control over the middle and upper reaches of the Yellow River and for control of the northern and southern parts of Yinshan Mountain region in the north, as well as for control for the area south of the Liao River and Greater Khingan Range in the northeast. Other such areas contested between the Western Han and the peoples of the Western regions or the Xiongnu in the west include swathes of territory stretching from Tianshan Mountain all the way to Lake Balkhash and the Ferghana valley and from the Pamirs all the way to the Yellow River. In areas where the coercive power of public authority was not exercised, where various rights had not been classified and where there were no peaceful legal relationships at play, i.e., before the so-called sovereignty issue was settled, property rights fundamentally did not exist. This situation is similar to the situation China finds itself in today, with regard to its maritime rights and interests vis-à-vis surrounding nations.[39]

However, through the implementation of the policy of *tuntian*, the Western Han eventually triumphed over the Xiongnu, first realizing property rights and then eventually sovereign rights in these border regions. Furthermore, the solution could not have been simpler.

On several occasions, the Western Han state also recruited more well-off individuals in mass migrations to border regions.

To recruit the earliest *tuntian* settlers, the Western Han state offered a bevy of attractive conditions to potential recruits, such as the provision of disaster relief, the mitigation of penalty, the granting of noble titles and monies, etc. In addition, settlers were also given residences and means of production. Spouses were even arranged for the bachelor settlers. With these conditions, the Western Han had no problems recruiting settlers in sufficient numbers. In this case, how did the state manage to entice the more well-off to move to the border regions?

There are only two reasonable explanations here: the first is that trade in the border regions was especially lucrative, and the second, the more well-off were attracted by future property rights with the *tuntian* policy. The Western Han attached great importance to agricultural practice and the use of land. Since *tuntian* was but a short-term state policy, once the military dispute was over the policy would become void and the management of *tuntian* lands would fall into private hands. As such, taking part in *tuntian* in border regions naturally became an excellent opportunity for entrepreneurship and investment. After all, many court officials and members of the royal family had made their fortunes on the back of land possession (Yang Shengmin 1990). For example, we have a letter written on a bamboo strip by a Han *tuntian* settler thanking a certain official for bringing him to the southwest as part of the *tuntian* migration. The writer, we learn, had been living in poverty, but in the southwest he was able to establish a household and become wealthy.

Apart from the aforementioned benefits granted to all *tuntian* settlers, the more well-off migrants also possessed the capability to perform land management on a more significant scale for even better development of such lands. These individuals

[39]Lattimore, Owen (2006). *The Inner Asian Frontiers of China*. (Tang, Xiaofeng. trans.) Nanjing: Jiangsu People's Publishing, pp. 37–68.

also received certain privileges from the state to do so. For instance, in the early days of the *tuntian* policy the state granted large swathes of land to these individuals at reduced prices or even for free, and even purchased agricultural products and livestock from these individuals. As a result, the fortunes of these individuals grew exponentially, creating many wealthy merchants and businessmen in the process.[40]

However, the enticing potential offered by *tuntian* does not mean that participating settlers were able to obtain easily what is akin to property rights today. At the very most what they obtained are "property rights on paper." Moreover, even if they were able to fill their coffers for a time did not mean that they would be able to provide for generations and generations of descendants to come. During the Western Han period, the borders between China proper and the lands of the grassland tribes were heavily contested, and control of these lands was continually in flux. However, as mentioned above, the *tuntian* settlers were happy to head to the border regions for these "property rights on paper." Some migrants engaged in both production and military defense, while others plowed the land and guarded the borders. Such multitasking by migrants eventually helped the state to realize "property rights on paper" into property rights proper, and for the state property rights were no longer contested and sovereign rights gained.

Lessons for us.

The Western Han government had, at a time it was unable to provide effectively the public good that is national defense, found a substitutive method: the policy of *tuntian*. Not only did implementation of the policy help the Western Han Empire tackle the problems of lack of skills in mountain warfare and cavalry action among its troops, it also resolved the problems of troop recruitment and mobilization and of supplies transport. Further, the policy was also unexpectedly helpful in relieving pressures on the state budget, in stabilizing the Western Han's borders, in assimilating different peoples, and in the clarification and classification of property rights, etc. The policy was certainly the stone that killed several birds, so to speak. So, how can we apply this experience to China's predicament on the seas today, and what lessons can we draw?

The most direct lesson we can draw is: the policy created a positive cycle where the economy, the local governments and military forces provided mutual aid to each other and reinforced each other's participation.

The fundamental idea behind the policy of *tuntian* is the creation of a positive cycle between the economy, the local governments, and military forces. Why did the Western Han Empire shift large numbers of migrants towards its land borders under the policy of *tuntian*?

[40]Zhu, Shaohou (2004). A Discussion of the *Mingtian* System and the Damage Caused by the System during the Han Dynasty. *Journal of Henan University*, no. 1.

The first reason would be to nurture the strong need amongst its people for land border security. As the number of people living in border regions increased, the desire of the people for border security and for a prosperous environment became even more aligned with the need for national unification. This alignment was the basis for the people's stronger desire for border protection by the state and for the maintenance of national borders.

Second, the policy would provide a steady stream of troops who have the right capabilities and were highly motivated. These troops, whose lives and families were also rooted in the border region, were more familiar with the local environment and terrain. Further, they were even stronger believers in the need for protecting the country and were more likely to put in their all during combat.

Third, the policy would also enhance the sense of honor amongst troops as well as underscore the importance of the local people they were meant to protect. Living with the border population meant that troops would have been able to witness the everyday joys of locals living in peace and abundance, joys which was their responsibility to protect. On the other hand, they would also recognize the importance of the local population when receiving supplies and other logistical support from locals.

China may wish to borrow from this line of thinking as it seeks to bring its development to the seas at a quicker pace and realize a complete set of maritime rights and interests. For instance, China can encourage its people to settle in coastal areas, as well as more investment into maritime-related industries. The Chinese navy can also look into focusing its recruitment efforts in coastal areas.

Care must be taken in the process to have all stakeholders fully motivated. During the Western Han, *tuntian* was realized with measures such as the granting of property rights gratis as well as settlement assistance. Troops and retired soldiers were granted land management rights for agricultural land, hence reassuring the troops, while the favorable conditions created for the businessmen led to the provision of much-needed logistic services and the development of border trade. In order to nurture the concept of maritime development among its people nationwide to the point that it becomes an integral part of national culture, China must also take the corresponding measures so that the high seas become a matter of survival for the local governments, enterprises, the civilians, and the military.

The biggest lesson we can draw here is: borders that can withstand the test of time are the result of continued competition between both disputing parties in border regions through a trial-and-error approach.

During the Western Han, the policy of *tuntian* was chiefly implemented in areas contested by the Han and the nomadic peoples. The state of flux in terms of Han/nomadic control of these areas can be, to a certain extent, regarded as a process of trial-and-error on both sides in terms of cost-and-benefit analysis.

There are two levels to this process: on one level, it was a contest in terms of the production efficiency between the agricultural ways of life versus the nomadic way of life. On another level, it was a contest between both parties in terms of their management (rule or war) efficiency.

Generally speaking, the latter is easily affected by the former.[41] Where the situation is unstable with the former, with no clear sign of resolution, the latter would also be in a similar state of disarray. This is because from the management perspective both parties typically had expectations of future benefits that vastly outstrip the realities. This gap between expectations and reality was expressed in the constant state of flux in terms of the party exerting control in these border regions. However, as the dust settled over the first level of trial-and-error, the trial-and-error process at the second level would also come to an end, as any comparison of both parties' management efficiency at this point would become rather straightforward: the measurement of one's overall political control capabilities and the cost of managing the border region in question based on a certain level of utility from such management.

In the latter part of the conflict between the Western Han Empire and the Xiongnu, both parties improved on what was the strength of its counterpart. That is to say, both parties made use of land resources in accordance with the principle of utility maximization.[42] At this point, whether either party chose to attack, retreat, fortify or abandon their positions were fully determined by whether they were able to mobilize for political control and consolidate sufficient resources to meet the cost of territorial management. "Without the Qilian Mountains, our livestock cannot multiply; without the Yanzhi Mountains, our women have no supply of rouge." The Xiongnu had decided to retreat north rather than counterattack despite Qilian and Yanzhi Mountains being so important to them precisely because they were not a match for the Western Han.

---

[41]If a particular region did well agriculturally under the control of the Western Han government, then during the cost-benefit "trial" process the Western Han Empire would have gained another reason to establish more institutions or implement more management measures in this region, as well as another reason to go to war for this region. The converse is also true. For the nomadic peoples, the logic for the cost-benefit analysis for territorial control was the inverse: for them, from the perspective of production utility the value of a piece of land lay in whether it was suitable for grazing.

Of course, in the cost-benefit analysis conducted by both parties, as to which mode of production is more advantageous in the border region in question was not the be-all and end-all of the issue. Both parties also had to consider other factors like the cost of implementing political control and the cost of going to war, whether the territory in question was geographically strategic, whether they had access to sufficient monetary and military resources to sustain political control, etc. As relative strength between the two changed repeatedly over the long term, so did the specifics of any cost-benefit analysis either party would conduct with regard to political control from one time to another.

[42]Huang, Jingyu (2006). The State Equine Breeding System during the Western Han Dynasty as Understood from Bamboo Slip Records. *Nandu Xuetan* (*Journal of the Nanyang Normal University Faculty of Humanities and Social Studies*), no. 3; An, Zhongyi (2006). Horse Breeding during the Han Dynasty and the Improvement of Equine Breeds. *Agricultural Archaeology*, no. 4; Zhang, Liren (2006). Historical Exchanges and Cultural Consolidation between the Peoples of the Hexi Corridor. *Journal of Chinese Historical Geography*, no. 3; Zhang, Zexian (1998). Description of Agricultural Production in the Hexi Corridor in the Han and Tang Dynasties. *Journal of Chinese Historical Studies*, no. 1.

The importance of a country's strength to its ability to put up an effective resistance can be seen in the importance the Western Han had attached to border regions. After the defeat of the Xiongnu by the Western Han, had the latter stuck strictly to the maximization of the profit-cost ratio it would have settled on a border with the Xiongnu along the 800 mm annual rainfall line—a line that delineates the two modes of production as well as respective political influences—as Owen Lattimore describes. However, the Western Han's borders were actually far beyond this line, with vast swathes of grasslands also brought under Han control. The reason for this is the strategic significance of the border region: one's control over the region is further entrenched with greater control in terms of scale and influence.

In border regions, the borders between the Western Han and the Xiongnu were determined in a series of production competitions in what was a long period of trial-and-error. This historical process provides us with a highly practical perspective on how the future may look like with regard to China's current position in international maritime competition, and its island and territorial disputes with other nations.

Though the impact of the oceans on a nation's social development is not completely obvious today, the strategic significance of the oceans and disputed islands and territories to a nation is closely related to the nation's overall strength as well as its maritime development and exploitation capabilities. A nation's overall strength determines the relative value of relatively fixed maritime interests such as the transport arteries, islands, specific maritime territory, etc., while its capabilities of developing and utilizing marine resources determine the extent to which it is possible for the country to obtain benefits from the oceans. These two factors also determine the degree of a nation's participation and long-term investment in international maritime competition (including disputes over islands and other maritime territory).

Therefore, if China wants to emerge on top in international maritime competition, it must score the final victory in the matters of disputed islands and waters. The fundamental way to achieving this for China is to continue its active development of its economy in general as well as its maritime economy in order to grow its national strength as well as develop the relationship between national strength and the maritime economy. At the same time, state guidance and support should also be augmented so that China may be able to enhance its maritime development and exploitation capabilities as soon as possible. This way, as long as the government is able to work towards consolidating our various strengths, we would be able to achieve a satisfactory outcome for China in terms of maritime development and the protection of our sea power and sovereignty.

The third lesson for us here is: we must introduce plans that meet both defensive and developmental needs, and to leave room for trade and cultural exchanges.

To ensure that the oceans can be harnessed fully for China's development and that China will be able to realize a complete set of sovereign sea power, it is best that apart from enhancing its marine resource development and exploitation capabilities China can also strengthen its maritime defense capabilities in a targeted fashion to provide security for national development and China's maritime rise. This corresponds with the dual functionalities of the *tuntian* approach, i.e., the people living in the border region were engaged in both production and border defense.

Hence, given that it would take time and significant resources for China to enhance its marine resource development and exploitation capabilities as well as strengthen its naval strength in terms of funding, human and material resources, technology, etc., and that the risks of China's move to take its development to the oceans must be minimized at the same time, here, we propose a strategy similar to that of *tuntian*. This strategy, which can be applied to the building of a maritime power, to the enhancement of the nation's marine resource development and exploitation capabilities as well as its defense capabilities to a certain degree, is therefore a practical option.

This proposed strategy must include trade and cultural exchanges as a component, or otherwise support such exchanges, as these were also part of the experiences accumulated by the Western Han as they practiced *tuntian* against the Xiongnu.

In the early days of the Han-Xiongnu conflict, Jia Yi had proposed the "Three Models and Five Baits" (*san biao wu er*) strategy wherein the Western Han would use its abundant material goods, comparatively luxurious lifestyle, and vibrant culture to win over the Xiongnu while at the same time converting them through the values of respect, sincerity and amicability as communicated by the throne. The idea was to split the Xiongnu from within through the offering of these "sugar-coated bombs" so that the Chanyu "would not be able to get to sleep or taste the sweetness in his food."[43]

Jia Yi also wrote on the importance of the trading cities in border areas: "The more we give them, the hungrier they get; the richer they get, the boxed in they are." As trade volume increased, the Xiongnu would become even more reliant on Western Han markets and goods. At the same time, because of the gains they have obtained they would place an even greater emphasis on peaceful relations and further refrain from the use of force.

History shows that the strategy of "Three Models and Five Baits" did become an excellent complement to the policy of *tuntian* during the Western Han period. The Xiongnu's "concerns over the peaceful evolution" of the Western Han,[44] the crumbling of the Xiongnu in the face of Western Han attacks and the surrenders of the Xiongnu King Hunye and the Huhanye Chanyu all had to do with the Xiongnu's cultural and trade reliance on the Western Han.[45]

---

[43]*Xinshu: The Xiongnu.*

[44]Kong, Zhiguo (2008). Property Rights on Paper. *Cenfortuna*, no. 12.

[45]Yu, Ying-shih (2005). *Trade and Expansion in Han China: A Study in the Structure of Sino-Barbarian Economic Relations*. (Wu, Wenling, trans.) Shanghai: Shanghai Ancient Books Publishing House, pp. 39–178.

The fourth lesson to be drawn is: the state should take the lead in organizing and planning, with sovereignty a priority over interests.

Maritime development involves a number of facets. Not only will a disorganized state of affairs slow down the rate of development, it will also complicate efforts to establish a strong institutional force for the enhancement of China's marine resource development and exploitation capabilities. Hence, in order to properly implement the proposed strategy and other strategies designed to support both China's defensive capabilities and maritime developmental needs, we must look to the practice of *tuntian* to craft an overall plan. Further, this plan must be implemented in an organized, step-by-step and well-timed manner[46] to fully harness the power of consolidated resources and to minimize the impact of various obstacles. Not only was the policy of *tuntian* during the Western Han period the result of in-depth discussion, planning, organization and design, it was also promoted, implemented and managed by dedicated agencies.[47] This was why the Western Han was able to implement the policy on a broad-based manner swiftly and develop it to its subsequent scale.

In addition, in view of the current state of international maritime competition as well as the specifics of China's move to take its development to the oceans, an organized effort, which aims to enhance our marine resource development and exploitation capabilities and realize complete sovereign sea power, will reduce the probability of maritime disputes, as well as better prepare China for various unforeseen circumstances on the high seas.

Of course, in the process of the government planning and implementing a maritime power scheme that is similar to *tuntian* and which can afford defensive and developmental benefits, we can learn from one principle or concept from the practice of *tuntian* during Western Han times: the process of weighing benefits. In this case, sovereignty rights are more important than economic interests, while diplomatic isolation is as effective a tactic as outright confrontation. Hence, we must be ready to work at, and invest in, obtaining recognition for our sovereign rights and the diplomatic isolation of our competitors.

The policy of *tuntian* in the Western regions was an inconspicuous yet integral component of the overall Western Han strategy of *tuntian*. In contrast to *tuntian* in other regions, the practice of *tuntian* in the Western regions was sometimes insufficient in producing enough rations for the soldiers that were ensuring the smooth implementation of *tuntian* policy. However, the *tuntian* settlers here were also expected to provide rations for officials and troops of local regimes. To express support for local rulers in the Western regions, not only did the Western Han state accept land offered by these rulers for *tuntian* purposes, it also rewarded officials under these rulers with various valuable gifts and even Western Han noble titles.

---

[46]This point is also corroborated by our cost-benefit analysis of China's maritime rights and interests.

[47]Zhu, Heping (2004). On Civilian *Tuntian* during Han Dynasty. *Agricultural Archaeology*, no. 1.

The practice of *tuntian* thus, also became a diplomatic measure. It was precisely the show of generosity made by the Western Han towards local rulers in the Western regions over the course of *tuntian*[48] that led to the diplomatic isolation of the Xiongnu and accelerated the defeat of the latter.[49] Moreover, these regions where *tuntian* was practiced also became economic and military bases for the Western Han, ensuring security for trade between the Western Han and India, Parthia (Anxi), Rome, etc., along the Silk Road. Although we do not have a specific figure for the profits generated for the Western Han by the Silk Road, anecdotes of a pound silk costing as much as a pound of gold in Rome can give us some idea of the scale. So, did the Western Han turn in a profit or loss from the practice of *tuntian* in the regions? The value of the Western Han's *tuntian* management in the Western regions is worth further reflection.

The final lesson we can draw is: peace is better than war, culture is better than conquest, and we must strengthen deterrence.

Although the practice of *tuntian* did produce positive effects in a number of areas, including in military and tax collection terms, and it did contribute to the Western Han's eventual prevailing over its border crisis, the *tuntian* victory did not belong to everyone. Fundamentally speaking, peace is better than war. The development of society as a whole aside, the costs of engaging in war is a senseless type of cost in what is a negative-sum game. For the victorious Western Han government, it was able to grow China's wealth by investing financial, military and human resources to the areas of transportation, large-scale irrigation projects, the promotion of new production technologies, etc., without having to provide for war against the Xiongnu any longer.

This conclusion is also applicable for the scenario of international maritime competition. When we limit our perspective most narrowly to the element of practical interests, we will see that individuals, peoples and nations are indeed competitors in the same game. However, if we are to cast our eyes to the future, and to future benefits, we see infinite space for growth. Then, clearly, a cooperation between all parties in seeking a better understanding, development and exploitation of the oceans which in turn will promote the interests and advancement of the human race as a whole should be the most optimal and ideal choice. From this perspective, peace must always be prioritized as China seeks maritime development. The military option should only be used when absolutely necessary.

However, the lack of desire to resolve issues through military means does not imply that one should not possess such means. The implementation of *tuntian* during the Western Han period proves that as long as there is a military threat to peace a deterrent would be needed. Such a deterrent serves to maintain justice and

[48]Yu, Ying-shih (2005). *Trade and Expansion in Han China: A Study in the Structure of Sino-Barbarian Economic Relations*. (Wu, Wenling, trans.) Shanghai: Shanghai Ancient Books Publishing House, pp. 118–124.

[49]Yu, Ying-shih (2005). *Trade and Expansion in Han China: A Study in the Structure of Sino-Barbarian Economic Relations*. (Wu, Wenling, trans.) Shanghai: Shanghai Ancient Books Publishing House, pp. 114–115.

peace and ward off belligerents who seek to mine additional benefits through the use of force. Without sufficient military preparation, not only would the implementation of *tuntian* present challenges, the Western Han would never have had prevailed over the Xiongnu and won themselves a longer timeframe for economic development.

Today, China faces all sorts of military threats and even provocations on the high seas. Whereas we must continue to focus on a peaceful maritime rise, in particular, the peaceful development and exploitation of marine resources, and the peaceful resolution of island and other maritime territorial disputes, unless we are able to exert a deterrent effect on the aforementioned threats and provocations, China must continue to enhance its military strength. This will ensure the fulfillment of both citizens' needs for public goods of maritime security as well as China's developmental needs.

Chapter 6
Peaceful Rise: Strategic Prospect and Recommendations

The background to the policy of *tuntian* is rather similar to the challenging scenario that China faces today as it seeks to take its development to the oceans. The effects of the policy of *tuntian* are also similar to what China seeks to achieve—or even exceeds its objectives—with its maritime development push. As such, it is necessary for China to introduce a *tuntian*-like strategy that can take care of both the defensive and developmental thrusts of its plan to become an important maritime nation. Further, China should also see to matters such as its positioning on international maritime issues, improve its domestic maritime management capabilities, and examine its corresponding military measures and planning in detail. To show that this proposed strategy is similar to that of the policy of *tuntian*, particularly in that it can take care of both China's defensive and developmental thrusts of its plan to become an important maritime nation just as the policy of *tuntian* did for the Western Han, we can name this strategy "tunhai."

6.1 The Strategy Must Come First

The policy of *tunhai* is to be in service to China's maritime development strategy. It is but a part of the strategy, perhaps a key part at a certain developmental stage. Therefore, prior to implementing *tunhai*, we must first determine China's strategic goals in the area of maritime development. That is, we must fully understand what kind of maritime nation China wants to become, and what it wishes to obtain from the oceans.

To a certain extent, China has little choice in terms of what it must achieve as it follows the process of maritime development. Globalization, the deepening of trade links between China and the rest of the world, rising expectations among global partners with regard to China's international role, and the emphasis of the United Nations Convention on the Law of the Sea (UNCLOS) on resources as well as

Z. Kong, *The Making of a Maritime Power*, Research Series on the Chinese Dream and China's Development Path, DOI 10.1007/978-981-10-1786-5_6

resource development and exploitation in international waters and "regional waters": all these factors mean that China must become a great maritime nation.

However, China can choose the path with which it achieves this status. Perhaps China can state its position as such: unless it suffers invasions or violations of its sovereignty, China will seek to accomplish a peaceful rise as part of its strategy to become an international maritime power based on persuasion rather than coercion. To this end, it would seek to become an international leader in maritime development and exploitation, as well as take up the corresponding international responsibilities in the maintenance of international maritime order and guaranteeing the sustainable development of maritime territory around the world.

To support this strategy, China must have a military force that can provide Chinese enterprises, assets and personnel worldwide with reliable protection in international waters. Further, China must also have a security support system that comprises domestic and overseas military bases with the requisite logistics supply and carrier/aircraft maintenance resources as well as a 360°, round-the-clock response system featuring the participation of the military, local communities, governments, and civilians.

Based on current circumstances, China is now on the cusp of change and upgrading as it works toward its strategic goals. Looking at its maritime development and exploitation capabilities, and in terms of its shipbuilding, research and manufacture for large-scale marine equipment, maritime resources exploration and exploitation, ocean shipping, and port-building capabilities, etc., it is clear that China is already capable of becoming a top-tier maritime nation. At the same time, China is also working gradually toward shaping its navy and corresponding naval combat capabilities for the challenges of global engagement in terms of its delivery and ocean combat capabilities. These efforts are designed to achieve a military influence that is commensurate with China's economic and political influence.

However, we should also note that currently, awareness of the importance of the oceans is not sufficiently high among the Chinese people. Moreover, we lack a tradition of maritime activities as well as maritime industries armed with advanced technologies. All these are factors that may impede China's pursuit of the status of an important maritime nation. Furthermore, China also lacks a long-range delivery capability as well as overseas naval bases. The professional state and combat capability of its naval forces still remain to be tested at this stage. All these factors mean that China can, at best, be considered as a mid-tier maritime nation at present.

Hence, as China seeks to take its development to the seas, it must achieve two strategic goals. On one hand, it must fight for survival, namely resolving the Taiwan question and the issues of sovereignty over the seas. On the other hand, it must seek development at the same time, namely expanding the overseas markets, enhancing its maritime development and exploitation capabilities, and finding room for further development while seeking to ensure its security. What is positive is that the scale of China's domestic market and international trade provides us with the room for fighting for survival and seeking development at the same time. Our missile capability forms an effective global deterrent and also provides the room for further development while seeking to ensure the security.

What this means is that China's foremost task in the maritime arena at present is to realize the return of Taiwan and to achieve common ground on the resolution of maritime sovereignty issues as soon as possible. To this end, apart from negotiation with various parties, we must also work to exert pressure in the form of military deterrence and competition and cooperation on the civilian front. We should note that while negotiation with various parties is a targeted process, the military deterrence as well as competition and cooperation on the civilian front are in no way limited by spatial or target considerations. An oceanic military deterrent may relieve defensive pressures in surrounding waters, while competition and cooperation among other nations on the civilian front may aid in the resolution of disputes between China and countries concerned. Alternatively, an increase in China's trade and cultural exchanges with other countries and regions can also exert pressure on some other counterparts to head to the negotiating table with China sooner rather than later.

A policy of *tunhai* would provide great help in this process. With reasonable design, guidance, and arrangements, not only will we be able to move China from the passive position it is currently in with regard to the standoff in surrounding waters, we will also be able to strengthen our ability to control island and other maritime territory as well as our global competitiveness. Before China becomes an important maritime nation, military and civilian resources will complement each other to address inadequate military support for oceanic security. This way, we will be able to establish a usable and tractable system of oceanic security that prioritizes global trade with global security in a close second place.

6.2 Prerequisites for the Implementation of *Tunhai*

Once China's maritime development strategy, as well as the place of the policy of *tunhai* within this strategy, has been made clear, we can then look at creating an overall *tunhai* plan which will lay out the respective responsibilities of the central government, local governments at various levels and other relevant entities and also look at the areas, industries, and methods appropriate for the implementation of *tunhai*.

What we can be sure of at this stage is: the plan must realize a virtuous cycle between the economy, local governments, and the military, a cycle that further reinforces active participation by all parties. The government should provide the appropriate leadership and guidance to establish a national action plan with strategic vision. We must, from beginning to end, remember that competition that can withstand challenges is competition that is rooted in peace. We must be clear about what our long-term and short-term interests are, as well as what is more urgent and important, our sovereignty or economic interests. Trade and culture are a key part of full-on competition, and also a key factor that will determine the final outcome. We must maintain an effective deterrent in order to carve out room and time for a peaceful growth. These are fundamental principles for the policy of *tunhai* that we can draw from the *tuntian* experience, and can certainly be used in the course of establishing an overall *tunhai* plan.

However, we must also recognize that times and circumstances have changed since the policy of *tuntian* was implemented during the Western Han period. Therefore, we must have a clear understanding of the possible differences between *tunhai* and *tuntian*, so that we will be able to establish a *tunhai* plan that is tailored to the specifics of China's maritime development and China's needs in modern maritime competition.

On one hand, generally speaking, the challenges that China now faces are even greater and more complex.

First of all, though the capability of the Western Han forces could not compete with that of the Xiongnu in the beginning, the Western Han Dynasty held greater overall strength. However, the gap between China and its key opponents today in maritime development is even wider. Data from the International Monetary Fund show that in 2013, the combined GDP of the United States and Japan (USD 21.70 trillion) was 2.36 times that of China (USD 9.18 trillion). Numbers from the Stockholm International Peace Research Institute (SIPRI) in Sweden indicate that in 2013, the combined military expenses by the United States and Japan (USD 688.825 billion) were 3.65 times that of China (USD 288.460 billion). If we are also to take into consideration China's low military spending over the years and the fact that the American and Japanese militaries are equipped at a standard that is far higher than China's, we see that the actual gap may actually be even bigger.

Second, from the perspective of social development, the policy of *tuntian* was a contest between the agricultural and nomadic cultures. The Western Han was able to successfully implement the policy in part due to the competitive advantages of advanced agricultural technologies. Similarly, a strategy of *tunhai* would be a contest of maritime attainment. Although China has long encountered and lived with the seas, its reliance on, and familiarity with, the seas still lag far behind when compared to traditional maritime nations. Therefore, any implementation of *tunhai* by China would be a process of enhancing its competitiveness as well as a cultivation of its relationship with the seas as it seeks to boost its maritime development and exploitation capabilities.

Third, while the Western Han was able to isolate the Xiongnu in diplomatic terms through strengthening of its trade and cultural ties with neutral parties in the Western regions, it is not the case with China today. Not only is China facing encirclement and blockade by an alliance comprising the United States and Japan, it also encounters challenges in the areas of cultural and trade exchanges with neutral parties. There are a number of US allies among nations that have a neutral attitude toward China's maritime enterprise; however, no nation is an open ally of China, and currently there are also very few nations that are potential allies of China.

Finally, with soldiers expected to have much higher professional standards and the specific modes of modern warfare today, the military aspects of *tunhai* will be very different from those of *tuntian*. It is unlikely that *tunhai* enterprise would be able to provide support to, or play a substitutive role in, defense matters the way *tuntian* settlers were able to. In contrast to the practice of *tuntian*, the strategy of *tunhai* would have a stronger emphasis on economic contributions, including a specific focus on the careful defense and management of islands as well as the provision of encouragement and support to the development of coastal regions and maritime industries. This will ensure that the maritime economy can contribute to the steady development of China and at the same time help the maritime economy to become one of the key pillars of Chinese economic development in the future. The enhancement of China's maritime development and exploitation capabilities on all fronts is the path to the realization of China's dreams of becoming an important maritime nation.

On one hand, the increasing rationality in competition and growing impact of international pressure will, to some extent, mitigate the challenges and issues that China will face when implementing the strategy of *tunhai*.

Although the international situation is comparatively more complex today, conflicts arising from differences in religion, ideology, or national interests can develop into political turmoil or war. However, from the trend of social development, with globalization accelerated by developments such as the Internet as well as aviation and high-speed rail technologies, as society is being reshaped by 3D printing, gene technology, energy revolution, and the like, and as the human race faces possible catastrophe in future disputes in the form of space wars, information wars, and the nuclear threat, it is no longer conceivable for the world to plunge into another conflict of a scale similar to that of the First or Second World Wars. Competition between modern states will instead be focused on the enhancement of their technological and innovation capabilities, their resource integrating capabilities, and their cultural creativity.

This change means that any country that tries to resolve issues using military means today can expect to face widespread criticism given the ubiquity of information and expression channels. The US has been criticized for engaging in military conflicts in Afghanistan, Iraq, and Libya without exhausting all avenues toward peaceful resolution. The trend toward peaceful competition in the international maritime order is clearly a result of this new development in human society. This also means that in contrast to the context of the policy of *tuntian*, the policy of *tunhai* will be implemented in an external environment that is more rational and less imbued with impulse.

In addition, the flaws of the maritime order and the fact that China is the largest trading partner of countries such as the United States and Japan also mean that although China is currently being constrained by the US, Japan, and some other countries, in political, economic, and military terms and hence needs to behave with extreme caution in waters near and far, the chances of actual military conflict with these nations are remote.

This is because: first, the resurgence of piracy, drug trafficking on the seas and terrorism have created a knotty problem for various Indian Ocean nations as well as the United States. To go up against China, a country that has put in effort in the maintenance of the maritime order and which is interested in further participation at this point would be an unwise move. Second, as Robert D. Kaplan puts it, trade is the true conquering power in the maritime world. To choose conflict would be to abandon trade, and to abandon trade would lead to lower employment rates, negative market growth, and a shrinking in the goods supply. It would also lead to pressures on domestic governance. To engage in conflict with China is probably unthinkable for the likes of the US and Japan, both of which are still recovering from the 2008 global financial crisis.

From China's point of view, as it seeks to achieve further development in a peaceful manner, the chances of it belligerently going head-to-head with nations that stand in the way of its maritime rise are even lower. Under such circumstances, for China the strategy of *tunhai* is undoubtedly a good way to enhance its maritime capabilities on all fronts and to grow its influence on the seas while mitigating the risk of severe conflict at the same time.

On the other hand, in terms of the perspective, logic, expected effect, and specific implementation measures, etc., of the strategy of *tunhai*, there are also differences compared to the policy of *tuntian*.

First of all, the starting point is different. Although the implementation of *tuntian* did resolve the Western Han's issues in providing for national defense, both its proposer Chao Cuo and its implementer (the Western Han) saw it as a means worth trying in the absence of better ideas. Although from the implementation process we can see that a number of characteristics are compatible with the modern concept of the public good, the utility of the intent stands out: the policy was meant as a "fire-fighting" measure at a time of unstable control over border regions rather than a deliberate move to improve the livelihood of the people. Hence, it was implemented focusing more on the Western Han's ability to conduct offensive campaigns on land.

Today, if we are to blindly implement a *tuntian*-like policy on military premises the same way the Western Han did, and ignore the important fact that the provision of public goods both domestically and abroad is critical in any maritime competition, then the implementation of *tunhai* may, as a result, become mired in difficulties and fail to unleash the full potential of the strategy.

It is important to note that the strategy of *tunhai* should be aimed at plugging the gap in the provision of public goods such as state management and services, and national defense, and that it is being implemented in a situation where China's maritime development and exploitation capabilities are still lacking. As such, the matters involved cannot be regarded or treated as any other common administrative, commercial or enterprise behavior. The strategy is chiefly centered on the idea to obtain complete maritime rights and interests through nonmilitary competition. Together, the combination of peaceful competition and military deterrence form the offensive posture for the strategy of *tunhai* as China seeks further maritime development.[1]

[1]We describe *tunhai* as an offensive move chiefly due to the regions involved. Regions where the policy of *tuntian* was implemented during the Western Han period consisted of the land borders of the time as well as surrounding areas. These areas are far more tangible. On the other hand, the regions where the policy of *tunhai* is to be implemented are more abstract: apart from China's maritime borders, we are also looking at areas where China's maritime influence and interests—as advocated by international law—are located.

Therefore, there are also differences in terms of the functions of *tunhai* and *tuntian*. The primary aims of the *tuntian* policy were of a military nature, i.e., the provision of logistics security and support for the troops. The policy was a part of the state's offensive and defensive efforts toward the securing of its land rights. However, under special circumstances the strategy of *tunhai* can also help provide for military goals in logistics, personnel, and intelligence terms, its focus is actually on the strengthening of China's maritime capabilities on all fronts, the development of China's comprehensive marine resource development and harnessing capabilities, and the development of its ability to protect and realize its sea power. The strategy is, in itself, an effective means for China to realize its sea power. In other words, the military objective here is secondary.

Furthermore, in terms of how the policy is implemented, *tunhai* encompasses a broader array of options than *tuntian* thanks to the development of governance skills and socioeconomic progress. *Tuntian* was more a government-led process in which the government was solely responsible for mobilization, organization, and implementation, and the possible policies were limited to state-granted permissions, tax waivers, and property use rights granted gratis. On the other hand, with the strategy of *tunhai*, in addition to similar measures carried out based on macroscopic planning and orientation of state policies, we can also—in the position of funder—encourage and invite civilian participation through means such as financial allocation in order to enhance China's maritime development and exploitation both in terms of scale and variety of methods used. This way, we will be able to develop an environment where both the people and the state of China are dependent on the seas, become closer to the seas, and are willing to protect our maritime territory.

These changes mean that the specific implementation the *tunhai* policy involves many factors: economy, market, public services, the principle of peace, and modern maritime competition. Of course, as any implementation of the strategy of *tunhai* is predicated on adjustments to, and the clarification of, China's maritime development plans, such implementation may pose a challenge to the current maritime law framework. Therefore, the institutional aspect of *tunhai* also needs to be noted. In this light, there will be changes to the system of maritime law, to maritime management functions, and to the corresponding institutional arrangements. The model of cooperation between the military and local governments, and between the government and private sectors, will also require planning and other arrangements beforehand.

Hence, whether the strategy of *tunhai* can become a success is determined by the importance that various parties attach to the strategy as well as whether the necessary changes can be made to perceptions of, and attitudes toward the oceans.

China must forge a consensus on the importance of the seas to national security and our social and economic progress and must work in response to the domestic needs for maritime development when faced with international competition and the country's economic transformation. We should avoid a single-minded pursuit of the balance in regional development by relying on the administrative strength[2] or the use

[2]Civil means of local protectionism, and the household registration policy.

of noneconomically viable state investments[3] to eliminate or diminish any developmental advantages coastal regions may have over non-coastal regions, advantages which have arisen for reasons of geographic location, environmental factors, etc.

The role of the state is to provide, as much as possible, the public goods that are needed for maritime development. If the state is unable to provide such public goods in sufficient quantities, then it must prioritize areas of greater interest, particularly areas that can have a catalytic effect on maritime development. These areas include: shipping, talent development in trade-related matters, the development of advanced maritime technologies, overall planning of the development of maritime industries, etc. The state should focus its energies and resources on providing quality and effective public goods that in turn can provide a boost to China's maritime development. For public goods that cannot be provided for one reason or another, the state can encourage civilian participation to make up for any gap and resulting negative impact on China's maritime development.

Enterprises and individuals should, both in their work in maritime-related areas as well as day-to-day life in coastal areas, comply with the relevant international and domestic laws to minimize the unnecessary costs by the state as it seeks to manage their behavior. This will allow the state to use its limited resources in the most critical areas. At the same time, it would be best that individuals are able to provide viable recommendations for, or criticism of, the state's maritime development plans based on their personal observations and reflections. This is critical to the development of a broad-based consensus on such development and a Chinese maritime philosophy that will be recognized by the world.

Most importantly, China's maritime development should be conducted in an organized and coordinated manner. First of all, we have to incorporate the strategy, principles, and measures of China's maritime development plans into the Constitution, Basic Law and corresponding laws, regulations and policies. Second, for the implementation of China's maritime development plans,we should establish an effective and high-quality maritime management entity that would coordinate or manage all relevant maritime matters and in so doing, minimize the negative impact of years of poor planning and unclear division of responsibilities on China's maritime development. Finally, a logically coherent, systematic, and detailed plan should be released to the public.

6.3 Establishing the *Tunhai* Policy

Correspondingly, the first step for the *tunhai* framework would be to establish or adjust the corresponding systems, laws, regulations, and policies.

---

[3]Such investments include commitments of hundreds of millions, or even billions, to projects without consideration of the costs of transport and human resources or the resulting economic benefits.

First of all, the maritime development strategy must be embodied in our Constitution.

Our Constitution should highlight the importance of China's efforts to become an important maritime nation, as well as provide the corresponding support. Recommendation: To amend the section of the preamble in the Constitution which reads: "Taiwan is part of the sacred territory of the People's Republic of China. It is the inviolable duty of all Chinese people, including our compatriots in Taiwan, to accomplish the great task of reunifying the motherland." to "Taiwan is part of the sacred territory of the People's Republic of China. China's territory includes both land territory and maritime territory to which it has placed sovereign claims. It is the inviolable duty of the entire Chinese people, including our compatriots in Taiwan, to accomplish the great task of reunifying the motherland and of achieving the integrity of our national territory." Further, it is recommended that we insert the concept of the "maritime development" in the General Principle of Constitution through the phrase "The state shall provide active support for, and guarantee, the development of various marine programs as well as to guide and facilitate the continued enhancement of our marine resource development and exploitation capabilities."

Second, with the aforesaid amendments to the Constitution serving as an opening, we can then spend a year or so to review and sort out policies of central and local governments concerning maritime development, and deal with the documents, regulations, and policies that impinge on China's development on the seas.

For instance, we should abandon the policy that suppresses the development of coastal regions in sole pursuit of balanced development between regions. Instead, we should launch policies that facilitate the flow of talent, the use of capital, technological innovation, entrepreneurship, etc., in coastal regions, with an emphasis on maritime development. In addition, we should also do away with the naval policy of "near-sea defense" and encourage our navy to establish a global defensive network over time with the help of other forms of military support. Further, we should move away from the current focus on trade of our foreign trade policy and encourage domestic enterprises and individuals to engage in the fishery business, island development, etc., in other coastal states.

Finally, we should consolidate all laws, regulations, and statutes concerning maritime development into a "Law of the Sea" as a basic law as soon as possible.

To deal with the current chaotic situation in terms of China's maritime law system and at the same time to establish a robust legal foundation for China's maritime supervision and management, the Standing Committee of National People's Congress can take the lead in the establishment of a Legislative Committee focused on the establishment of a "Law of the Sea." The Committee's task would be to propose the consolidation and amendment of existing maritime laws, regulations, and statutes in line with China's strategic trajectory, goals, and principles for its maritime development to create a basic law that would cover all aspects of China's maritime development. The proposed Law should then be approved and enacted by the National People's Congress.

The second step is to further refine our maritime governance structure to provide solid institutional support.

In 2009, the author of this book called for the establishment of a high-level National Maritime Development Commission that would be engaged in maritime affairs in areas including national defense, technology, environmental protection, and maritime law enforcement. The author also called for the establishment of a strong Bureau of Maritime Development Commission and an Administration of Maritime Development Commission, with the former responsible for the stage-by-stage drafting and implementation of China's maritime development plans, such as the layout of marine industries, the provision of technological support, personnel training, and coordination between the military and local governments. On the other hand, the latter would be responsible for administrative management and the enforcement of various maritime laws to provide various enterprises and individuals with a standard suite of maritime services.

On March 10, 2013, at the Third Plenum of the First Session of the 12th National People's Congress, then Secretary General of the State Council, Ma Kai, when explaining the reform of State Council bodies and the efforts to transform its functions, disclosed that China was planning to establish a National Maritime Commission as well as restructure the State Oceanic Administration that would incorporating fishery administration from the Ministry of Agriculture, coast guard and anti-smuggling work from the Ministry of Public Security, as well as the existing law enforcement responsibilities of the original Oceanic Administration. The State Oceanic Administration would also command the newly established China Coast Guard, which would take on these duties. In 2013, the General Office of the State Council of the People's Republic of China released the Notice on Printing and Issuing of the Guidelines for the Departments and Personnel of the State Oceanic Administration [GBF (2013) No. 52], marking the completion of the transformation of the State Oceanic Administration.

Based on the current situation, the proposed National Maritime Commission may be modeled after the National Energy Commission. That is to say, just as the National Energy Administration, the executive arm of the National Energy Commission, is managed by the National Development and Reform Commission, the possible executive arm of the proposed National Maritime Commission, the State Oceanic Administration, would be managed by the Ministry of Land and Resources. However, such an arrangement would place the National Maritime Commission at the risk of becoming a white elephant.

This is because the National Energy Commission, which was founded in January 2010, held its first general meeting on April 22, 2010 and only held its second meeting subsequently 4 years later on April 18, 2014. Given that energy industries such as the coal, electrical power, and petroleum industries have operated for at least half a century and that both the domestic and international energy situation is fairly stable, such an interval is acceptable for the development of China's energy sector. However, if the National Maritime Commission were to operate along the same line, the Commission would not be able to effectively tackle the rapidly changing maritime landscape that China finds itself in, particularly in surrounding sea. What China urgently needs at this point is a high-level, permanent and dynamic maritime administration agency and not an ad hoc deliberative body.

Therefore, in terms of the institutions and mechanisms of maritime governance, China has two choices: it can continue with its plans for the National Maritime Commission and ensure effective implementation on the basis of the State Oceanic Administration, or it can transfer the coordination and deliberative functions of the proposed National Maritime Commission to the Central Leading Group for Comprehensively Deepening Reform or the National Security Commission so that the issues that have an impact on China's maritime development would be tackled in a timely manner. At the same time, the status of the State Oceanic Administration should be further elevated and its authority expanded, so that it becomes a permanent department or direct subsidiary of the State Council. Doing so will help it better guide, manage, and serve the maritime development.

The third step is to be clear about the focus of the implementation of *tunhai*.

The implementation of *tunhai* should be focused on the strengthening of the weak links in China's maritime development, with a specific emphasis on the extensive development and exploitation of marine resources. What this means is that emerging or high-tech maritime industries such as the development of far-flung islands, deep-sea resource exploration and development, the consolidation of coastal resources, high-yield manufacturing and processing, marine biology, marine chemicals, deep-sea tourism, etc., as well as activities or services that cater to such industries covering technology, education, public services, finance, insurance, etc., can be fully included in such implementation.

Of course, as these industries have varying levels of impact on national defense and the security of the national economy, the amount of financial, personnel, and material resources needed also vary. However, the average investment cost is still hefty while the state's resources in these areas are all limited. Therefore, when implementing the strategy of *tunhai*, the state must be able to set priorities for the work in accordance with policy and with an emphasis on the delivery of public services. With the exception of infrastructure projects that are directly related to national economy and people's livelihood, national defense and security, and projects where the return on significant investment is likely to take some time, in general the state should not engage in the implementation of specific projects. What it should do is to encourage the movement of private capital toward maritime and other related industries and to encourage and support its participation in, and management and organization of industries and projects that are important to the country but cannot be adequately developed by the state's efforts alone.

The fourth step is to introduce specific *tunhai* measures.

With a standardized national maritime development strategy and the agencies to implement this vision, we can then look at the issue of specific implementation. The basic principles of *tunhai* implementation can be described as "integration of peacetime and wartime operations, coordination between the military and local governments, and state management with civilian operations." The *tuntian* experience has already given us insights into how "integration of peacetime and wartime operations" and "coordination between the military and local governments" would work. "State management with civilian operations" is listed here as another implementation principle in consideration of the various flaws in state-owned enterprises (SOEs) that have emerged to the fore after years of development. Studies by Zhang Weiying, Fan Gang, Liu Shijin, Zhang Jun, and all show that although legally speaking the property rights of SOEs that had borne the burden of carrying out national policies appear to be very clear, the transfer of these "property rights" to the market is fraught with issues due to principal-agent problems, the absence of supporting market mechanisms and the need for improvements to the legal system. The ownership of a large number of SOEs by the state makes supervision a tremendous challenge and is also incompatible with the state's primary role as the provider of public services. Furthermore, countries that have had multiple conflicts with China due to sea power disputes such as Japan and Malaysia have also practiced "state management with civilian operations" in the following ways: they import advanced technologies and foreign investment in the joint development of oil and gas fields or the building of power plants or fisheries in disputed seas or around disputed islands, or they allow civilian entities to organize trips to disputed islands or to build on these islands. At the same time, the state provides only public goods such as policy support and the guarantee of safety. They have chosen this path most probably because of consideration of the various possible disadvantages of state operations in these instances. Therefore, in the implementation of the *tunhai* strategy, the government must stay focused on its role as provider of public services and hence only stay in control of key enterprises that have an impact on critical industries concerning national defense, national economy and the livelihood of the people. These are but a small number of the total. The rest of the enterprises should be controlled by private capital although the state may use policy and legal tools to prompt these enterprises to be compliant with, and to work in service of, the strategic objectives established by the government.

Now that we have established the operating principle, we will now examine how the specific implementation of *tunhai* should look like as follows:

1. **Civilian *tunhai* as the mainstay, with military measures as a supplement.**

This is the specific formulation of "integration of peacetime and wartime operations, coordination between the military and local governments, and state management with civilian operations." It is best that the implementation of the strategy of *tunhai* be mainly conducted in the civilian realm. Civilian *tunhai* entities can be classed into four categories: the first are individuals and small enterprises, such as individual fishermen or various types of consortia formed by these fishermen; the second are private enterprises of a certain economic scale, those that can engage in enterprises such as fishing, oceanic exploration, oil drilling, and even island management or maritime tourism development; the third are state-owned enterprises (again, of a certain scale); and the last are foreign-owned and foreign-invested enterprises. These *tunhai* entities can go about their efforts singly or work together in groups. What the state needs to do here is to delineate maritime territories and to establish specific policies suited to the specific circumstances of the territory in question as well as the characteristics of the businesses or industries that certain *tunhai* entities are in. This way, various rents and taxes can be collected when the resources in these territories are handed over for development and use.

Of course, although civilian *tunhai* must be the key thrust here, sometimes when necessary and under special circumstances "military *tunhai*" can also be implemented. Since some islands and waters over which China has sovereignty are tyrannically occupied by others, we should station troops of a certain number in these areas, or otherwise set up long-term regular patrols. Where suitable, we can also arrange a certain level of production activity in these areas. However, the main purpose of modern military *tunhai* is the display of one's sovereign status. When implementing military *tunhai*, the state can also consider the use of military resources as a means of protecting the development and exploitation in these islands and waters by civilian entities. Another possible measure would be for the protected entities or individuals in question to provide such troops with subsidies, depending on the prospects of the territory in question and the specific circumstances of the troops deployed. Strictly speaking, this defensive service is actually a "mixed model" of civilian and military *tunhai* rather than pure military *tunhai* per se.

2. **Give full play to the potential of ex-service personnel.**

The most direct way of doing so would be to settle all discharged or retired military personnel to coastal areas so that the country can make full use of their skills and experiences. In this instance, the state can use measures such as subsidies, tax waivers, and skills education for these personnel to encourage local governments and enterprises in coastal areas as well as various *tunhai* entities to provide employment for ex-naval personnel. This way, the hired personnel would be able to make use of their experiences in their new positions, as well as ensure that their production environments can be linked smoothly to the military environment at times of war without affecting normal production as much as possible. For instance, these personnel can participate in the ship-design process or serve as security staff on ocean-going vessels. On one hand, this will provide effective support to battle units in times of war; and on the other hand, doing so will also minimize the impact on production when conflict breaks out.

In addition, to enhance the military capabilities and fitness levels of residents along the coastline, the state can also arrange for ex-service personnel from other branches of the military to work at local governments or enterprises in varying capacities. These personnel can, after work, help to organize and participate in civilian military training. This way, not only will coastal regions benefit from the building of a strong civilian militia, individuals of the right age range in these areas can also enhance their fitness levels and pick up a certain level of soldiering skills in case of emergency.

Military personnel are able to bear hardship, are disciplined, and are also trained to work as part of a team. As long as the government or enterprises provide the ex-service personnel with business or skills training, they will be able to take on their civilian vocations quickly. Such personnel should be in demand at various employing units.

3. **Shift away from the single-minded pursuit of equal regional development and work to establish a coastal economic belt.**

The economic advantage that coastal regions have over inland regions means that the state does not have to encourage migration to the former for *tunhai* purposes. What the state needs to do is to respect the natural flow of resources and provide the right facilitation for enterprises and individuals to settle down and engage in business in coastal regions. As such, it should abolish the policy artificially suppressing the development of coastal regions to ensure equal development between coastal and inland regions, and allow various coastal cities to develop to form a "belt" that would tie the people of China together with the oceans. This "belt" can also become a demonstration zone for China's move to take its development to the seas and further highlight the attraction of the seas and coastal regions to enterprises and individuals.

Studies by some experts show that America's modern prosperity is inextricably linked to the rise of cities on its west coast.[4] It is possible that China will undergo a similar process.[5] China can consider developing the more than 50 coastal cities with access to deepwater ports into an urban coastal zone with booming economy and large population.[6] Examples of municipal governments that have successfully developed their respective cities through efforts in living environments, talent introduction, industry planning, etc., are the local governments of Shenzhen, Dalian, Ningbo, Rizhao, and Yangshan.

If China is able to build another two or three cities like Shenzhen, and another dozen or so cities like Ningbo, Qingdao, and Dalian, the vast majority of Chinese would not hesitate about China's path to becoming a maritime nation. And this is not impossible. The emergence of some port cities that used to be relatively unknown, such as Caofeidian, Huanghua, Qinzhou, Fangchenggang, and Weifang is undoubtedly a positive sign.

---

[4]Refer to: Abbott, Carl (1998). *The Metropolitan Frontier: Cities in the Modern American West.* (Wang, Xu, et al. trans.) Beijing: The Commercial Press, p. 184.; and: He, Shunguo (2007). *Fifteen Lectures on American History.* Beijing: Peking University Press, pp. 85–87 and 92–96.

[5]Wang, Fang (2006). Reflections on Including Seas in the Nation's Territorial Planning. *Latest Trends in the Study of Maritime Development Strategies*, no. 4; Xu, Zhiliang (2002). An Essay on Planning for China's Maritime Economy in the "New East." *Study of Maritime Development Strategies*, no. 9; Gao, Zhiguo (2000). On the Strategy of Developing the Great Ocean in the East in the Twenty-First Century. *Study of Maritime Development Strategies*, no. 3.

[6]In China, there are a total of 53 medium-to-large sized coastal cities as well as 238 coastal counties (county-level cities and districts). However, the collective economic effect of these cities has yet to be realized, perhaps due to the impact of existing household registration policies. Xu, Zhiliang, Fang, Kun, et al. (2008). *The "New Eastern Region" for China: An Overall Vision for Land and Sea Planning.* Beijing: National Ocean Science Press, pp. 19.

4. **Encourage the scientific development of islands.**

Many islands can serve a defensive purpose in coastal areas similar to that of aircraft carriers. China has 6961 islands with an area of 500 m^2 and above (not including the islands of Taiwan, Hong Kong, Macao). Of these islands, only 433 are inhabited. However, the development of these islands is unsatisfactory.[7] In fact, more than 140 of these islands are yet to be named. Thankfully, the situation has improved somewhat with the Notice on Ensuring Service for Expanding Domestic Demand and Promoting Steady and Robust Economic Development by the State Oceanic Administration at the end of 2008 and particularly after the promulgation of the Island Protection Law at the end of 2009. However, the "island development fever" that appeared around 2011 has subsided. In addition, the problem of predatory exploitation of islands is also rather severe.

As such, the government of China should strengthen its legal supervision and recognize or recall unauthorized island development. It may use measures such as the assessment of island development plans and prospective developers' strength, capabilities, and qualifications, to introduce various incentives to promote the development of different islands and ensure the sustainable development and exploitation of resources in these territories.

The government should ensure the people benefit from the policy and seek their advice. Here, possible measures include political measures (promoting public participation in the decision-making process, guaranteed security and salvation, reducing government review and approval procedures) and economic measures (tax incentives, preferential loan terms, business support). As long as developers are compliant with existing agreements and are willing to accept supervision by the state, they should be encouraged to participate in developing the islands in the manner that is most compatible with the specific characteristics of the islands, which would hence maximize benefits.

For islands that have begun to show signs of economic and social benefits, or which require relatively little investment to obtain such benefits, competitive bidding can be used to select the best possible investor based on various criteria. These investors should generally be large domestic or foreign corporations that are able and willing to shoulder the corresponding social responsibility to develop such islands to the best of their capabilities.

For far-flung islands, the state can grant developers use rights gratis for a given period before they would be returned to the state. Further, in the case of special developers who have particular expertise in the development of islands, which are confident of doing well and already have a detailed plan in hand, the state can also provide financial support.

As for islands with military significance, the state can consider having the military and corresponding local governments (such as the Sansha municipal

[7]Refer to: Liu, Rongzi and Qi, Lianming (2006). *A Study of Value Systems of Uninhabited Islands in China*. Beijing: China Ocean Press; and: Zeng, Jin (2010). Why the Awareness of Island is So Poor among the Chinese. *Chinese National Geography*, no. 10.

government) to establish a joint Island Construction Corps made up of retired naval personnel for the development of such islands. This approach can help meet the security requirements of the military as well as maximize the economic and social value of these islands.

5. **Provide support for certain marine programs.**

The state can provide appropriate financial and policy support to specific maritime industries and programs that have a critical role to play in China's maritime development.

For fishermen who are willing to work in far-off marine territories, the state should assist them in the building of stronger sea-going vessels and in the acquisition of new tools and equipment. Further, the state can also finance and then lease out such equipment to these fishermen, with the labor output and hours put in by these fishermen as the payment for such concessions.

In addition, the government can also establish startup hubs and science parks for maritime industries and promising high-tech projects, which will provide centralized support for further development as well as an environment conductive to the comprehensive development of marine resources. Further, support can also be given in terms of the establishment of a favorable financing environment and the provision of government services.

High-caliber personnel can be remunerated at levels slightly higher, or even significantly higher, than their peers working on land.

6. **Enhance cooperation with, and minimize conflict against, other nations with an interest in disputed maritime territories.**

First of all, in terms of the use of waters and islands, China can allow the use of these territories by the relevant nations, if they are relatively closer to those territories or have sufficient development capability, either for free or at concessionary rates as long as they recognize China's sovereign claims over these territories. In special cases only token fees may be charged. This measure should be used chiefly with countries that are keen on undersea oil and gas resources.

Second, for waters and islands where China recognizes the sovereign rights of other countries but where Chinese parties are better able to develop, China can also negotiate with the country concerned for Chinese organizations or enterprises to lease these territories. This measure is to be used chiefly with countries with undersea oil and gas resources or fishery resources but which are less equipped to develop and exploit these resources.

Finally, with disputed waters and islands, China can first establish a cooperation framework with its counterparts that allows for joint development and risk- and benefits-sharing in the disputed territory, with responsibilities and rights to be borne in accordance with the proportion of one's contributions. The framework can be designed thusly: first, disputes over sovereign rights would be put aside for the time being. The disputed water/islands is declared to be under the state of concurrent control as it was in (with the participation of non-disputing parties eliminated) prior to the announcement of UNCLOS. The counterpart acknowledges China's historical claim to the territory, and China also acknowledges that the territory is being controlled by its counterpart currently (This means that the opposing party must receive approval from China if it wishes to legalize its control of its territory.). Then, both parties can begin to engage in the development and exploitation of resources in the area in question to the best of their respective capabilities. This state is to last until both parties reach an agreement on the sovereignty status of the disputed islands or waters in question.

The bottom line is, China should seek to maintain friendly relations in the international arena and refrain from engaging in conflict as far as possible. China must try its utmost to do so by means of trade relations and the attractions of the Chinese market, and try as much as possible to convert opposing parties to its point of view with regard to its sea power position. We should try to resolve disputes through negotiation rather than resorting to military deterrence. As for powers from outside the region, we must be able to put forth our best arguments so that they would understand that it is in their interests for China to serve as a regional power capable of maintaining regional stability.

7. **Expand the scope of Maritime Silk Road plans, and provide means of security by conducting *tunhai* along main maritime passages and in key trading countries.**

China attaches great importance to the safety of ocean shipping and the safety of Chinese citizens and enterprises abroad as well as their properties due to the importance of international trade and overseas investments to China's development, as well as the continued growth in the numbers of Chinese citizens traveling and working abroad.

Here, China may look back on how the Western Han implementation of *tuntian* in the Western regions provided security for Silk Road trade. Similarly then, we can conduct marine resource development and exploitation activities with *tunhai* characteristics in areas where China's ocean-going vessels frequently berth or pass through, where Chinese enterprises have made significant investments, and where Chinese citizens visits in large numbers. These activities, which can include the building of ship repair bases, the establishment of joint fishery companies or service enterprises targeted at Chinese enterprises and citizens, can be done either through the leasing of use rights or in joint partnership. Such activities can also be further developed to become part of larger cultural, educational, entertainment, and exchange hubs, etc., with a specific maritime theme.

China has already proposed a partnership with the Association of Southeast Asian Nations (ASEAN) to build the Maritime Silk Road. This undoubtedly is a rare opportunity for China to engage in *tunhai* overseas. China should expand the scope of its Maritime Silk Road plans, and invite its key maritime trading partners in South America, Africa, and Europe to take part in the establishment of the Maritime Silk Road. Further, the Maritime Silk Road should be regarded as a key link upon which an overseas security network designed to protect Chinese interests and connected by means of *tunhai* can be build over time.

8. **Work actively to develop plans for alternatives to existing ocean navigation routes.**

China should work actively, based on the existing ocean navigation routes, to develop various plans and plan combinations in order to mitigate the pressures caused by tension in surrounding waters. Doing so will also give China more options in terms of ocean routes as well as strengthen its strategic initiative against any encirclement by the likes of the US and Japan.

On one hand, China can choose to increase the number of routes it uses, improve existing routes, and minimize risk. Current partnerships with Thailand to develop the Kra Isthmus Canal (that would connect the Gulf of Thailand and the Indian Ocean) and with Bangladesh and Pakistan to jointly build and operate seaports as well as explorations with these partners into the possibility of using the Gulf of Thailand, Bay of Bengal and the waters around Pakistan in Arabian Sea as possible entry points into the Indian Ocean have already drawn public discussion. As these options would all dramatically shorten shipping routes, if they can be achieved there would be significant economic benefits to gain. When emergencies occur, another possible alternative route toward the Pacific Ocean would be via Huichun in Jilin, through the Tumen River into the Sea of Japan.

On the other hand, new transcontinental and transnational overland shipping routes and pipelines can also help in the transport of goods, persons, and energy resources. Alternatively, these routes can be connected to sea routes in parts for the same purpose. Both these options can help to reduce China's reliance on existing shipping routes. In this vein, the establishment and opening of Sino-Russian and Sino-Kazakhstan oil pipelines, the China-Central Asia gas pipeline, the China-Myanmar oil and gas pipeline, the Chittagong-Myanmar-Kunming road (railway), the China-Laos-Thailand and the China-Myanmar road links, and China-Europe rail links, etc., are in fact all ways around the "Malacca dilemma" caused by the South China Sea sovereignty problem. In fact, China can work even harder in this respect. For instance, it can improve on its established oil and gas supply network and international overland links as well as capitalize on its technical capabilities in terms of long-distance electrical power transmission via transnational and transcontinental high-voltage lines to minimize any negative impact caused by the cutting off of China's "maritime energy lifeline."

9. **Make as many friends as possible, and keep away from enemies. Establish a clear position, and create a diplomatic environment that can keep threats in the South China Sea in check.**

Not only must China work to refine its land and sea links, it must also keep an eye on the international diplomatic situation. China must be able to look at the South China Sea dispute from a broader perspective, and make the correct judgments on the geopolitical situation and maritime competition. Further, it must be adept at looking past disputes centered on interests to harness the advantages offered by changes in the international scene in order to facilitate the smooth implementation of *tunhai* and to create a macro environment that is as favorable as possible to its hopes of achieving victory on the seas.

First, it must no longer have an unclear position in the international arena. China must clearly identify its allies, friends, and opponents, and establish standards and bottom lines for its international engagement. It should provide unconditional support for its friends and allies and be as good a friend as possible, and at the same time distance itself from the opponents and their ironclad allies ("The friend of my enemy is my enemy").

Second, China as a friendly and peace-loving country should rally all the forces that can be rallied to strengthen the international united front. Mutually beneficial trade and mutual political trust are the links connecting China and European countries, while in the case of African and Latin American nations common development and mutual respect are key. China's effort to ensure regional stability and achieve regional prosperity can serve as a banner under which Asian nations can be mobilized. Doing so can help to isolate hegemonic powers in Asia, restrain such powers in Europe and Latin America, and put a stop to hegemony altogether in Africa.

Further, China should objectively assess the pressures it faces, work gradually to resolve antipathy towards China, neutralize hostile actions, and break up the opposition. The US alliance in China's surrounding waters is not ironclad.

The fact is, the US is not part of Asia, which means that its long-term leadership of this alliance lacks legitimacy. For certain nations, relying on and fawning over the US is not a long-term solution, and may even do more harm than good.

The painful memories that Asian nations have of Japan from the Second World War as well as the negative impact wrought far outweigh any unhappiness brought on by disputes with China on the subject of disputed islands or waters.[8]

Putting its maritime disputes over islands and waters with China aside, Vietnam and China have similar positions in terms of ideology, geopolitical concerns, and economic and social development. India and Australia, on the other hand, are but bit players as they do not have direct interests in the region.

Therefore, while on one hand China must be able to communicate the pros and cons of engaging in conflict to the corresponding nations and the international community; on the other hand it must take a tough stance to let the US know that without China's support it will not be able to achieve much in Asia and even accelerate its disassociation from Asia. "Cold politics and cold economy" between China and Japan as well as Asian countries' wariness toward Japan all have let Japan know that it no longer has the right to lead Asia for historical reasons, that its predicament in terms of seeking routes to the Indian Ocean is worse off than China's, and that it should work together with other countries rather than engage in fantasy and try to seek the jockey's seat and cause trouble. China must also be able to communicate to Vietnam the pros and cons of conflict and allow Vietnam to

[8]Jacques, Martin (2010). *When China Rules the World: The End of the Western World and The birth of a New Global Order*. (Zhang, Li and Liu, Qu, trans.) Beijing: Citic Press, p. 241.

weigh the matter and come to a decision on future action on its own. For India, apart from conveying an attitude of openness toward its strategic move eastwards, China should also convey to India that it hopes India can take the same attitude of openness towards China's effort to gain access to the Indian Ocean. As for Australia, China should clearly state that it can only choose one of two options: prosperity with China, or hard times with the US.

6.4 Implementation and Examples

For the strategy of *tunhai,* although China has not openly described how it would establish the system, it has already made, or is making, the relevant efforts in the meantime. For instance, after 2008 it has placed an emphasis on the development of islands, and promulgated the Island Protection Law at the end of 2009. In 2012, Sansha City was formed, and the "981" large-scale deepwater drilling rig began operating in the South China Sea. After 2012, a number of civilian militia organizations have also emerged in coastal areas, and in 2013 the mandate of the State Oceanic Administration was broadened. Further, the National Maritime Commission was established after years of planning and drafting work on the Law of the Sea began. In another vein, Chinese operators have also built and/or now run overseas ports such as Karachi Port and Gwadar Port in Pakistan, the Port of Hambantota and the Port of Colombo in Sri Lanka, Chittagong Port in Bangladesh and the Port of Piraeus in Greece. Of course, China has also proposed the concept of the Maritime Silk Road. All these efforts are worth noting.

However, compared to the ultimate objective of *tunhai*, China has but just begun with the possible specific *tunhai* measures that can be taken. Some of these efforts have just commenced, while others are still in the deliberation or planning stages; others are but concepts at this point and would require in-depth exploration and further thinking in order to work. Clearly, there is much more to be done, particularly in terms of the groundwork for implementation.

In addition, although *tunhai* is still a rather new concept, there have already been specific examples of implementation both within China and overseas. For instance, as early as the 1950s there have been civilian maritime militias that had been recognized by the Chinese government. Other examples include the introduction of Special Zones and the establishment of pilot economic zones centered on certain coastal cities following the opening-up of China. All these measures are actually large-scale *tunhai* measures. On the other hand, the global network of US military bases and the management of disputed islands by Japan, Vietnam, the Philippines, etc., are indubitably examples of *tunhai* by international parties.

In terms of the specific implementation of *tunhai,* China has much to learn from its history as well as from international players and its opponents in terms of perseverance, techniques, etc.

For example, **Japan's careful and sustained management of the Rock of Okinotori is a typical case of *tunhai* at work.**

Given the size of potential benefits to be gained if the Rock of Okinotori were to be recognized as an island proper, the Chinese mainland, the Republic of Korea, the Democratic People's Republic of Korea, the Taiwan region and Japan have engaged in intense conflicts over the years over the question of whether the Rock of Okinotori should be recognized as an island or a coral reef.

In the opinion of the Chinese mainland, the Republic of Korea, the Democratic People's Republic of Korea, and the Taiwan region, the Rock of Okinotori, which is 600 km away from the Japanese mainland, had five reefs that were above the water in 1933, while only four remained in 1982. Currently, only two reefs have remained above the water: the eastern islet and the northern islet. We can foresee that the forces of marine erosion will eventually place the whole of Rock of Okinotori underwater in time to come. Hence, according to Article 121(3) of the United Nations Convention on the Law of the Sea (UNCLOS) which states that: "rocks which cannot sustain human habitation or economic life of their own shall have no exclusive economic zone or continental shelf," the Rock of Okinotori should not be taken as a basis for the definition of Japan's exclusive economic zone or continental shelf. Japan may claim 12 nautical miles of territorial waters at most.

However, Japan has pointed to Article 121(1) of the same document, which states that: "An island is a naturally formed area of land, surrounded by water, which is above water at high tide" to argue that the Rock of Okinotori should be regarded as an island proper and hence may be taken as a basis for the definition of Japan's exclusive economic zone or continental shelf. Japan has even marked the Rock of Okinotori on its maps as the southernmost point of its land territory, while the eastern islet named "Okinotori Island" and the northern islet named "Kita-Kojima." Since 1983, Japan has also taken a series of measures such as reinforcement of the reef, building an airport, a weather station, and a fishery, and exclusive exploration surveys in spite of the high cost to cultivate the image of an "island" that is "in use." Although in May 2012 the United Nations Commission on the Limits of the Continental Shelf (CLCS) did not approve Japan's application for its outer continental shelf based on the premise that the Rock of Okinotori is an island, Japan has not slowed down in terms of its efforts to have the Rock of Okinotori recognized as one. The latest open move by Japan in this matter is its effort to build a port at the Rock of Okinotori beginning in August 2013.

These efforts by Japan to develop, manage, and use the Rock of Okinotori, indicate Japan's desire to cultivate grounds for sovereignty through productive activities and competitions. Here, the thrust of *tunhai* is extremely clear.

Further, **Vietnam's move to organize civilian maritime self-defense force is also a reflection of *tunhai* thinking**.

In November 2009, Vietnam launched the establishment of civilian maritime self-defense force as a key state measure, with the force regarded as part of a larger national defense network that also comprises the border defense force, navy, the coast guard, and other regular forces. In peacetime, the self-defense force is to engage in tasks such as taking part in sea rescues, intelligence gathering, etc., while during wars it would be drafted as part of the military force.

The history of the self-defense force, which is both civilian and military in nature, can be traced to the armed organizations formed by fishermen in the 1970s. These organizations once played a significant role in Vietnam's occupation of the Nansha Islands.[9] The Vietnamese government has chosen to recycle this tactic, and also to define these self-defense troops as an integral part of its maritime security strategy based on "the people's defense" and "the people's maritime war," precisely because it has recognized that it would be able to supplement its thin naval and coast guard numbers as well as to ensure external support for regular forces during times of conflict. These are characteristic of the *tunhai* strategy, the basic principle being "the integration of peacetime and wartime operations and coordination between the military and local governments."

In addition, **the United States can also be regarded as practicing *tunhai* in various forms with its overseas naval bases, military exercises on the high seas, naval diplomacy, international political interactions, rescue efforts in international waters, cultural exchanges, and relevant international charitable moves. All these form an intricate mesh that maintains and even expands its maritime influence around the world.**

Just as it is shown in the game played by the US in key maritime territories around the world (including the South China Sea), its naval power stems from its network of naval bases around the world, a network that provides points for mobilization, replacement, and support. Its frequent maritime military exercises and other naval engagements with other nations are in fact extensions of its naval power. On the other hand, its international political interactions, participation in rescue missions on the high seas, cultural engagements, and other related charitable efforts serve to extend its maritime influence and strengthen the legitimacy of its activities. All these create the US maritime presence. The mix of military deterrence, exchanges, and the establishment of physical nodes together with high coordination of political, military, and cultural activities at various levels might serve as a refined *tuntian* policy, with many similarities as well to the ideas of the *tunhai* strategy.

It is worth noting that the conduct of US cultural exchanges and charitable work in the relevant nations serve as a catalyst and promoter of US sea power in a subtle manner. Robert D. Kaplan's description of his interactions with US intelligence personnel and NGO workers over several occasions in Myanmar in his book *Monsoon: The Indian Ocean and the Future of American Power* vividly illustrates this point. According to these intelligence personnel, the benefits (to US national interests) from Myanmar thanks to US support for the building of schools, the

[9]Cheng, Hanping (2011). Vietnam's Maritime Security Strategies and China's Countermeasures. *Forum of World Economics & Politics*, no. 3.

establishment and running of clinics, and the building and improvement of irrigation systems by NGOs far exceed benefits gained from defense programs that come with an exorbitant price tag.[10]

The effect of international diplomacy and engaging in rescue missions in international waters is similar. The US has increased its influence in Myanmar politics through its support for Aung San Suu Kyi, while it has also created greater distance between China and Vietnam due to its growing ties with the latter. Its efficient emergency response shown in the wake of the 2004 Indian Ocean tsunami has changed the political landscape in South Asia somewhat, enhanced the image of the US within the region, and has certainly helped to expand US influence in the Pacific and Indian Oceans.

6.5 However, *Tunhai* Is not the Be-All and End-All

By examining existing examples of *tunhai* measures both by China and other nations, we can see that the development and implementation of *tunhai* requires an open and systematic approach.

On one hand, the form and effect of measures taken can change in tandem with the situation and are not merely limited by specific design and objectives, and a number of effects would be possible, even unintended positive ones. When China's naval strength becomes sufficient for the defense of its territory,[11] *tunhai* can be used solely for the enhancement of its marine resource development and exploitation capabilities. *Tunhai*, when used as a transitional measure in a situation with few other choices to accelerate the realization of China's sea power and enhance China's marine resource development and exploitation capabilities, should be implemented with the ultimate objective of respecting and complying with the professional division of labor in society. That is, work that is in the governmental realm should be performed by the government, work in the civilian realm performed by civilians, work in the military realm performed by the military, and work in the business realm performed by enterprises. Any implementation of *tunhai* must work toward this division over time.

On the other hand, we must be clear that *tunhai* only serves certain functions, and is not the be-all and end-all of China's maritime policy. The purpose of *tunhai* is to facilitate China's rise as an important maritime nation. Although the implementation of *tunhai* can help enhance China's various maritime capabilities and powers, and is helpful in mitigating the issue of inadequate sea defense capabilities

[10]29. Kaplan, Robert D. (2013). *Monsoon: The Indian Ocean and the Future of American Power*. (Wu, Zhaoli, and Mao, Yue, trans.) Beijing: Social Sciences Academic Press, pp. 268–288.

[11]Lin, Heli (2009). China Changes Diplomatic Tack with Enhanced Strength. *National Defense Journal*, 16 May.

in an indirect manner, the problems faced during the implementation of *tunhai* are not the sum total of problems faced by China as it seeks to take its development to the seas. Further, the implementation of *tunhai* alone will not make China a successful and great maritime nation. If China wishes to become an important maritime nation that would leave a mark in history, it would need to achieve the following:

First: Remain committed to the development and growth of its naval power.

Unless the fact that the nation-state is the basic unit of human society changes, China being a nation-state as well as home to the world's largest population and second-largest economy—and forecast to become the world's largest economy in 2015 by the World Bank—must have the fundamental naval power to protect its basic interests, including maritime interests. Due to the political, economic, and military encirclement of China led by the US and comprising other nations such as Japan and Vietnam, any such naval power must be of a certain scale and level, with standards higher than what China possesses currently.

Therefore, China must at the same time also be able to convince the world that for the future it should be prepared for an increase in China's military expenditure and the swift growth of China's naval power. China must be prepared to handle the relation between this change and normal economic development, so that it may avoid the fate of the former Soviet Union, which saw a decline due to its arms race with the US. Within a specific timeframe, China can consider using most or even all of the tax revenue generated from the value-added of marine economy due to the implementation of *tunhai* on military purposes including the strengthening of its navy, air force, and missile troops to minimize the financial burden of its efforts on the state.

China must enhance its resistance capabilities with the aid of technology, enhance the battle capabilities of its troops, and make sure that its weapons are up-to-date. It must also enhance the readiness of its troops psychologically, so that they would not be complacent, would not shy away from conflict, and have the capabilities to fight well. This is undoubtedly the fundamental path China must walk in order to build up its naval power. Apart from engaging in professional training and exercises, in order to strengthen its naval power China should also make use of rare opportunities to engage in naval diplomacy and participate in rescues on the sea. Through such exchanges, it can gain a better understanding of modern naval warfare and test its responsiveness and battle readiness when extending services during emergencies.

Second, place an emphasis on technological innovation by enhancing the R&D capabilities for homegrown technology.

The use of aircraft and tanks in battle during the First World War, the appearance of the atomic bomb and the broad use of the aircraft carrier during the Second World War, and the arms race between the former Soviet Union and the US in the aviation realm are all illustrations of the power of technology. For modern maritime competition, technological innovation is undoubtedly crucial. Without technological innovation, it would not be possible for China to develop its naval strength or to enhance its marine resource development and exploitation capabilities.

Furthermore, in today's combat environment where "the air and space are one" and where various nations are competing with each other for control of deep-sea and oceanic resources, nations cannot afford to possess technological advantages in only one field. Indeed, such competition is fundamentally that of nations' technological capabilities as a whole.

Therefore, whether China can successfully achieve its maritime rise depends on its R&D capability, which determines the upgrading of its maritime industries and weapons, as well as on the kind of support such a move can expect to receive from the domestic R&D system in terms of basic science research and peripheral technologies. As such, China needs to build a robust system that is oriented toward autonomous and fundamental innovation and which at the same time is focused on maritime concerns and which is able to facilitate applications from basic science research in the maritime realm as soon as possible.

In addition, the intersectional role of maritime technologies in the maritime and technological realms will not only help to promote technological innovation from a cause-driven point of view but also bring about a similar effect in the development of maritime education. Technological innovation requires the existence of a strong talent pool. On the other hand, China would also need R&D talent with a keen eye on maritime developments to engage in maritime technology research long-term in order to uncover China's latent needs in terms of maritime technology. If we do not work on the education aspect, any talk of cultivating a talent pool should simply be building castles in the air.

Third, and perhaps most importantly, have the courage to showcase a maritime philosophy that can withstand challenges on the international stage as well as scrutiny for developmental purposes domestically.

A maritime nation with brute power and no fundamental maritime philosophy will find it difficult to become a maritime power that enjoys international recognition. Even if it does ascend to the position of maritime power, it may not stay there for long. This is the root cause of the constant churning of global maritime leadership since the fifteenth century.

The reason for Britain's broader influence compared to Portugal, Spain, and Holland which had come before is that it had understood the importance of the global maritime order from the onset and sought to draw a clear line between itself and pirates. However, perhaps due to the fact that early on in history European sea forces were also pirates, even after Britain became lord of the seas it continued to transact with pirates.[12]

America's maritime rise has very much to do with its belief that the maritime order was a public good provided by the state. America did not believe that the maritime order could be obtained through trade with illegal organizations or through compromise with individuals (such as pirates and unreasonable nations). It

[12]Konstam, Angus (2010). *Piracy: The Complete History*. (Yang, Yujie, Zhao, Guomei, et al., trans.) Beijing: People's Liberation Army Press, pp. 241–260.

was the first nation in the world to have the courage to stand against piracy and nations which engaged in the same kind of behavior.[13]

However, the problem is that it is overly reliant on the use of military force. Not only does it want to be the sheriff of the world, it also wishes to be the world hegemon. America's military deployment around the world far exceeds what it needs to reasonably defend its interests and to maintain the world order. The negative consequences of this approach have already emerged: the attitudes of superiority on the part of the US has led to volte-faces, and its spying, threats, and acts of coercion against other countries have met with opposition even by its allies. Although the US does count a military superiority in various regions, it has found itself stuck in a morass of regional conflicts on several occasions as engagement typically occurs on the cultural and economic fronts over time. Furthermore, although the US does have impressive troop sizes, such troops are distributed around the world, causing a great drain on US finances while only serving to provide the illusion of security, rather than substantial security, for US interests. Therefore, the motivation for the US to continue its expansionist policy in terms of global sea power is shrinking, which means that its military expenditure is set to decrease in the future.

Therefore, if China wishes to surpass the US, or at least become a maritime nation of its stature, it must have a maritime philosophy that is more in line with the world today compared to the US. Further, it must also be better at international diplomacy than the US. For example, China must make it clear that it will effect its rise through fair competition rooted in the peaceful development and exploitation of marine resources, that it only seeks a global security presence commensurate with its interests, and that its global naval deployments are targeted at ensuring the security of international trade and will be based on where Chinese citizens are. Further, it will not seek the outright control of the maritime territories in question, and only wishes to erect an effective deterrent for the establishment of an environment wherein nations work together to maintain the international maritime order. China must also clearly state its opposition to hegemonic behavior and piracy in all forms.

At the same time, China should push for amendments to the United Nations Convention on the Law of the Sea (UNCLOS) so that its provisions would be more aligned with the logic of peaceful competition and to reduce the sovereign interests associated with disputed islands and waters. As for islands and waters that are not being disputed, China should continue to maintain various rights, such as its territorial seas, adjacent waters, its exclusive economic zone, and continental shelf in accordance with UNCLOS. As for disputed territories, it should advocate that disputing nations put away the dispute for the time being, and set up a system where all disputing parties are of joint management and production rights in such territories and encourage them to resolve the issue through competition in production as well as through negotiation.

[13]Ibid., pp. 264–268.

6.6 Possible Scenarios for Dispute Resolution

Although the strategy of *tunhai* will help China to enhance its maritime capabilities, it is not the direct means to realizing a full set of maritime sovereignty rights for China. Therefore, in the course of China's maritime rise, several questions remain: just how would Taiwan return to the motherland, and what possible solutions are there with regard to territorial disputes? These are issues that we must still address and surmount.

There are two possible scenarios for the reunification of the two sides of the Taiwan Straits:

First, China resorts to force to resolve the Taiwan question following a declaration of independence by the Taiwan authorities; or second, the two undergo peaceful reunification as cross-straits cultural and trade links increase and Taiwan becomes more understanding, and reliant on, the mainland.

Based on the current situation, the chances of the first scenario happening are low. Although Taiwan has maintained the momentum of its pro-independence faction with the instigation and support of the US and Japan, this faction can only effectively exist if the mainland and Taiwan maintain the status quo. If the faction were to push their luck to try for Taiwan's independence, the US and Japan are unlikely to provide assistance and hence run the risk of conflict with China. In this scenario, there is only one probable outcome: Taiwan will be unified with the mainland by force. At this juncture, the matter would no longer simply in the hands of the Chinese government. It would also be determined by the nationalist sentiments unleashed by the people of China, who will throw themselves behind the effort to realize the reunification of the country.

Conversely, the possibility of the second scenario is higher. Not only would the outcome be a win-win situation for the mainland and Taiwan, for Japan, and the US—particularly the US—this would be an acceptable outcome as they have already benefited from Taiwan for over seven decades with scant input. Of course, as to whether Taiwan would retain a certain degree of autonomy in terms of foreign matters, home affairs, judicial matters and even defense or whether it would return to the motherland as a province following mutual agreement on reforms to the existing Chinese political system would depend on the sentiment of the people on both sides of the Taiwan Straits and following deep negotiation between both sides.

As for the resolution of territorial disputes between China and surrounding nations, there are four possibilities:

The first possibility would be peaceful resolution following amicable negotiation between disputing parties. This form of resolution would be the best possible outcome for international society, for China, and for its counterpart.

In the second case, China seeks—with other partners—amendments to UNCLOS to reduce friction during dispute resolution due to the interests attached to sovereign rights and to promulgate the requirement that disputing parties seek resolution through cooperative competition as they jointly develop the disputed territory in question. This would be the second-best outcome.

The third possibility would be the resolution of disputes through the means of local wars or limited military force. The fundamental requirement here is that the intensity and form of the war must be kept within limits. While the outcome here would certainly exhilarate the victorious party, over the long term, the complex nationalist sentiments stirred up as a result of conflict will have a negative impact on bilateral relations and even lead to a downwards spiral. Therefore, the zero-sum game would not result in the resolution of the issue at hand.

With the fourth possibility, the outcome is even worse: the predictions of certain Western commentators are fulfilled, with China engaging in local wars with countries like Japan or Vietnam and slipping into broader-based wars with participation from the US and other outside players, eventually making the South China Sea the powder keg that ignites a Third World War.

A close analysis of all four possibilities will tell us that with the first possibility, the difficulty is working with the pressures of nationalist sentiment, while with the fourth possibility the risk of destructive war exists. Therefore, both these two scenarios are unlikely to happen. Comparatively speaking, the chances of the second and third scenarios happening are greater.

However, history tells us that the third scenario would not lead to a full resolution of the problem, as animosity would remain between the disputing nations even after the conflict is over. The wariness toward Japan on the part of other Asian nations and Vietnam's preference to keep the US at arm's length can be attributed to precisely this cause. Hence, when comparing the second and third possibilities, mere politicians may opt for the latter as all that is needed is courage. On the other hand, statesmen would opt for the former, the choice of which requires both courage and wisdom.

Of course, it must be emphasized that while we may have the best intentions, plans, and visions, history is sometimes shaped by the unforeseen and the accidental. No matter it be Taiwan's return to the motherland, or the resolution of China's maritime territorial disputes with surrounding nations, the least probable scenario may take place after all. Hence, we must prepare ourselves for all possibilities with China's move to take its development to the seas.

Although it may be way too early to draw conclusions, we can expect much gains for China as long as it implements the strategy of *tunhai* as soon as possible, and as widely as possible, and that it would be able to confront any scenario head-on no matter what the eventual means of dispute resolution would be.

MIX
Papier aus verantwortungsvollen Quellen
Paper from responsible sources
FSC® C105338

If you have any concerns about our products,
you can contact us on
ProductSafety@springernature.com

In case Publisher is established outside the EU,
the EU authorized representative is:
Springer Nature Customer Service Center GmbH
Europaplatz 3, 69115 Heidelberg, Germany

Printed by Libri Plureos GmbH
in Hamburg, Germany